VOLUME

CHUB—DEPUTY

The LIVING ENCYCLOPEDIA

This family library serves both adult and younger readers.
It combines THE ZONDERVAN PICTORIAL BIBLE DICTIONARY,
stories and narrative accounts from the KNOW YOUR BIBLE PROGRAM,
a gallery of 480 paintings based on Bible themes,
and the most fascinating photographs of contemporary
scenes and archaeological finds in the Holy Land.

BIBLE

in Story
and
Pictures

VOLUME 4

CHUB—DEPUTY

H. S. STUTTMAN CO., INC.
New York, New York 10016

"And there followed him great multitudes of people from Galilee, and from Decapolis, and from Jerusalem, and from Judaea, and from beyond Jordan."

(MATTHEW 4:25)

Cover illustration: Here is Jerash, one of the original of the Decapolis league of ten cities listed by the Roman historian Pliny. Multitudes from the Decapolis region followed Christ.

"After this did Sennacherib
king of Assyria send his
servants to Jerusalem, (but
he himself laid siege against
Lachish, and all his power
with him)...."
(II CHRONICLES 32:9)

This detail from an Assyrian relief depicts an Assyrian in the
act of beheading a Jew during the conquest by King Sennacherib
of the Judaean city of Lachish in 701 B.C.

CHUB (kŭb, Heb. *kûv*), a land mentioned with Ethiopia, Libya, and Lydia in Ezekiel 30:5. The Hebrew text may here be corrupt. The LXX has *Lud*.

CHUN (kŭn, Heb. *kûv*), an Aramean city taken by David (I Chron. 18:8). In II Samuel 8:8 *Berothai* is given as the name of the city. The identification is uncertain.

CHURCH. The English "church" derives from the Greek *kuriakós* (belonging to the Lord), but it stands for another Greek word *ekklesía* (whence "ecclesiastical"), denoting an assembly. This is used in its general sense in Acts 19:32, but had already been applied in the LXX as an equivalent for the "congregation" of the Old Testament. Stephen's speech makes this equation (Acts 7:38), and in this sense it is adopted to describe the new gathering or congregation of the disciples of Jesus Christ.

In the Gospels the term is found only in Matthew 16:18 and 18:17. This paucity is perhaps explained by the fact that both these verses seem to envisage a situation still future. Only after the saving work of Christ is effected will the Old Testament Church be reconstituted as that of the New. Yet the verses show that Christ has this reconstitution in view, that the Church thus reconstituted will rest on the apostolic confession, and that it will take up the ministry of reconciliation.

When we turn to Acts, the situation changes. The saving work has been fulfilled, and the New Testament form of the Church can thus have its birthday at Pentecost. The term is now used regularly to describe local groups of believers. Thus we read of the churches at Jerusalem in Acts 5:11, Antioch in 13:1, and Caesarea in 18:22. At the same time the word is used for all believers in universal fellowship, as is possibly the case in 9:31. From the outset the Church has both a local and a general significance, denoting both the individual assembly and the world-wide community.

This twofold usage is also seen in Paul. He addresses his epistles to specific churches, e.g., Corinth (I Cor. 1:2) or Thessalonica (I Thess. 1:1). Indeed, he seems sometimes to localize further by referring to specific groups within the local community as churches, as though sending greetings to congregations within the one city (cf. Rom. 16: 5). Yet Paul also develops more fully the conception of a Church of all believers embracing the local churches, as in I Corinthians 10:32 and I Timothy 3:15, and with an even grander sweep in Colossians 1:18 and especially Ephesians. The other New Testament books give us mostly examples of the local usage, as in III John 9 and Revelation 1:4; 2:1, etc.

A point to be emphasized is that there is no tension between the local and the universal sense. Each church or congregation is the Church in its own setting, and each a manifestation or concretion of the whole church. This means that there is scope for great flexibility in organization and structure according to particular and varying needs. At the world-wide level it is unlikely that there can ever be more than the loosest practical interconnection. Varying degrees of integration are possible at national, provincial or municipal levels. But the basic unity is always the local church, not in isolation or as a parochially-minded body, but as a concretion of the universal fellowship with a strong sense of belonging to it.

This leads us to the further consideration that the Church is not primarily a human structure like a political, social or economic organism. It is basically the church of Jesus Christ ("my church" Matt. 16:18), or of the living God (I Tim. 3:15). The various Biblical descriptions all emphasize this. It is a building of which Jesus Christ is the chief corner-stone or foundation, "an holy temple in the Lord," "an habitation of God through the Spirit" (Eph. 2:20f). It is the fellowship of saints or people of God (cf. I Pet. 2:9). It is the bride of Jesus Christ, saved and sanctified by Him for union with Himself (Eph. 5:25f). Indeed, it is the body of Jesus Christ, He being the head or whole body, and Christians the members (Rom. 12:5; I Cor. 12:12f; Eph. 4:4,12,16f). As the body, it is the fulness of Christ, who Himself fills all in all (Eph. 1:23).

It is to be noted, as opposed to many commentators, that the Bible does not call this being of the Church as Christ's temple, bride or body, its ideal or mystical reality. While there is an element of imagery in the terms, this is its true reality as the company of those who believe in Christ, and are thus dead, buried and raised in Him as the Saviour-substitute. The various local concretions in this sinful age do not conform to their new and true reality any more than does the believer to what he now is in Christ. The visible life which it must also have, and which should be conformed to its true reality, may fall far short of it. Yet the Church invisible is not just ideal or mystical, but the real fact of the Church is in Christ, as the new man of faith is the real fact of the believer. In every manifestation, there should thus be the aim, not of conformity to the world, but of transformation by renewal into the likeness of Him in whom it has its true life (cf. Rom. 12:2).

In this connection appears the relevance of the traditional marks or "notes" of the Church. It is one (Eph. 4:4), for Jesus Christ has only one temple, bride and body, and all divisions are overcome in death and resurrection with Him, and by endowment of His Spirit. In all its legitimate multiformity, the visible Church should thus seek a unity corresponding to this reality. It is holy, for it is set apart and sanctified by Himself (Gal. 1:4; Eph. 5:26). Even in its pilgrimage in the world, it is thus to attest its consecration by the manner of its life and the nature of its service (cf. I Pet. 1:15). It is catholic, constituted from among all men of all races, places and ages (Eph. 2:14; Col. 1:6; 3: 11; Rev. 5:9). For all its diversity of membership and form, it is thus to maintain its universality of outreach, yet also its identity and relevance in every age and place. It is apostolic, for it rests on the foundation of the apostles and prophets (Eph. 2: 20), the apostles being raised up as the first authoritative witnesses (Acts 1:8) whose testimony is basic and by whose teaching it is called, instructed and directed. In all its activity it is thus to "continue steadfastly in the apostles' doctrine and fellowship" (Acts 2:42), not finding apostolicity in mere externals, but in conformity to apostolic teaching and practice as divinely perpetuated in Holy Scripture.

This brings us to the means of the Church's life, and its continuing function. It draws its life from Jesus Christ by the Holy Spirit, but it does so through the Word of which it is begotten (James

1:18), and by which it is nourished and sanctified (Eph. 5:26; I Pet. 2:2). Receiving life by the Word, it also receives its function, namely, to pass on the Word that others may also be quickened and cleansed. It is to preach the Gospel (Mark 16:15), to take up the ministry of reconciliation (II Cor. 5:19), to dispense the mysteries of God (I Cor. 4:1). Necessarily, therefore, it is the Church of the divine Word and sacraments first received by believers and then passed on to others; hence the Reformation insistence that the marks of the visible Church are preaching of the Word and administration of the Gospel sacraments.

The ministry of the Church arises in this connection. The apostles were first commissioned, and they ordained others, yet no rigid form of ministry arises in the New Testament. Rather, we have patterns, notably of speech, action and rule as historically focused in the elders, deacons and overseers or bishops. The Bible's concern is that there should be real ministry, i.e., service, not in self-assertion and pride, but in humility, obedience and self-offering conformable to the example of Him who was among us as one who serves (cf. Matt. 23:11f; Phil. 2:5f; I Pet. 5:1f).

Finally, the Church's work is not merely for men's salvation, but to the praise of God's glory (Eph. 1:6; 2:7). Hence neither the Church nor its function ceases with the completion of its earthly task. There is ground, therefore, for the old distinction between the Church triumphant and the Church militant. All the Church is triumphant in its true reality. But the warring and wayfaring church is still engaged in conflict between the old reality and the new. Its destiny, however, is to be brought into full conformity to the Lord (I John 3:2) with all the saints. Towards this it moves hesitantly yet expectantly, confident in its future glory when it will be wholly the Church triumphant as graphically depicted in Revelation 7:9ff, enjoying its full reality as the bride and body of the Lord.

CHUSHAN RISHATHAIM (kū'shăn rĭsh'à-thā'ĭm), a Mesopotamian king who held the Israelites in bondage for eight years. Othniel, Caleb's younger brother, put an end to his rule (Judg. 3:5-11).

CHUZA (kū'zà, Gr. *Chouzás*), the steward of Herod Antipas. In Luke 8:3 we read that his wife Joanna, "and Susanna, and many others," ministered to Christ and His disciples of their substance. He was undoubtedly a man of rank and means.

CILICIA (sĭ-lĭsh'ĭ-à, Gr. *Kilikía*), a country in SE Asia Minor, bounded on the N and W by the Taurus range, on the E by the Amanus range, and on the S by the Mediterranean. It had two parts, the western one called the Rugged; the eastern one, the Plain Cilicia, the chief city of which was Tarsus, the birthplace of Paul (Acts 21:39; 22:3; 23:34). The early inhabitants must have been Hittites. Later, Syrians and Phoenicians settled there. It came under Persian sway. After Alexander, Seleucid rulers governed it from Antioch. It became a Roman province in 100 B.C., and was reorganized by Pompey, 66 B.C. One of its governors was Cicero, the orator (51-50 B.C.). Cilicia is accessible by land only by way of its two famous mountain passes, the Cilician Gates and the Syrian Gates. Jews from Cilicia disputed with Stephen (Acts 6:9). The Gospel reached it early (Acts 15:23), probably through Paul (Acts 9:30; Gal. 1:21). On Paul's second missionary journey he confirmed the

churches which had been established there (Acts 15:41), and on his way to Rome as a prisoner he sailed over the sea of Cilicia (Acts 27:5). S.B.

CINNAMON (See Plants)

CIRCUMCISION (sĭr kŭm sĭ shŭn, Lat., *a cutting around*), the cutting off of the foreskin, a custom that has prevailed, and still prevails, among many peoples in different parts of the world — in Asia, Africa, America, and Australia. In ancient times it was practiced among the western Semites — Hebrews, Arabians, Moabites, Ammonites, Edomites, and Egyptians, but not among the Babylonians, Assyrians, Canaanites, and Philistines. Various theories are held regarding the origin and original significance of circumcision, but there can be no doubt that it was at first a religious act.

Among the Hebrews the rite was instituted by God as the sign of the covenant between Him and Abraham, shortly after the latter's sojourn in Egypt. God ordained that it be performed on Abraham, on his posterity and slaves, and on foreigners joining themselves to the Hebrew nation (Gen. 17:12). Every male child was to be circumcised on the eighth day. Originally the father performed the rite, but in exceptional cases a woman could do it (Exod. 4:25). In later times a Hebrew surgeon was called in. The child is named at the ceremony. Nowadays the rite is performed either in the home of the parents or in a synagogue. In former times flint or glass knives were preferred, but now steel is usually used.

According to the terms of the covenant symbolized by circumcision, Jehovah undertook to be the God of Abraham and His descendants, and they were to belong to Him, worshiping and obeying only Him. The rite effects admission to the fellowship of the covenant people, and secures to the individual as a member of the nation his share in the promises God makes to the nation as a whole. Circumcision reminded the Israelites of God's promises to them and of the duties they had assumed. The prophets often reminded them that the outward rite, to have any significance, must be accompanied by a "circumcision of the heart" (Deut. 30:6; Lev. 26:41; Ezek. 44:7; Jer. 9:25, 26). Jeremiah says that his countrymen are no better than the heathen, for they are uncircumcised in heart. Paul uses the word *concision* for this outward circumcision not accompanied by a spiritual change. In the early history of the Christian church Judaizing Christians argued for the necessity of circumcising Gentiles who came into the Church, over against Paul, who held that Christ made an end of all Jewish rites. The Apostolic Council took up the problem and decided against them (Acts 15). S.B.

CISTERN (sĭs'têrn, Heb. *bō'r* or *bôr*), an artificial tank or reservoir dug in the earth or rock for the collection and storage of rain-water, or, sometimes, of spring water brought from a distance by a conduit. A cistern is distinguished from a pool by being always covered. Cisterns were very numerous in Palestine. The long, dry, rainless summers, lasting from May to September, and the small annual precipitation, together with a lack of natural springs, made the people largely dependent upon rain water. Cisterns were fed from surface and roof drainage by gutters and pipes. The hilly character of the land allowed little rain to penetrate the soil. Most of it flowed down the steep hillsides

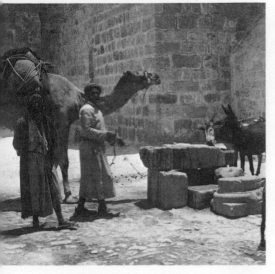

A COVERED WELL, or cistern, near the entrance to the Church of the Nativity in Bethlehem. The Temple area in Jerusalem had at least 37 cisterns, one of which held between two and three million gallons of water.

through the many ravines and water-courses, and it was easily brought by conduits to pools and cisterns. Cisterns in Palestine varied in size and character. Some were cut wholly in the rock, often in the form of a bottle-shaped tank, with a long stairway leading to the surface of the ground. They were frequently of great depth, some more than a hundred feet deep. Very large ones were supported by rock pillars. The Temple area in Jerusalem had at least 37 great cisterns, one of them holding between two and three million gallons. Public rock-cut cisterns were made within the city walls so that the inhabitants could hold out in time of siege.

Where the substratum of the soil was earth and not rock, cisterns of masonry were built. Some of these were large and had vaulted roofs supported by pillars. Besides the large public cisterns, there were many smaller private ones. Ancient sites are honeycombed with them. All cisterns had one or more openings for drawing water to the surface. They needed periodic cleaning because of the impurities washed in from the outside. Empty cisterns were sometimes used as prisons. Joseph was cast into one (Gen. 37:22), and Jeremiah the prophet was let down into one with a miry bottom (Jer. 38:6). Zechariah 9:11 alludes to the custom of confining prisoners in an empty cistern. S.B.

CITIES OF REFUGE, six cities, three on each side of the Jordan, set apart by Moses and Joshua as places of asylum for those who had accidentally committed manslaughter. Those E of the Jordan were Bezer in Reuben, Ramoth-Gilead in Gad, and Golan in Manasseh (Deut. 4:41-43); those W of the Jordan were Hebron in Judah, Shechem in Ephraim, and Kedesh in Naphtali (Josh. 20:7,8). To aid the killer in escaping the pursuit of the avenger of blood, provision was made that the principal roads leading to these cities should always be kept open. No part of Palestine was more than 30 miles away from a city of refuge — a distance that could easily be covered in one day.

In Semitic lands, if a man were slain it was regarded as the duty of his nearest relative to avenge him. Only in that way could justice be satisfied. Almost no distinction was made between intentional and unintentional killing. Many a man was therefore killed in revenge for what was an accident. Cities of refuge were provided to protect a man until his case could be properly adjudged. The right of asylum was only for those who had taken life unintentionally. Wilful murderers were put to death at once.

The regulations concerning these cities of refuge are found in Numbers 35, Deuteronomy 19:1-13, and Joshua 20. If a manslayer reached a city of refuge before the avenger of blood could slay him, he was given asylum until a fair trial could be held. The trial took place where the accused had lived. If proved innocent of wilful murder, he was brought back to the city of refuge. There he had to stay until the death of the high priest. After that he was free to return to his own home. But if during that period he passed beyond the limits of the city of refuge, the avenger of blood could slay him without blame. The temple at Jerusalem could also be used as a place of refuge. S.B.

CITIES OF THE PLAIN (Heb. *kikkar ha-yardēn, circle of the Jordan*), cities near the Dead Sea, including Sodom, Gomorrah, Admah, Zeboiim, and Zoar; first referred to in Genesis 13:10-12, where Lot, after Abraham had given him the choice of where he wanted to live, decided to dwell in the cities of the plain, and pitched his tent toward Sodom. In Genesis 14 it says that they were royal cities, each with its own king, and that Abraham delivered Lot when the cities were attacked and Lot taken captive. The story of the destruction of the cities because of their wickedness is given in Genesis 19. It is thought that God may have accomplished this by causing an eruption of gases and petroleum to ignite. Only Lot and his two daughters were spared. The exact site of the cities is unknown; but although there are weighty arguments for believing that they were at the N end of the Dead Sea, scholars favor the S end, especially since asphalt in large quantities has been found only at the S. It is believed that the sea covers the site. In the Bible, Sodom and Gomorrah are often used as a warning example of sin and divine punishment (Deut. 29:23; Isa. 1:9, 3:9; Jer. 50:40; Ezek. 16:46; Matt. 10:15; Rom. 9:29, etc.). S.B.

CITIZENSHIP (Gr. *politeuma, commonwealth*). In the NT the word for citizen often means nothing more than the inhabitant of a country (Luke 15:15; 19:14). Among the ancient Jews emphasis was placed on Israel as a religious organization, not upon relationship to city and state. The good citizen was the good Israelite. Non-Israelites had the same protection of the law as native Israelites, but they were required not to perform acts hurting the religious feelings of the people. The advantage of a Jew over a Gentile was thus strictly spiritual. He was a member of the theocracy.

Among the Romans, citizenship brought the right to be considered as equal to natives of the city of Rome. Emperors sometimes granted it to whole provinces and cities, and also to single individuals, for services rendered to the state or to the imperial family, or even for a certain sum of money. Roman citizens were exempted from shameful punishments, such as scourging and crucifixion, and they had the right of appeal to the emperor with certain limitations.

Detail from the famous mosaic-standard found on the tombs of the kings of Ur (*ca.* 2400 B.C.), showing a harpist playing before the king.

"And it came to pass, when the evil spirit from God was upon Saul, that David took an harp, and played with his hand:
so Saul was refreshed, and was well, and the evil spirit departed from him."
(I SAMUEL 16:23)

The above mosaic-standard from Ur, and this one, which depicts the servant before his king, measure less than 3″ in height.

422

PROBABLE SITE of the Cities of the Plain, at the southern end of the Dead Sea. The cities included Sodom, Gomorrah, Admah, Zeboiim, and Zoar. Their destruction, recounted in Genesis, may have been caused by an eruption of gases and petroleum that ignited.

Paul says he had become a Roman citizen by birth. Either his father or some other ancestor had acquired the right and had transmitted it to his son. He was proud of his Roman citizenship, and, when occasion demanded, availed himself of his rights. When writing to the Philippians, who were members of a Roman colony, and therefore Roman citizens, Paul brings out that Christians are citizens of a heavenly commonwealth, and ought to live accordingly (Phil. 1:27; 3:20).   S.B.

CITY. In ancient times cities owed their origin not to organized manufacture, but to agriculture. When men left the pastoral life and settled down to the cultivation of the soil, they often found their cattle and crops endangered by wandering tribes of the desert; and it was to protect themselves from such enemies that they created first the village and then the city. Cities were built in areas where agriculture could be carried on, usually on the side of a mountain or the top of a hill, and where a sufficient supply of water was assured. The names of cities often indicate the feature that was determinative in the selection of the site. For example, the prefixes Beer, meaning "well," and En, meaning "spring," in such names as Beer-sheba and En-gedi, show that it was a local well or spring that determined the building of the city. Names like Ramah, Mizpah, and Gibeah (all from roots indicating height), which were very common in Palestine, indicate that a site on an elevation was preferred for a city. A ruling family sometimes gave its name to a city (Beth, meaning "house of").

Ancient farmers did not have their own farmsteads. At the end of a day's work they retired for the night to the village or city. Smaller villages sought the protection of nearby cities. That is the meaning of the expression "cities and their villages" and "cities and their daughters," in Numbers 21:25; 32:42; Josusha 15 and 19. In return for the protection offered against nomadic depredations, the cities received payment in service and produce. Sometimes a city was protected by a feudal lord around or near whose fortress the city was built. Often it depended entirely upon the strength of its walls and the bravery of its men.

The chief feature distinguishing a city from a village was that it had a wall (Lev. 25:29f). Walls 20 and 30 feet thick were not unusual. Sometimes it was also surrounded by a moat (Dan. 9:25, "wall" in KJV), and even by a second smaller wall acting as a rampart (II Sam. 20:15, "trench" in KJV). The wall had one or more gates which were closed during the night (Josh. 2:5,7), and in later times on the sabbath (Neh. 13:19). The gates were strengthened with iron or bronze bars and bolts (Deut. 3:5; Judg. 16:3), and had rooms overhead (II Sam. 18:24). From the roof of the wall or from a tower by the gate, a watchman was on the lookout for approaching danger (Jer. 6:17). The gates were approached by narrow roads easy to defend. From a distance, usually all that could be seen of a city was its walls, except possibly its inner stronghold.

Within the walls, the important features of a city were the Tower or Stronghold, the High Place, the Broad Place by the Gate, and the streets. The Tower was an inner fort protected by a garrison to which the inhabitants could flee when the outer walls were taken by an enemy. The people of Shechem tried unsuccessfully to hold out against Abimelech in such a tower (Judg. 9:49), and the king was afterwards killed by a stone thrown by a woman from the tower within the city of Thebez (Judg. 9:53). When David captured the stronghold of Zion, the whole city came into his possession (II Sam. 5:7). Sometimes towers abutted against the inside of the city wall.

The High Place was an important part of every Canaanite city and retained its place in Palestine to the time of Solomon's reign (I Sam. 9:12 ff). There sacrifices were offered and feasts held.

Originally they were on an elevation, but the term became the general one for any local sanctuary even when it was on level ground.

The Broad Place was an open area — not a square, but only a widening of the street, just inside the city gate, serving the purpose of social intercourse in general. It was the center of communal life. Here justice was administered, deliberative assemblies were held, news was exchanged, and business was transacted. Strangers in the city passed the night there if they had no friends in the city. It had a defensive value in time of war, as it permitted the concentration of forces in front of the city gate.

The streets in ancient cities were not laid out on any fixed plan. They were narrow, winding, unpaved alleys. The streets of Jerusalem were not paved until the time of Herod Agrippa II. Cities built on steep hillsides had streets on the roofs of houses. Streets were rarely cleaned and were unlighted. Certain streets were allocated to particular trades and guilds—for bakers, cheese-makers, gold smiths, etc.

Little is known about the way city government was administered. In Deuteronomy 16:18 and 19:12 mention is made of elders and judges. Samaria had a governor (I Kings 22:26). Jerusalem must have had several high officials (II Kings 23:8). S. B.

CITY OF DAVID. 1. The Jebusite stronghold of Zion captured by David, and named by him the city of David. It stood on a ridge near the later site of the temple. David made it his royal residence.

2. Bethlehem, the home of David (Luke 2:4).

CLAUDA (klô'dà), a small, unimportant island off the SW coast of Crete. Paul's ship was driven under its lee by a storm on his way to Rome (Acts 27:16).

CLAUDIA (klô'dĭ-à), a member of the Christian church at Rome, who, along with other members of that church, joined with Paul in sending Timothy greetings (II Tim. 4:21).

CLAUDIUS (klô'dĭ-ŭs), the fourth Roman emperor (41-54). He was nephew of Tiberius, the second Roman emperor. A weak, vacillating man, he was under the influence of unprincipled favorites and his wife Messalina. His second wife, Agrippina, poisoned him in 54. Herod Agrippa I, the grandson of Herod the Great, had assisted him much in his advancement of the throne, and in consequence was given the whole of Palestine. Claudius also gave to the Jews throughout the empire the right of religious worship, but later he banished all Jews from Rome (Acts 18:2; cf. Suet. *Claud.* 25). The famine foretold by Agabus took place in the reign of Claudius (Acts 11:28). Ancient writers say that from various causes his reign was a period of distress over the whole Mediterranean world.

CLAUDIUS LYSIAS (klô'dĭ-ŭs lĭs'ĭ-ăs), a chief captain who rescued Paul from fanatical Jewish rioters at Jerusalem (Acts 21:31; 24:22). He was a chiliarch (i.e. leader of 1,000 men), in charge of the Roman garrison at Jerusalem, stationed in the Castle of Antonia, adjoining the temple. When Paul informed him that he was a Roman citizen, and therefore could not legally be scourged, he told Paul that he had purchased his Roman citizenship with a great price. To protect Paul, he soon afterward sent him to Caesarea, to Felix, the Roman governor.

CLAY, a word that renders a number of different Hebrew words and one Greek word, and is frequently used in the Bible in a literal or metaphorical sense, in the latter sense meaning *dust* or *flesh* (as made from earth). Clay was widely used in OT times for the making of brick, mortar, and pottery, and, in some countries, for the making of tablets on which inscriptions were impressed. Mud bricks were not always made of true clay, but of mud mixed with straw. True clay was variable in composition, giving variety to quality and color, and thus was suited for different uses. As a building material, clay has been used from very ancient times. Babylon was made wholly of brick, either baked or dried in the sun. Nineveh, the capital of Assyria, was made mostly of brick. The villages of Egypt were constructed of sun-dried clay.

CLAY TABLETS. In ancient times writing was done on papyrus, parchment, potsherds, and clay tablets. Clay tablets were made of clean-washed, smooth clay. While still wet, the clay had wedge-shaped letters (now called "cuneiform" from the Latin *cuneus,* meaning "wedge") imprinted on it with a stylus, and then was kiln-fired or sun-dried. Tablets were made of various shapes — cone-shaped, drum-shaped, and flat. They were often placed in a clay envelope. Vast quantities have been excavated in the Near East. It is estimated that of those that have been found, about a half million are yet to be read, and that 99 per cent of the Babylonian tablets have yet to be dug. The oldest ones go back to 3,000 B.C. They are practically imperishable; fire only hardens them the more. Personal and business letters, legal documents, books, communications between rulers are represented. One of the most famous is the Code of Hammurabi, a Babylonian king who lived long before the time of Moses. They reveal intimate details of everyday life in the Near East and shed light on many obscure customs mentioned in the Old Testament. Some tell the story of the Creation, the Fall, and the Deluge. They do much to verify the truthfulness of the Biblical record. S.B.

CLEANTHES (klē-ăn'thēz), son of Phanius of Assos and head of the Stoic school from 263 to 232 B.C. He infused religious fervor into Zeno's Stoicism. He taught that the universe was a living being and God its soul. He taught disinterestedness in ethics, maintaining that doing good to gain advantage was like feeding cattle for meat. He taught, too, that evil thoughts were worse than evil deeds. His *Hymn to Zeus,* a surviving poem, contains the words quoted by Paul in Athens (Acts 17:28).

CLEMENT (klĕm'ĕnt), a Christian who labored with Paul at Philippi (Phil. 4:3). It is uncertain whether he was in Philippi when Paul wrote. Origen (Comm., John 1:29) identifies him with the church father who afterwards became bishop of Rome and wrote an epistle to the Corinthian church, but if he is right, Clement must have lived to an extreme old age.

CLEOPAS (klē'ō-pàs), one of the two disciples to whom the Lord appeared on the afternoon of the resurrection day. They walked with Him from Jerusalem to Emmaus, about seven miles away (Luke 24:18). Nothing more is known about him. He is not to be confused with the Cleophas mentioned in John 19:25, although some Christian fathers assumed that the two were identical.

CLEOPHAS (klē'ō-făs), mentioned in John 19:25 as the husband of Mary, one of the women who stood beside the cross, and is described as a sister of the mother of Jesus. He is not the same as the Cleopas who walked with Jesus to Emmaus (Luke 24:18).

CLERK (See Occupations, Professions)

CLOAK (See Dress)

CLOSET (Gr. *tameíon*), found in Matthew 6:6 and Luke 12:3, and referring most probably to a special store closet in which bedding was stored during the day. If required, it could also be used as a sleeping-room or for private conference. Our Lord advised that it be used for private prayer.

CLOTH, CLOTHES, CLOTHING (See Dress)

CLOUD. There are few references in the Bible to clouds having to do with actual weather conditions, the reason for this being that the weather in Palestine is not very varied. There were two recognized seasons, a rainy one from October to April, and one of sunshine from May to September. The Hebrews were not much given to making comments upon the weather. In Scripture there are, however, many references to clouds in a metaphoric and figurative sense. They symbolize transitoriness. God says Judah's goodness is like a morning cloud (Hosea 6:4), and Job compares his prosperity to the passing clouds (Job 30:15). Sometimes they are used as a type of refreshment, for they bring shade from the oppressive sun and give promise of rain. Clouds without water, therefore, symbolize a man who promises much but does not perform (Prov. 16:15; 25:14; Jude 12). The darkness of clouds is the symbol of mystery, especially that of creation (Job 3:5; 38:9; Ps. 97:2). Their distance from the earth is made to typify the unattainable (Isa.:14:14; Job 20:6; Ps. 147:8). One of the most frequent and suggestive uses of the figure is in connection with the presence of God. Clouds both veil and reveal the divine presence. Jehovah rides upon the cloud (Isa. 19:1; Nah. 1:3); He is present in the cloud (Exod. 19:9; 24:16; 34:5). The pillar of cloud symbolized God's presence and guidance to the children of Israel in their wilderness journeys (Exod. 40:36; Ps. 78:14). The cloud appears at our Lord's transfiguration (Matt. 17:5) and at His ascension (Acts 1:9), and it has a place in His prediction of His coming again (Matt. 24:30; 26:64). S.B.

CLOUD, PILLAR OF, was a symbol of the presence and guidance of God in the 40 years wilderness journey of the Israelites from Egypt to Canaan (Exod. 13:21,22). At night it became fire. When God wanted Israel to rest in any place, the cloud rested on the tabernacle above the mercy seat (Exod. 29:42,43) or at the door of the tabernacle (Exod. 33:9,10; Num. 12:5), or covered the tabernacle (Exod. 40:34-38).

CLOUT (See Dress)

CNIDUS (nī'dŭs), a city of Caria, at the SW corner of Asia Minor, past which Paul sailed on his journey to Rome (Acts 27:7). It was situated at the end of a long, narrow peninsula projecting between the islands Cos and Rhodes, and had two excellent harbors. It had the rank of a free city. Jews lived there as early as the second century B.C. Only ruins are left of a once flourishing city, especially noted for its temple of Venus and a statue of the goddess by Praxiteles.

COAL, often found in the English Bible, but it never has reference to true mineral coal, which has not been found in Palestine proper, where the geological formation as a whole is recent. Coal of a poor quality has been found at Sidon, and for a time some was mined at Lebanon. The half dozen Hebrew and Greek words rendered "coal" refer either to charcoal or to live embers of any kind. Charcoal was used by the Hebrews to provide warmth in winter (Isa. 47:14; John 18:18), for cooking (Isa. 44:19; John 21:9), and by the smith (Isa. 44:12; 54:16). It was made by covering a carefully stacked pile of wood with leaves and earth and then setting fire to it. After several days of burning and smoldering, the wood was converted into charcoal and the pile was opened.

In Psalm 120:4 there is mention of "coals of juniper," doubtless a kind of broom abundant in Judaea. In Isaiah 6:6 and I Kings 19:6 the Hebrew word denotes a hot stone (RVm). Frequently the word is used metaphorically. "As coals are to burning coals . . . so is a contentious man to kindle strife" (Prov. 26:21), means that quarrelsome men add fuel to a flame. In Proverbs 25:22 and Romans 12:20, where we are told to give to an enemy good in return for evil, for so coals of fire will be heaped upon his head, the coals of fire are not meant to suggest the pain of punishment to the guilty, but the softening of his heart as he thinks with burning shame of his unworthy hatred. Love will melt and purify. In Lamentations 4:8 the literal meaning of the Hebrew word translated "coal" is "blackness" (RVm). S.B.

COAT (See Dress)

COCK (See Birds)

COCKATRICE (See Animals)

COCK CROWING, when referring to time, is the third of the four watches into which the Romans divided the night: evening, midnight, cock crowing, morning. Cock crowing was between 12 and 3 a.m. (Matt. 26:34; Mark 13:35).

COCKLE (See Plants)

COELE SYRIA (sēl'ē-sēr'ĭ-à), in KJV Celosyria, Gr. *Koíle Syría, hollow Syria*), the name for that part of Syria that lay between the Lebanon and Anti-Lebanon Mountains, but it was often used to cover all the Syrian possessions as far S as Egypt and as for E as the Euphrates. The term frequently occurs in the OT Apocrypha.

COFFER (kŏf'ẽr), a word occurring only in I Samuel 6:8,11,15, and probably referring to a small box in which the Philistines put their golden mice and other offerings when they returned the Ark. The exact meaning of the term is obscure.

COFFIN, used only in Genesis 50:26. The literal meaning of the Hebrew word is "chest" or "box," but in this case may mean "mummy-case." Coffins were unknown among the Israelites, who were carried to the grave upon a bier, a simple flat board with two or three staves. In Egypt, where Joseph died, the dead were embalmed and put in a mummy-case.

COIN (See Money)

COL-HOZEH (kŏl-hō'zĕ, *all-seeing one*), a Judahite of Nehemiah's day whose son Shallum rebuilt the fountain gate of Jerusalem (Neh. 3:15; 11:5).

COLLEGE, a mistranslation of the Hebrew *mishneh* in the KJV of II Kings 22:14 and II Chronicles 34:22. The Hebrew word also appears in

Zephaniah 1:10, where it is correctly rendered "the second," and denotes the second quarter of the city of Jerusalem, which was not far from the Fish-Gate.

COLLOP (kŏl'ŭp, Heb. *pîmâh*), an old English word meaning a *slice of meat* or *fat*. It is used only in Job 15:27, where the wicked man is said to gather fat upon his loins.

COLONY (Gr. *kolonía*, a transliteration of the Latin *colonus, farmer*), in the only occurrence of the word in the NT, Acts 16:12, it says that Philippi was a colony. A colony was a settlement of Roman citizens, authorized by the government, in conquered territory. The settlers were usually retired Roman soldiers, settled in places where they could keep enemies of the empire in check. They were the aristocracy of the provincial towns where they lived. Such colonies had the rights of Italian cities: municipal self-government and exemption from poll and land taxes.

COLOSSAE (kŏ-lŏs'ē, Gr. *Kolossaí*), an ancient city of Phrygia, situated on the S bank of the Lycus river. It was about 11 miles from Laodicea and 13 from Hierapolis. Colossae stood on the most important trade route from Ephesus to the Euphrates, and was a place of great importance from early times. Xerxes visited it in 481 B.C., and Cyrus the Younger in 401 B.C. The city was particularly renowned for a peculiar wool, probably purple in color (*colossinus*). The church at Colossae was established on Paul's third missionary journey, during his three years in Ephesus, not by Paul himself (Col. 2:1), but by Epaphras (Col. 1: 7,12,13). Archippus also exercised a fruitful ministry there (Col. 4:17; Philem. 2). Philemon was an active member of this church, and also Onesimus (Col. 4:9). During Paul's first Roman imprisonment Epaphras brought to him a report of the religious views and practices in Colossae which called forth his epistle, in which he rebuked the church for its errors. Colossae lost its importance by the change of the road-system. Laodicea became the greater city. During the seventh and eighth centuries its openness exposed it to the terrible raids of the Saracens, and the people moved to Chonae (now called Chonas), a fortress upon the slope of Mt. Cadmus, about three miles farther south. In the 12th century the Turks destroyed the city. Archaeologists have unearthed ruins of the ancient church.   S.B.

COLOSSIANS, BOOK OF (kŏ-lŏsh'ănz), an epistle written by the Apostle Paul when he was a prisoner (Col. 4:3,10,18), about the year 62, probably during his first imprisonment in Rome (Acts 28:30, 31), although Caesarea (Acts 23:35; 24:27) and Ephesus have also been suggested. The external and internal evidence for its genuineness is all that can be desired. The church was very likely founded during Paul's three year stay in Ephesus on his third missionary journey. It appears from Colossians 2:1 that Paul himself had never preached in Colosse. Epaphras, a native of Colossae (Col. 4:12), was probably converted under Paul's ministry at Ephesus, and was then sent by the apostle to preach in his native city (Col. 1:7). He also appears to have evangelized the nearby cities of Laodicea and Hierapolis (Col. 4:13). At the time Paul wrote this epistle, the minister of the church at Colosse was Archippus (Col. 4:17), who may have been Philemon's son (Philem. 2). Epaphras had recently come to Paul with a dis-

turbing report of the condition of the church and this led Paul to the writing of the letter. The bearer of the letter was Tychicus (Col. 4:7,8), to whom Paul also intrusted the epistle to the Ephesians (Eph. 6:21), which was probably written at the same time. With him went Onesimus (Col. 4:9), a runaway slave converted by Paul, bearing Paul's letter to Philemon, a resident of Colossae, who was also one of Paul's converts, perhaps made at Ephesus.

In the few years since Paul had been in the province of Asia an insidious error had crept into the church at Colossae. Who the false teachers were we do not know; but it is clear that the trouble was different from that faced by Paul at Galatia, where Judaizers had tried to undermine his work. The teaching attacked by Paul is described in 2:8,16-23. It was, at least in part, Judaistic, as is seen in his reference to circumcision (2:11; 3:11), ordinances (2:14), meats and drinks, feast days, new moons, and sabbaths (2:16). There was also in it a strong ascetic element. Special self-denying rules were given (2:16, 20,21) which had as their purpose the mortification of the body (2:23). Some sort of worship of angels was practiced — a worship which continued for several centuries, as we know from the fact that in the fourth century the Council of Laodicea in one of its canons condemned it, and in the fifth century Theodoret said that the archangel Michael was worshiped in the area. This heresy claimed to be a philosophy, and made much of wisdom and knowledge (2:8). Plainly, the Colossians were beguiled by this religious syncretism and even took pride in it (2:8). The exact origin of this false teaching is unknown. Some find it in Essenism; others in incipient Gnosticism or in contemporary Judaism with a syncretistic admixture of local Phrygian ideas.

Paul met these errors, not by controversy of personal authority, but by presenting the counter truth that Jesus Christ is the image of the invisible God (1:15), in whom are hid all the treasures of wisdom and knowledge and in whom the fulness of the divine perfections find their perfect embodiment (1:19). He is the creator of all, and all power is from Him. On the cross He revealed the impotence of all the powers that had tried to thwart His purposes (2:15). Freedom from the corruption of human nature is found in the newness of life which the death and resurrection of Christ provide. The epistle may be divided into four parts: 1. The salutation and thanksgiving (1:1-8); 2. The doctrinal section (1:9-2:5); 3. Practical exhortations (2:6-4:6); 4. Concluding salutations 4:7-18). Towards the end of the epistle (4:16), Paul asks that the Colossian church exchange epistles with the church at Laodicea, to which he has also written. It is likely that this letter to the Laodiceans is our epistle to the Ephesians, sent as a circular letter to various churches in the Roman province of Asia.   S.B.

COMFORTER, THE (See Holy Spirit)

COMMANDMENT, used in the English Bible to translate a number of Hebrew and Greek words meaning law, ordinance, statute, word, judgment, precept, saying, charge, etc. The idea of authority conveyed by these words comes from the fact that God as sovereign Lord has a right to be obeyed. The instruction of Jesus is full of ethical teachings which have the force of divine command-

PLAIN OF THE LAW, Wady Er-Raha, at the foot of Mt. Sinai, from which Moses brought the Ten Commandments. The commandments, which constituted in part a ratification of the Israelites' covenant with God, are not to be confused with the elaborate system of law known as the Mosaic.

ments. What He says is as authoritative as what was said by Jehovah in OT times. That is true even when He does not use the word "commandment" or its equivalents, as He often does. But what is said of Jehovah and Jesus Christ is also true of the apostles. Paul, for example, does not hesitate to say, "the things that I write unto you are the commandments of the Lord" (I Cor. 14:37) The Bible makes it abundantly clear that God is not satisfied with mere external compliance with His commandments, but expects willing and joyful obedience, coming from the heart.

COMMANDMENTS, TEN The OT is distinctly a religion of law, with creed, cult, and conduct prescribed minutely by Jehovah. Judaism glories in the Torah (Rom. 9:4), the revelational instruction which has come to the elect nation as a gift of grace and which has come to it invested with divine authority and sanction. Torah is revered because it embodies the will and wisdom of the Creator. Expressing God's own nature, it demands of the creature only what the Creator's holiness necessitates for fellowship with Himself. The apex and quintessence of Torah is the Decalogue, the Code of the Ten Words, received by Moses on Mt. Sinai. That it is unique among the several Codes found in the OT can scarcely be disputed. Originally spoken by God in a context calculated to produce unforgettable awe (Exod. 19:9-25), it was afterward inscribed by His finger on two tables of stone (Exod. 31:18); in fact, it was inscribed by Him a second time after Moses in anger had shattered the first two tables (Deut. 10:1-4). It was placed in the Ark of the Covenant (Exod. 25:21) and thus enshrined at the very center of Israel's worship. All of its precepts, with the exception of sabbath-keeping, are repeated in the NT. Hence the Code of the Ten Words is indeed *sui generis,* a statement which gives the distillation of religion and morality: these principles, so simply phrased, are remarkably comprehensive and universally valid. Mt. Sinai, therefore, was the scene of an epochal event in human history; from a religious standpoint, only Mt. Calvary surpasses it.

Before examining this Code in any detail we must answer several questions concerning it. First, How explain the two somewhat dissimilar versions of it which the Pentateuch contains, one in Exodus 20:1-17, the other in Deuteronomy 5:6-21? In the Exodus version the Fourth Commandment grounds sabbath-keeping in God's sabbath-rest after His six days of creation; in the Deuteronomic version, however, sabbath-keeping is grounded in the Egyptian deliverance. Moreover, the two versions do not agree with respect to the Tenth Commandment, which forbids covetousness; different verbs are used and the order of clauses varies. But surely these are trivia which fade into nothingness when we remember that the Deuteronomic version is part of an address Moses delivered. In an oral recital one scarcely expects notarial precision. Not only so: Moses, because of the Spirit's guidance, was free to introduce new elements and slight changes.

Second, How are the Ten Words to be numbered? W. S. Bruce helpfully clears away the complexities of this question. "These commandments are not numbered by Moses, and consequently different schemes of arrangement have been common. The most ancient of these is that found in Josephus and in the writings of Philo. It is accepted by the Greek Church and by the Reformed Churches, and is that most commonly known among English-speaking communities. In it the preface is not made a commandment or part of one: but the first commandment simply forbids the worship of false deities, and the second prohibits the use of idols; while all the prohibitions of covetousness are included under the last command. Among the Fathers this division is supported by Origen. The Jews, on grounds that do not appear to be very trustworthy, regard the first commandment as containing only Exodus xx.2: 'I am the Lord thy God, which have brought thee out of the land of Egypt.' This they interpret as a command to believe in Jehovah as their God, because of His gracious deliveries of their forefathers from bondage. Then, to preserve the number ten, they include in one our first and second commandments; and they justify this by regarding the prohibition of images as an extension of the idea of the unity of God. On the other hand, the Roman and the Lutheran Churches reverse this order and include the first and second commandments in one; while to preserve the number ten, they divide the last commandment into two, thus combining two separate and dividing two similar things" (*The Ethics of the Old Testament*, Edinburgh: T. & T. Clark, 1909, pp. 101-102).

Third, How are the Ten Words to be divided between the two tables? The Roman Catholic Church puts three commandments on the first table, seven on the second. The Reformed Church adheres to a four and six classification. Josephus, however, gives the traditional five and five arrangement, the first table dealing, as he says, with piety, the second with probity. Taking Josephus as his guide, C. E. Luthardt in his *History of Christian Ethics* gives what seems to be the most satisfactory division:

First Table

1. No other gods.
2. No image of God.
3. No dishonouring of God's name.
4. No desecration of God's day.
5. No dishonouring of God's representatives (parents).

Second Table

1. No taking away of a neighbour's life.
2. No taking away of his wife — his home — his dearest good.
3. No taking away of his goods.
4. No taking away of his good name.
5. Nor even coveting of his good or his goods. (Quoted in Bruce, *op. cit.*, pp. 103-104).

Fourth, Is there any significance to the fact that the Ten Words are inscribed on two tables rather than one? Apparently so. The first table is devoted to the worship of God, the second to the service of man. We gather, accordingly that in OT thought a right relationship with God is essential for a right relationship with man. In other words, religion is the basis and dynamic of morality. Our Lord Jesus in His master-simplification of Torah (Matt. 22:37-40) teaches that love to God and love to man are the two all-inclusive imperatives; actually, love is the sole imperative since neighbor-love is derived from and sustained by our love for God.

Fifth, Is this Code merely negative or does it have a positive aspect as well? Admittedly, the only commandment couched in positive terms is the Fifth Law which enjoins respect for one's parents. But the seeming negativism of the Ten Words is only superficial. Whenever an evil is forbidden, the opposite good is implicitly demanded. Here we have far more than a forbidding: we have a requiring as well. So, as we have noticed, when Jesus interprets and epitomizes this Code, He reduces it to the positive virtue of love. Paul does

exactly the same thing in Romans 13:8-10. This Law cannot be fulfilled only by concern and care; it calls for loving obedience to God and loving service to man.

Sixth, Is this Code really to be viewed as "a yoke of bondage" (Gal. 5:1) or as a wise provision which God graciously made for His people? Undeniably in the course of the centuries rabbinic traditionalism perverted Torah into a grievous legalism; undeniably, too, the Law as a whole had a pedagogic function, revealing as it did — and still does — man's need of Jesus Christ (Rom. 7:7; Gal. 3:24). Yet the primary purpose of the Ten Words was to enable the Israelites, as Jehovah's redeemed and peculiar treasure, to enter into a life of joyful fellowship with their Redeemer. This Code issued from God's sovereign and saving relationship with His elect nation. It was imposed at His initiative and as the result of His covenantal activity. Passages like Exodus 20:2 and Deuteronomy 4:32-40 show that Israel's Saviour was Israel's Legislator. This Law, then, was designed to bring Jehovah's saving deed to its fulfillment by creating a holy community, a community reflecting His own nature, a community in which He could dwell and by which He could be magnified (Lev. 11:44; 20:8). Hence, used lawfully (I Tim. 1:8), this Code, which guided life rather than gave it, was a source of beatitude (Ps. 19:8-9; 119:54).

With these six questions answered, let us now analyze briefly each of the Ten Words. The First Commandment (Exod. 20:3) enjoins a confession of Jehovah's singularity, His absolute and exclusive deity. It predicates faith in Him as the one and only God. Though not expressly teaching monotheism, it inferentially denounces polytheism as treason and unbelief. It demonstrates that God is not a class term but a proper Name.

The Second Commandment (Exod. 20:4-6) enjoins the adoration of Jehovah's spirituality. Forbidding His worship by any false means, it rebukes the gross idolatry which surrounded Israel. It shows that because of His very Being (John 4:24) no visible or material representation of true Deity is possible. Thus it prevents wrong concepts of God from taking root in man's mind (Rom. 1:21-23).

The Third Commandment (Exod. 20-7) enjoins the reverence of Jehovah's Name. Since in the OT name and person are equivalent, with the name practically a reification of the person, this Law prohibits blasphemy and profanity. It also interdicts immorality, any conduct which causes God's honour to suffer defilement by the sinner who bears His Name (Rom. 2:24-25). With respect to the sacredness and significance of God's Name, Malachi 3:16-17 is instructive.

The Fourth Commandment (Exod. 20:8-11) enjoins the observance of Jehovah's day. For both humanitarian (Amos 8:5-6) and religious (Isa. 58:13-14) reasons, one day of rest in every seven is a blessed necessity. A sabbath — whether on Saturday as commemorating a finished creation or on Sunday as commemorating a finished redemption — serves man's physical and spiritual welfare simultaneously (Mark 2:27).

The Fifth Commandment (Exod. 20:12) enjoins the honor of God's surrogates, parents to whom He grants a kind of co-creatorship in the begetting of children and to whom He grants a kind of co-rulership in the governing of children. Let any nation abandon respect for the mystery, dignity, and authority of parenthood, and before long the moral fibre and social fabric of that nation are bound to disintegrate. That is why the OT statutes on this score are so severe (Exod. 21: 15; Deut. 27:16; Prov. 20:20).

The Sixth Commandment (Exod. 20:13) is a prohibition of murder. A man's life is, patently, his one utterly indispensable possession; but, more than that, man is God's image-bearer, and murder wantonly destroy's God's image. Hence capital punishment is the penalty affixed to a breaking of this law (Gen. 9:5-6).

The Seventh Commandment (Exod. 20:14) is a prohibition of adultery, a stringent prohibition which safeguards the sanctity of marriage and throws a bulwark around the home. In our day we are beginning to see what happens when the home is undermined by marital infidelity.

The Eighth Commandment (Exod. 20:15) is a prohibition of theft in any and all forms. Property is essentially an extension of a man's personality, and thus this law indicates that the rights and achievements of one's neighbor must not be ignored.

The Ninth Commandment (Exod. 20:16) is a prohibition of falsehood in its many varieties, whether perjury, slander, or defamation. Truth is the cement of community, the *sine qua non* of enduring interpersonal relationships on every level. Consequently, the OT like the NT stresses the need for a sanctified tongue (Ps. 5:9; 15:1-4; Prov. 18:21; Jer. 9:1-5).

The Tenth Commandment (Exod. 20:17) is a prohibition of covetousness, and as such reveals that the Ten Words are not simply a civil code, but form a moral and spiritual code which strikes beneath the surface of the overt act (and the overt act is the exclusive province of civil law), tracing evil conduct to evil desire, probing the hidden motives of men (and motive is the province of morality and religion, God's province). This Tenth Commandment, therefore, highlights the pivotal importance of wrong appetites and intentions; it agrees with Paul that covetousness is idolatry (Col. 3:5), since inordinate craving means that man's ego has become man's god.

Except as the NT deepens and extends its principles, the Decalogue represents the high-water level of morality.   V.C.G.

COMPEL, in English, suggests the idea of force, though not necessarily physical. When Jesus, in Luke 14:23, says "compel them to come in," He means that Christians should use the utmost zeal and moral urgency to get people to enter the kingdom of God.

CONANIAH (kŏn'à-nī'à, Heb. *kônanyāhû, Jehovah has founded,* in KJV twice *Cononiah.* 1. A Levite in charge of tithes and offerings in the reign of Hezekiah (II Chron. 31:12,13).

2. A Levite in Josiah's reign (II Chron. 35:9).

CONCISION (kŏn-sĭzh'ŭn, Gr. *katatomé, mutilation, cutting*), a term used only once in the Bible, in Philippians 3:2, to designate circumcision that is wholly ceremonial and without regard for its spiritual significance. Paul distinguishes it from true circumcision (verse 3).

CONCUBINE, in the Bible, not a paramour, but a woman lawfully united in marriage to a man in a relation inferior to that of the regular wife. No moral stigma was attached to being a concubine. It was a natural part of a polygamous social system. Concubinage is assumed and provided for in

the law of Moses, which tried to prevent its excesses and abuses (Exod. 21:7-11; Deut. 21:10-14). Concubines were commonly taken from among Hebrew or foreign slave girls, or Gentile captives taken in war, although free Hebrew women might also become concubines. They enjoyed no other right but lawful cohabitation. They had no authority in the family or in household affairs. Their husbands could send them away with a small present, and their children could, by means of small presents, be excluded from the heritage (Gen. 25:6). The children were regarded as legitimate, although the children of the first wife were preferred in the distribution of the inheritance. In patriarchal times, at least, the immediate cause of concubinage was the barrenness of the lawful wife, who herself suggested that her husband have children by her maid-servant (Gen. 16 and 30). Prominent OT figures' who had concubines were Nahor (Gen. 22:24), Abraham (Gen. 25:6), Jacob (Gen. 35:22), Eliphaz (Gen. 36:12), Gideon (Judg. 8:31), Saul (II Sam. 3:7), David (II Sam. 5:13; 15:16; 16:21), Solomon (I Kings 11:3), Caleb (I Chron. 2:46), Manasseh (I Chron. 7:14), Rehoboam (II Chron. 11:21), Abijah (II Chron. 13:21), and Belshazzar (Dan. 5:2).   S.B.

CONCUPISCENCE (kŏn-kū'pĭ-sĕns, Gr. *epithumía*), a word meaning intense longing or yearning for what God would not have us to have or be. It does not refer to sexual desire only. (Rom. 7:8; Col. 3:5; I Thess. 4:5).

CONDUIT (kŏn'dū ĭt), a channel, either cut out of solid rock or made of masonry, for conveying water from its source to the place where it was delivered. It was covered with stones to keep the water pure and cool. Conduits were used to deliver water to towns or for purposes of irrigation. One of the oldest in Palestine was about 13½ miles long and brought water from the Pools of Solomon, beyond Bethlehem, to the temple in Jerusalem. Tradition ascribes its construction to Solomon. Hezekiah constructed a conduit in anticipation of Sennacherib's invasion (II Kings 20:20). Other conduits mentioned in the Bible are one where Isaiah was commanded to meet Ahaz (Isa. 7:3), and beside which the messengers of Sennacherib stood when they spoke to the people on the wall (II Kings 18:17; Isa. 36:2), and another referred to in II Chronicles 32:30.

CONFECTION, found only in Exodus 30:35, it refers to a compound of perfume or medicine, not sweetmeats.

CONFECTIONARY, a perfumer; found only in I Samuel 8:13. RVm has "perfumers."

CONFECTIONER (See Occupations, Professions)

CONFESSION (Heb. *yādhâh,* Gr. *homologéo,* and their derivatives). Both the Hebrew and Greek words are capable of the same twofold meaning as the English. To confess is openly to acknowledge one's faith in anything, as in the existence and authority of God, or the sins of which one has been guilty. Occasionally it also means to concede or allow (John 1:20; Acts 24:14; Heb. 11:13), or to praise God by thankfully acknowledging Him (Rom. 14:11; Heb. 13:15). In the Bible confession of sin before God is recognized as a condition of forgiveness. Christ taught the necessity of confessing offenses committed against other men (Matt. 5:24; Luke 17:4). The Bible gives no instruction about the mode of confession.

CONGREGATION (Heb. *'ēdhâh* and *qāhāl,* Gr. *ekklesía* and *sunagogé*), a word used in Scripture mainly to refer to the Hebrew people; in its collective capacity regarded as God's people, or as an assembly of the people summoned for a definite purpose (I Kings 8:65) or met on a festal occasion (Deut. 23:1). Sometimes it refers to an assembly of the whole people; sometimes, to any part of the people who might be present on a given occasion. Occasionally it conveys the idea of "horde." Every circumcised Hebrew was a member of the congregation and took part in its proceedings probably from the time he bore arms. He had, however, no political rights as an individual, but only as a member of a house, a family, or a tribe, which was usually represented by its head, known as an elder or a prince. The elders, summoned by the supreme governor or the high priest, represented the whole congregation, served as a national parliament, and had legislative and judicial powers. They sat as a court to deal with capital offenses (Num. 15:32, 33), declared war, made peace, and concluded treaties (Josh. 9:15). The people were strictly bound by their acts, whether they approved of them or not (Josh. 9:18). Occasionally the whole body of people was assembled for some solemn religious occasion (Exod. 12:47; Num. 25:6; Joel 2:15) or to receive some new commandments (Exod. 19:7,8; Lev. 8:4). After the conquest of Canaan, the congregation was assembled only to consider very important matters.   S.B.

CONIAH (kō-nī′a, Heb. *konyāhû, Jehovah is creating*). A form of the name Jehoiachin, found in Jeremiah 22:24,28; 37:1. See JEHOIACHIN.

CONSCIENCE (Gr. *syneídesis*), a word is not found in the OT, but the idea frequently appears, as when Adam and Eve hide from God (Gen. 3:8) and Joseph's brothers confess their guilt regarding him (Gen. 42:21). In ancient religion and philosophy the word seldom appeared in its modern meaning of the moral sense of the individual applied to his conduct, but it was never thought of as having any religious connection. Jesus never used the word.

In the NT outside of Paul's epistles, where it is found with fair frequency, it is used only in Acts (in speeches by Paul) and in Hebrews and I Peter. Nowhere in the NT is there a clearly defined doctrine of conscience, or even a description of it. The most illuminating passage in the NT on the nature of conscience is Romans 2:14,15, where Paul declares that all men, both Gentiles and Jews, are responsible for their actions before God, because all have a revelation of God's moral law as their standard for right living, the Jews in the law of Moses, and the Gentiles in the law written on their hearts. Heathen Gentiles, moreover, know that they ought to obey it, for their conscience tells them to. I Corinthians 8-10 is the passage where "conscience" occurs most often. There Paul says that the Christian whose conscience allows him to eat meat offered to idols has no right to disregard the conscience of a less well-instructed Christian brother who thinks it wrong to eat it (I Cor. 8:7,12), or the ignorant conscience of a heathen (I Cor. 10:27). In II Corinthians 4:2 and 5:11 he applies the word "conscience" to the approval of his conduct by others. Repeatedly, Paul, Peter, and the author of Hebrews stress the need of having a good conscience toward God. Hebrews, which emphasizes the effects of the atonement on the individual, declares that the OT sacrifices did not produce a conscience free from the sense of guilt, because only the blood of Christ can do that.   S.B.

CONSECRATION, an act by which a person or thing is dedicated to the service and worship of God. It is the translation of several Hebrew and Greek words of different meanings. 1. Heb. *hāram,* "devote"; "I will consecrate ("devote") their gain unto the Lord" (Micah 4:13). 2. Heb. *nāzar, nēzer,* "separate" (Num. 6:7,9,12). 3. Heb. *qādhēsh,* "to be set apart," i.e., set apart from that which is common or unclean (Exod. 28:3; 30:30; Josh. 6:19; II Chron. 26:18; 29:33; 31:6; Ezra 3:5). 4. Heb. *millē′ yadh,* lit. "to fill the hand," a peculiar idiom usually used for the installation of a priest into his office or of the installation offerings put into his hands (Exod. 28:41; 29:9; 29:29; Lev. 8:33). 5. Gr. *teleióo,* "to make perfect" Heb. 10:20).

CONVERSATION, a word often used in the KJV to render various terms signifying conduct or manner of life, especially with respect to morals. The Greek words rendered "conversation" in Philippians 1:27 and 3:20 refer to "civil life" or "citizenship." Paul means that we should live like citizens of heaven.

CONVERSION (kŏn-vêr′zhŭn, Heb. *shûv,* Gr. *epistrophé*), occurs only once in the Bible (Acts 15:3). The words commonly used in the English Bible as equivalent with the Hebrew and Greek words are "turn," "return," and "turn back," "turn again." Thus "conversion" is synonymous with "turning." The turning may be in a literal or in a figurative, ethical or religious, sense, either from God, or, more frequently, to God. It is to be noted that when the turning refers to a definite spiritual change, it almost invariably denotes an act of man: "Turn ye, turn ye from your evil ways (Ezek. 33:11); "Except ye turn" (Matt. 18:3). Since the word implies both a turning *from* and a turning *to* something, it is not surprising that in the NT it is sometimes associated with repentance (Acts 3:19; 26:20) and faith (Acts 11:21). That is, conversion on its negative side is turning from sin, and on its positive side is faith in Christ, "Repentance toward God, and faith toward our Lord Jesus Christ" (Acts 20:21) expresses the content of the idea, although the word turning is not found in the verse. Although conversion is an act of man, Scripture makes clear that it has a divine ground. The turning of sinful man is done by the power of God (Acts 3:26). In the process of salvation, conversion is the first step in the transition from sin to God. It is brought about by the Holy Spirit operating upon the human mind and will, so that the course of man's life is changed. It is not the same as justification and regeneration, which are purely divine acts. It may come as a sudden crisis or as a process more or less prolonged.

CONVICTION (kŏn-vĭk′shŭn, Gr. *elégcho, to convince* or *prove guilty*). Conviction is the first stage of repentance, experienced when in some way the evil nature of sin has been brought home to the penitent, and it has been proved to him that he is guilty of it. Although the word "conviction" is never used in the KJV, both Testaments give many illustrations of the experience. In the OT one of the most notable is found in Psalm 51, where David, realizing he has sinned against God, is overwhelmed with sorrow for his transgression and cries out to God for forgiveness and cleansing. In the NT the central passage bearing on this theme is John 16:7-11, where Jesus says that when the Holy Spirit comes "He will reprove the world of sin, and of righteousness, and of judgment." Here the word "reprove" means "convince" or "prove guilty." The thought is that the Holy Spirit addresses the heart of the guilty and shows how inadequate ordinary standards of righteousness are. The purpose of conviction is to lead to godly repentance.   S.B.

CONVOCATION (kŏn-vō-kā'shŭn, Heb. *mikrā'*), used in the expression "Holy Convocation," but it is sometimes used alone (Num. 10:2; Isa. 1:13; 4:5). A convocation was a religious festival during which no work could be done. The holy convocations were the sabbath days (Lev. 23:1-3), Pentecost (Lev. 23:15-21), the first and seventh days of the feast of unleavened bread (Exod. 12:16; Lev. 23:6,7), the first and tenth days of the seventh month, the latter being the great day of atonement (Lev. 23:24-28), and the first and eighth days of the Feast of Tabernacles (Lev. 23:34-36). The phrase "solemn assembly" is applied only to the concluding festivals at the end of Passover and Tabernacles.

COOS (Kō'ôs, Gr. *Kós, summit*), a long, narrow island off the coast of Caria in S Asia Minor, mentioned in connection with Paul's third missionary journey in Acts 21:1. It was the birthplace of Hippocrates (the father of medicine), the famous painter Appelles, and Ptolemy Philadelphus.

COPING (kōp'ĭng), a word used only in I Kings 7:9 and probably referring to the customary parapets on Oriental house roofs, which were always flat.

COPPERSMITH (kŏp'êr-smĭth, Gr. *chalkeús*), found in the NT only in II Timothy 4:14: "Alexander the coppersmith did me much evil." The word should be rendered "worker in brass."

COR (See Weights & Measures)

CORAL (kŏr'ăl, Heb. *rā'môth*), the Hebrew word, the meaning of which is not entirely certain, is twice rendered "coral" (Job. 28:18; Ezek. 27:16), and, once, "too high" (Prov. 24:7). Red coral, which is the calcareous skeleton of a branching colony of polyps, was highly prized in ancient times, and was obtained in the Mediterranean and Adriatic seas at various depths down to about 100 fathoms. It differs much from the white coral which forms coral reefs. It was made into beads and charms.

CORBAN (kôr'băn, Heb. *qorbān, an offering*), occurs in the Hebrew text of the OT and refers to an offering or sacrifice, whether bloody or unbloody, made to God (Lev. 1:2,3; 2:1; 3:1; Num. 7:12-17). It is found in the NT in Mark 7:11, where it has reference to money dedicated to God. The Talmud says that the Jews were much given to making rash vows to God, without any intention of carrying them out. By Christ's time the reprehensible practice arose of children avoiding the responsibility of looking after their parents' material needs by telling them that their money was dedicated to God and that it would be wrong to divert it from this sacred purpose. This could be done by simply pronouncing the votive word "Corban." Ideally, the money thereafter belonged to God, but actually the one who made the vow might keep it in his possession. By referring to this custom Christ demonstrated the sophistry of tradition which enabled the Jews to disregard plain commandments of God, like the one requiring children to honor their parents.

CORD (kôrd, Heb. *hevel, yether, mêthār,* Gr. *schoiníon*). Throughout the East in ancient times ropes and cords were made of goat's or camel's hair spun into threads and then plaited or twisted into the larger and stronger form. Sometimes they were made of strips of skin from goats and cows twisted together. Ropes for temporary fastenings were sometimes made from vines twisted together, and also from the bark of the branches of the mulberry tree. Frequently the word is used in a figurative sense in the Bible. Thus Job speaks of being "holden in cords of affliction" (Job 36:8), and Solomon says that the wicked "shall be holden with the cords of his sins" (Prov. 5:22). Other illustrations of this figurative use are Psalm 2:3; 129:4; 140:5; Ecclesiastes 4:12; Isaiah 5:18; 54:2.

CORIANDER (See Plants)

CORINTH (kôr'ĭnth, Gr. *Kórinthos, ornament*), a city of Greece on the narrow isthmus between the Peloponnesus and the mainland. Under the Romans, Athens was still the educational center of Greece, but Corinth was the capital of the Roman province called by them Achaia, and the most important city in the country. Land traffic between the N and S of Achaia had to pass the city, and much of the commerce between Rome and the East was brought to its harbors.

Corinth occupied a strategic geographical position. It was situated at the southern extremity of the isthmus, at the northern foot of the lofty (2000 ft.) and impregnable Acrocorinthus, which commands a wonderful view over the Saronic Gulf on the E and the Corinthian Gulf on the W, as well as over central Greece and the Peloponnesus. From the Acrocorinthus it is possible on a clear day to see the Acropolis of Athens 40 miles away. Corinth had three harbors: Lechaem, 1½ miles to the W, Cenchreae, 8½ miles to the E, and Schoenus, also to the E, but much less used than Cenchrea. Lechaeum was connected with Corinth by a double row of walls. Because of its highly-favored commercial position, in ancient times the city was known as "two-sea'd Corinth."

Ancient sailors dreaded making the voyage round the southern capes of the Peloponnesus, and this, as well as the saving of time effected, caused many of the smaller ships and their cargoes to be hauled across the narrow isthmus on a track. Sometimes the cargo of large ships was removed at the harbor, carried across the isthmus, and then loaded on another ship on the other side. Several attempts were made in ancient times to cut a ship-canal across the isthmus, notably one by Nero about A.D. 66, but none was successful. One was opened in 1893, and is now in use.

Corinth had an ancient and very interesting history. Phoenician settlers were early attracted to it. They introduced many profitable manufactures and established the impure worship of the Phoenician deities. Later, Greeks from Attica became supreme. They probably changed the name of the city to Corinth, and glorified the games held there in honor of Poseidon, the god of the sea. About 1074 B.C. the Dorians conquered the city. After the invention of triremes, about 585 B.C., a series of important colonies was founded, and Corinth became a strong maritime force. The city was lukewarm in the Persian wars, and opposed Athens in the Peloponnesian war. Except for a brief period, the Macedonians held the city from 335-197 B.C. The Romans declared Greece and Corinth free in 196 B.C., but in 146 B.C., in consequence of a rebellion against Rome, the city was totally destroyed by the Roman consul Mummius, and its famous art treasures taken as spoil to Rome. Julius Caesar rebuilt it as a Roman colony and made it the capital of Achaia in 46 B.C., and after that it rapidly came into prominence again. The Goths raided it in the third and fourth centuries; the Normans sacked it in 1147; the Venetians and Turks held it in the Middle Ages; from 1715 until 1822 it remained with the Turks. A severe earthquake in 1858 caused the abandonment of the city and the building of a new town a few miles from the ancient site. Modern Corinth has a population of about 9000 people. Until, in recent times, archæologists began excavating the ancient city, nothing marked its site except seven columns of an old Doric temple.

In Roman times Corinth was a city of wealth, luxury, and immorality. It had no rivals as a city of vice. "To live like a Corinthian" meant to live a life of profligacy and debauchery. It was customary in a stage play for a Corinthian to come on the scene drunk. The inhabitants were naturally devoted to the worship of Poseidon, since they drew so much of their wealth from the sea, but their greatest devotion was given to Aphrodite, the goddess of love. Her temple on the Acrocorinthus had more than a thousand *hierodouloi*—priestesses of vice not found in other shrines of Greece, and she attracted worshipers from all over the ancient world. Besides drawing vast revenues from the sea, Corinth had many important industries, its pottery and brass, especially, being famous all over the world. The Isthmian games, held every two years, made Corinth a great center of Hellenic life.

At the height of its power, Corinth probably had a free population of 200,000, plus a half million slaves. Its residents consisted of the descendants of the Roman colonists who were established there in 46 B.C., many Romans who came for business, a large Greek population, and many strangers of different nationalities attracted to the city for various reasons. In the last group was a considerable body of Jews, and also some Gentiles brought under the influence of Judaism because of its monotheism and lofty morality.

Paul visited Corinth for the first time on his second missionary journey (Acts 18). He had just come from Athens, where he had not been well-received, and he began his work in Corinth with a sense of weakness, fear, and trembling (I Cor. 2:3). A special revelation from the Lord in a night vision altered his plans to return to Thessalonica (Acts 18:9,10; I Thess. 2:17,18), and he was told to speak freely and boldly in the city. At his first arrival, he became acquainted with Aquila and Priscilla, fellow Christians and, like himself, tent-makers. During his stay of a year and a half he resided in their home. He labored with his own hands, so that his motives as a preacher would be above suspicion. Soon after his arrival, Silas and Timothy rejoined him, Timothy bringing news from the church at Thessalonica (I Thess. 3:6).

Every sabbath Paul preached in the synagogue, but before long he met with strong opposition from the Jews, so that he turned from them and for the rest of his stay in Corinth gave his attention to the Gentiles (Acts 18:6). He was then offered the use of the house of Titus Justus, a God-fearing Gentile, who lived next door to the synagogue. Many turned to Christ and were baptized as a result of Paul's preaching, among them Crispus, the ruler of the synagogue, and all his house. None of the baptisms in Corinth were performed by Paul himself, except those of Crispus, Gaius (Paul's host on his later visit (Rom. 16:23), and the household of Stephanas, who were Paul's first converts (I Cor. 16:15).

During Paul's stay in Corinth, Gallio, the elder brother of the Roman philosopher, Seneca, came to govern Achaia as proconsul. This was about the year 51, as an inscription found at Delphi in 1908 shows. The Jews brought an accusation before him against Paul, charging that he was preaching a religion contrary to Roman law. Gallio, however, refused to admit the case to trial and dismissed them. It is evident that he looked upon Christianity as being only an obscure variety of Judaism and that to him the quarrel between the Jews and Paul had its origin in nothing more than differing interpretations of the Jewish law. Following Gallio's decision, the Greek bystanders vented their animus against the Jews by seizing and beating Sosthenes, the ruler of the synagogue, and Gallio paid no attention to them. Gallio's action was highly important, for it practically amounted to an authoritative decision by a highly-placed Roman official that Paul's preaching could not be interpreted as an offense against Roman law; and from this experience Paul gained a new idea of the protection the Roman law afforded him as a preacher of the Gospel. After many days, Paul left Corinth to go to Jerusalem and Antioch, on his way stopping off briefly at Ephesus.

Luke tells little of the subsequent history of the church at Corinth. Apollos, a convert of Aquila and Priscilla at Ephesus, was sent from Ephesus with a letter of recommendation, and he exercised an influential ministry in Corinth (Acts 18:27,28; I Cor. 1:12). There is evidence that during Paul's stay in Ephesus on his third missionary journey he paid a brief visit to Corinth (II Cor. 12:14; 13:1), although some hold that he did this later from Macedonia. While at Ephesus he wrote a letter to Corinth which has not been preserved (I Cor. 5:9). A reply to this, asking advice on important problems facing the church, and an oral report brought to him that all was not well in the church, led to his writing I Corinthians. This was probably sent by the hands of Titus: at least he was sent to Corinth by Paul about this time (II Cor. 7:13). Timothy was also sent to Corinth on some mission (I Cor. 4:17). After the silversmiths' riot at Ephesus, Paul went to Troas, hoping to meet Titus there with news from Corinth, but he was disappointed and went on to Macedonia, where he did meet him. On getting a largely favorable report, Paul wrote II Corinthians, and probably sent Titus to deliver it. After some time in Macedonia, Paul went to Greece, spending three months there (Acts 20: 2,3), chiefly, no doubt, in Corinth. On Paul's third missionary journey he had been much occupied with getting offerings of money for the poor Christians in Jerusalem from the various churches he had founded. The Corinthian church responded to this appeal generously (II Cor. 9:2-5). It was during this visit to Corinth that Paul wrote his Epistle to the Romans (Rom. 16:23). Whether he ever returned to the city is unknown.

About the year 97, Clement of Rome wrote an epistle, which survives, to the church at Corinth. It shows that in his time the Christians there were still vexed by divisions. S.B.

CORINTHIANS (kô-rĭn'thĭ-ănz), First and Second Epistles. The First Epistle to the Corinthians was written by the Apostle Paul in Ephesus on his third missionary journey (Acts 19; I Cor. 16: 8,19), probably in 56 or 57. He had previously written a letter to the Corinthians which has not come down to us, in which he had warned against associating with immoral persons (I Cor. 5:9); and in reply had received a letter, (alluded to several times in I Corinthians 5:10; 7:1; 8:1), in which they declared it was impossible to follow his advice without going out of the world altogether, and submitted to him a number of problems on which they asked his opinion. This letter from Corinth was probably brought by three of their number, Stephanas, Fortunatus, and Achaicus (I Cor. 16:17), who came to visit Paul at Ephesus, and undoubtedly told him about the condition of the church. Meanwhile, Paul had heard of factions in the church from the servants of Chloe (1:11), probably from Corinth, and this news caused him much pain and anxiety. It was these various circumstances that led to the writing of I Corinthians.

The following are the subjects discussed in the epistle, after the introductory salutation (I Cor. 1:1-9):

1. In the first four chapters the apostle takes up the reported factionalism in the church, and points out the danger and scandal of party spirit. He reminds them that Christ alone is their Master, their Christian teachers being only servants of Christ and fellow-workers with God.

2. In chapter 5 the apostle deals with a case of incestuous marriage, and prescribes that the offender be put out of the church so that his soul may be saved.

3. In chapter 6 Paul comes to their practice of bringing disputes between themselves before heathen judges for litigation, and shows that this is morally wrong and out of harmony with the spirit of love by which they as Christians should be animated.

4. Various phases of the subject of marriage are considered in chapter 7. While commending a celibate life, Paul holds marriage to be wise and honorable. He forbids divorce between Christians and separation of Christians married to heathen partners.

5. The eating of meat offered to idols was a problem of conscience to many Christians, and ch. 8-10 are devoted to it. Paul points out (ch. 8) that while there is nothing inherently wrong in a Christian's eating such food, the law of love requires that it be avoided if it will offend another who regards the eating of it as sin. In ch. 9 he illustrates this principle of self-control in his own life; lest his motives in preaching the Gospel be misunderstood, he refuses to exercise his undoubted right of looking for material aid from the church. In ch. 10 he warns against a spirit of self-confidence and urges them to be careful not to seem to countenance idolatry.

6. Paul next takes up certain abuses in public worship: first, the matter of appropriate head apparel for women in their assemblies (11:2-16), and then the proper observance of the Lord's Supper (11:17-34), in the administration of which there had been serious abuses.

7. There then follows a long discussion of the use and abuse of spiritual gifts, especially speaking in tongues (chs. 12-14), and the apostle, while commending the careful exercise of all the gifts, bids them cultivate above all God's greatest gift, love (chs. 13).

8. In ch. 15 Paul turns to a consideration of one of the most important of their troubles — the resurrection of the dead, which some were inclined to doubt. He meets the objections raised against the doctrine by showing that it is necessitated by the resurrection of Christ and that their salvation is inseparably connected with it.

9. The epistle concludes with directions about the collections being made for the saints in Jerusalem, the Mother-Church, and with comments about Paul's plans and personal messages to various of his friends.

The Second Epistle to the Corinthians was written by Paul on his third missionary journey somewhere in Macedonia, where he had just met Titus, who had brought him a report concerning the church at Corinth.

The epistle reveals that Judaising teachers — perhaps recently arrived from Jerusalem — had sought to discredit the apostle, and had succeeded in turning the church as a whole against him. Paul was denounced as no minister of Christ at all. This revolt caused Paul to make a brief visit to Corinth in order to restore his authority (II Cor. 12:14; 13:1,2), but the visit did not have its expected effect.

The report Titus brought Paul was, on the whole, most encouraging. The majority had repented of their treatment of Paul and had cast out of the church the man who had led the attack on him. Paul's authority was acknowledged once more. Titus seems to have helped greatly in bringing about this happy change. It was the report of Titus that chiefly occasioned the writing of this epistle.

Paul's mention of a severe letter which had caused him great sorrow of heart to write (2:3,4, 9; 7:8-12) has naturally caused scholars to wonder what he had in mind. Some think he refers to I Corinthians; others hold that this letter, like the one referred to in I Corinthians 5:9, is wholly lost; while still others believe that it is preserved in II Corinthians 10-13, which, they say, was written by Paul at Ephesus sometime after the writing of I Corinthians.

II Corinthians is the least methodical and the most personal of Paul's epistles. It is very autobiographical, and falls naturally into three main divisions:

1. In chs. 1-7 Paul, after giving thanks to God for his goodness to him in trial (1:1-11), gives some thoughts on the crisis through which the church has just passed. 2. In chs. 8 and 9 he treats of the collection for the poor in Jerusalem. 3. Chs. 10-13 are a defense of Paul's ministry against the attacks of his enemies and a vindication of his apostleship. S.B.

CORNELIUS (kôr-nēl'yŭs, Gr. *Kornélios, of a horn*), a name of ancient and honorable standing among the Romans. Before the NT age, it was borne by such distinguished families as the Scipios and Sulla. He was a centurion of the Italian cohort. While being stationed at Caesarea, in obedience to instructions received in a vision, he sent for Simon Peter, who was staying at Joppa, to learn from him the message whereby he and his household should be saved (Acts 11:14).

As to his moral character, he is described as *díkaios kaì phoboúmenos*, "upright and god-fearing." His exact religious status prior to Peter's visit is ambiguous, but the likelihood is that Cornelius was a pious Roman, who, disillusioned by polytheism and disappointed by philosophy, had gravitated spiritually towards Judaism, and was now a "proselyte of the Gate" (Acts 11:2). Any doubts that Peter was acting improperly by sharing the message with this first Gentile convert are obviated by the twofold consideration of Peter's preparatory vision (10:9-16) and the subsequent outpouring of the Holy Spirit upon Cornelius' household (Acts 10:44-47). On these grounds, Peter defended his conduct before his critics at Jerusalem (Acts 11:1-18).   J.F.G.

CORNERSTONE (Heb. *pinnâh, akrogoniaíos*), a term that has both a literal and figurative use in Scripture but is usually used figuratively (Ps. 118: 22; Job 38:6; Isa. 28:16; Zech. 10:4, etc.). Among the Canaanites, before the conquest of the land of Joshua, the laying of the foundation stone was accompanied by the dreadful rite of human sacrifice. Numerous skeletons have been unearthed, especially those of tiny babies in earthen jars.

Following rabbinical practice, which understood the term "cornerstone" in a Messianic context, the Synoptics validate the claim of Jesus of Nazareth to Messiahship by citation of Psalm 118:22 (Matt. 21:42; Mark 12:10; Luke 20-17). In a similar fashion must be understood the Pauline and Petrine usage of the word (see Rom. 9:33, quoting Isa. 28:16 and 8:14, following LXX; also Eph. 2:20 et. al., I Peter 2:6, etc.).   J.F.G.

CORNET (Heb. *shôphār, qeren*). The musical instruments mentioned in the OT fall into three groups: the stringed, the percussion, and the wind. The instrument known as the "cornet" is to be found in the last class. It was a curved horn, the sound being a dull monotone. Some translators have understood the term to imply a musical instrument akin to the bagpipe or oboe (I Chron. 15:28; Ps. 98:6; Dan. 3:5,10,15; Hos. 5:8).

COS, COOS (kŏs, KJV Cō ŏs), an island off the coast of Asia Minor, one of the Sporades; mountainous in terrain, especially in the southern sector. The birthplace of Hippocrates, the father of medicine and of Ptolemy Philadelphus. The name of its capital is also Cos. A large Jewish settlement was located here. It is mentioned in connection with Paul's third missionary journey (Acts 21:1).

COSAM (kō'săm), an ancestor of Christ (Luke 3:28).

COSMETICS, any of the various preparations used for beautifying the hair and skin. Such practices are regarded with disfavor by the writers of Holy Writ. Jezebel, Ahab's wicked queen, painted her face immediately prior to her slaying by Jehu, son of Nimshi (II Kings 9:30). The practice of

CORNELIUS THE CENTURION prostrated himself before Peter. But Peter said, "Stand up; I myself also am a man." Then Cornelius told Peter of the angel's instructions, and Peter's eyes were opened. Now he knew that God wanted him to teach the Gospel to all who would believe, not just to the Jews.

painting the eyes is referred to by Ezekiel in an uncomplimentary vein in the parable of Aholah and Aholibah (Ezek. 23:40b). The "painted stare" is referred to by Jeremiah (Jer. 4:30). See Perfume.

COTTON (Per., *karpas*), originally designated muslin or calico. Its use was gradually extended to include linen. The plant was imported to Palestine shortly after the Captivity. Cotton was spun into cloth by weavers in Egypt. The mummies of Egypt were wrapped in this material. It is mentioned but once in the Bible (Esth. 1:5,6), where the word "green" should be rendered "cotton," as in the RSV. See PLANTS.

COUCH, a piece of furniture for reclining. The couch became so ornate that Amos rebuked the rich for the costly display of their couches (Amos 6:4). Sometimes, however, the couch was no more than a rolled-up mat which could be easily transported (Matthew 9:6). See BED.

COULTER (kōl'têr), a plowshare (I Sam. 13:19-21). The plows used in eastern lands today are very similar to those used in ancient times. At first, a plow was nothing more than a sturdy branch of a tree; later it was improved so that a pair of oxen could be attached to it. The sharp end of the plow scratched rather than turned over the soil so that the seed might be sown. In later times, the plowman steered the plow with one hand, while guiding the oxen with the other. See PLOW.

COUNCIL (koun'sĕl, Heb. *rigmâh,* Gr. *sumboúlion, sunédrion*), a Jewish governing body, more or less informally held. David speaks of "the princes of Judah and their council" (Ps. 68:27); but he does not mean the Sanhedrin, which did not come into existence until after the Captivity. Except for Matthew 12:14 and Acts 25:12, the word "council" in the KJV always refers to the Sanhedrin, as the Greek shows.

COUNSELLOR (koun'sĕ-lêr). The modern English spelling, "counselor," is not found in the KJV. The word refers to one who gives counsel. It is found in both Testaments. A counsellor (Gr. *bouletes*) was a member of the Sanhedrin. The word is applied to Joseph of Arimathea (Mark 15:43; Luke 23:50).

COURSE OF PRIESTS AND LEVITES. David divided the priests and Levites into 24 groups, called courses in Luke 1:8, each with its own head (I Chron. 24:1 ff). These courses officiated for a week at a time, the change being made on the sabbath before evening sacrifice.

COURT. At the advice of Jethro, Moses instituted a system of jurisprudence for the Israelites. He appointed judges over tens, fifties, hundreds, and thousands; and finally a Supreme Court under himself and his successors. There was no opportunity of appeal to a higher court (Exod. 18:25, 26). The office of judge was an elective one (Deut. 1:13). Eventually judges were usually chosen from among the Levites, although this was not necessary. They were held in very high regard. In time, the profession of law developed among the Hebrews, its members being called "Lawyers," "Scribes," or "Doctors of the Law" (Luke 2:46). These men studied and interpreted the law, decided questions of the law, and taught Hebrew boys the law. Technical knowledge of the law was not a prerequisite to become a judge. Under the Romans the supreme legislative and judicial body was the Sanhedrin. Its judgment was final except in cases involving capital punishment, when the consent of the procurator had to be secured. The Sanhedrin met in Jerusalem.

COVENANT, translates the Hebrew noun *berîth.* The verbal root of *berîth* means either "to fetter" or "eat with," which would signify mutual obligation, or "to allot" (I Sam. 17:8), which would signify a gracious disposition: compare the Hittite "suzerainty covenant," in which a vassal swore fealty to his king, out of gratitude for favors received (E. J. Young, *The Study of Old Testament Theology Today,* London: J. Clarke, 1958, p. 62).

In the OT, *berîth* identifies three differing types of legal relationships. 1. A two-sided covenant between human parties, both of which voluntarily accept the terms of the agreement (for friendship, I Sam. 18:3-4; marriage, Mal. 2:14; or political alliance, Josh. 9:15, Obad. 7). God, however, never "enters in" to such a covenant of equality with men. The closest approximation is the "covenant of redemption" between Jehovah and Christ (mentioned in certain of the Psalms, 2:7-8; 40:6-8), under which the Son agrees to undertake man's salvation. But the actual term *berîth* is not employed. 2. A one-sided disposition imposed by a superior party (Ezek. 17:13-14). God the Lord thus "commands" a *berîth* which man, the servant, is to "obey" (Josh. 23:16). In the original "covenant of works" (Hos. 6:7 ASV), He placed Adam on probation, bestowing life, should he prove faithful (Gen. 2:17). Humanity failed; but Christ, the last Adam (I Cor. 15:45), did fulfill all righteousness (Matt. 3:15, Gal. 4:4), thereby earning restoration for all who are His. 3. God's self-imposed obligation, for the reconciliation of sinners to Himself (Deut. 7:6-8, Ps. 89:3-4). As He stated to Abraham, "I will establish My covenant between Me and thee . . . to be a God unto thee and to thy seed after thee" (Gen. 17:7).

The LXX avoided the usual Greek term for covenant, *synthéke* (Meaning a thing mutually "put together"), as unsuitable for the activity of the sovereign God, and substituted *diathéke* (a thing, literally, "put through"), the primary meaning of which is "a disposition of property by a will." The LXX even used *diathéke* for the human-agreement type of *berîth.* NT revelation, however, makes clear the wonderful appropriateness of *diathéke,* testament, for describing the instrument of God's redemptive love: "For, where a testament is, there must of necessity be the death of him that made it . . . [Christ's] death, for the redemption of the transgressions that were under the first covenant" (Heb. 9:16). "Testament," indeed, signifies a specific form of covenant, the bequest; and it well describes God's OT *berîth,* because apart from the death of Christ the OT saints "should not be made perfect" (11:40; see J. B. Payne, *An Outline of Hebrew History,* Grand Rapids: Baker, 1954, pp. 220-228).

The covenant then constitutes the heart of all God's special revelation: when put into writing, "the book of the covenant" becomes the objective source for man's religious hope (Exod. 24:7); and, as E. J. Young has summarized it, "The subject matter with which [Biblical] theology is concerned is that covenant which God has made with man for man's salvation" (*op. cit.,* p. 61). Scripture consists of "the Old Testament" and "the New Testament." For while there can be but one testament, corresponding to the one death of Christ ("My blood of *the* testament," according to the better MSS of Matt. 26:28), revelation yet organizes itself under the older testament, with its anticipatory symbols of Christ's coming (Jer. 31-32, II Cor. 3:14), and the newer testament, commemorative of His accomplished redemption (Jer. 31:31, II Cor. 3:6).

The following aspects compose the testamentary arrangements: the testator, God the Son, "the mediator" (Heb. 9:15); the heirs, "the called" ones (9:15); the objective method of effectuation, a gracious bequest (9:16); the subjective conditions by which the heir qualifies for the gift, namely, commitment (9:28: it is "to them that wait for Him"); and the inheritance of reconciliation, "eternal salvation" (9:15,28). Certain specific features then characterize this covenant. Its objective effectuation is always marked by a monergism, "one worker," God exercising pure grace (*cf.* Gen. 15:18, Exod. 19:4), unassisted by man's works (Eph. 2:8-9); b. the death of the testator (Exod. 24:8, Heb. 9:18-22); c. the promise, "I will be their God, and they shall be My people" (Gen. 17:7 to Rev. 21:3); d. the eternity of the inheritance (Ps. 105:8-10. Num. 18:19 thus mentions "a covenant of salt"; compare Lev. 2:13, "the salt [eternal preservation] of the testament of thy God"); and e. a confirmatory sign, such as the rainbow to Noah (Gen. 9:12-13), the exodus to Moses (Exod. 20:2), or Christ's resurrection to us (Rom. 1:4). Subjective appropriation of the covenant is likewise marked by unchangeable features of human response: a. faith (Gen. 15:6, Deut. 6:5; Heb. 11:6) and b. obedience, both moral (Gen. 17:1, Matt. 7:24, Eph. 2:10) and ceremonial (Gen. 17:10-14, Acts 22-16, I Cor. 11:24); for genuine faith must be demonstrated by works (James 2:14-26).

Yet God's revelations of His covenant also exhibit historical progression (covenants, plu., Rom. 9:4). Under the older testament appear 1. the Edenic (Gen. 3:15), God's earliest promise of redemption, though at the cost of the "bruising of the heel of the seed of woman"; 2. the Noachian (9:9), for the preservation of the seed; 3. the Abrahamic (15:18), granting blessing through Abram's family; 4. the Sinaitic (Exod. 19:5-6), designating Israel as God's chosen people; 5. the Levitical (Num. 25:12-13), making reconciliation through priestly atonement; and 6. the Davidic (II Sam. 23:5), with Messianic salvation promised through David's dynasty. Each of these covenants anticipated the same redemptive death; yet differences appear, particularly in their ceremonial response. A "dispensation" may thus be defined as a covenantal period during which faith in Christ is manifested by a distinct form of ceremonial obedience. Even our own, newer testament thus exhibits two stages: 7. the present new covenant in Christ, which is internal, "in their heart"; reconciling (as always, "I will be their God"); direct, "They shall all know Me"; and with finished atonement, "For I will forgive their iniquity" (Jer. 31:33-34, Heb. 8:6-13). But its ceremony, the Lord's Supper, possesses a dispensational limit, exhibiting "the Lord's death *till He come*" (I Cor. 11:26). For Ezekiel speaks of 8. the future covenant of peace, when our internal salvation will reach out to embrace external nature (Ezek. 34:25), when direct spiritual communion will become "face to face" (20:35; 37:27), and when divine forgiveness will achieve the goal of peace among all nations (34:28).   J.B.P.

COVERING THE HEAD, mentioned only in I Corinthians 11:15, where Paul says that a woman's hair is given her for a covering. In the preceding verses he says that women should have their heads covered in public worship. At that time in Greece only immoral women were seen with their heads uncovered. Paul means that Christian women cannot afford to disregard social convention; it would hurt their testimony. In giving them long hair, a natural veil, nature teaches the lesson that women should not be unveiled in public assemblies.

COVETOUSNESS, (kŭv′ĕt-ŭs-nĕs), has various shades of meaning, among the most important the following: 1. The desire to have something (I Cor. 12:31; 14:39). 2. The inordinate desire to have something (Luke 12:15 ff; Eph. 5:5; Col. 3:5). 3. Excessive desire of what belongs to another (Exod. 20:17; Rom. 7:7). A great deal of OT law was intended to counteract the spirit of covetousness. Outstanding examples of covetousness are: Achan (Josh. 7); Saul (1 Sam. 15:9,19); Ananias and Sapphira (Acts 5:1-11).

COZBI (kŏz′bī), a Midianite woman slain by Phineas, Aaron's grandson, because through her the plague had come upon Israel in the wilderness (Numbers 25:16-18).

CRACKNEL, cakes cooked in a pan, corresponding to our pancakes (I Kings 14:3).

CRAFT, CRAFTSMAN (See Occupations, Professions)

CRAFTINESS, CRAFTY, ability that stops short of nothing, however bad, to attain its purpose; guile; cunning (Dan. 8:25; Luke 20:23).

CREATION, does not occupy a great deal of space in the Bible, but is clearly presented in Genesis 1-2, and in Hebrews 11:3, and is emphasized in Isaiah 40-51 and in the latter part of Job. The Bible clearly teaches that the universe, and all matter, had a beginning, and came into existence through the Will of the eternal God. In Genesis 1:1, the words "the heaven and the earth" summarize all the various materials of the universe. This verse has been interpreted in various ways, but all agree in its essential significance. This is true even of the new interpretation that takes it as a mere introduction to what follows, rendering it: "When God began to create heaven and earth," for even on this interpretation v.2 would describe the situation that came into existence shortly after God began to create, rather than to contradict Hebrews 11:3 by implying that there was pre-existing matter.

Some hold that there is a long gap between verses 1 and 2, in which God's perfect creation came into chaos through a great catastrophe. Hebrew syntax permits such a view but does not require it.

The length of the creative days of Genesis 1 is not stated in the Bible. The Hebrew word "day" may mean a period of light between two periods of darkness, a period of light together with the preceding period of darkness, or a long period of time. All three usages occur frequently in the Bible, including Genesis 1-2. No one of them is exactly 24 hours, though the second one is near it. There is no indication as to which of the three is meant, though the type of expression used in the third, fifth and sixth days seems to suggest a long period. The Bible gives no information as to how long ago the original creation of matter occurred, or the first day of creation began, or the sixth day ended.

On the seventh day (Gen. 2:2-3) God ceased from His labors. This is given as an example for man in his life of six days of labor followed by one day of rest (cf. Exod. 20:11). No end to the seventh day is mentioned. As far as the Bible tells us, the cessation of God's creative activity still continues.

There is much discussion about the question of "evolution" in relation to creation, but the word "evolution" is used in many different ways. If taken in its historic sense, to indicate the theory that everything now existing has come into its present condition as a result of natural development, all of it having proceeded by natural causes from one rudimentary beginning, such a theory is sharply contradicted by the divine facts revealed in Genesis 1-2. These chapters indicate a number of specific divine commands bringing new factors into existence. God's activity is indicated throughout the entire creation. It is explicitly stated several times that plants and animals are to reproduce "after their kind." Moses nowhere states how large a "kind" is, and there is no ground for equating it with any particular modern definition of "species." Yet it is clear that Genesis teaches that there are a number (perhaps a large number) of "kinds" of plants and of animals, which cannot reproduce in such a way as to evolve from one into the other. Nothing in the Bible denies the possibility of change and development within the limits of a particular "kind."

Moreover, the creation of man is sharply distinguished from the other parts of the creation, and the creation of woman is described as a distinct act of God. Genesis 2:7 (in the Hebrew) clearly teaches that man did not exist as an animate being before he was a man, created after the image of God.

It is sometimes said that the Bible begins with two contradictory accounts of creation. To say that it begins with two creation accounts is like saying that an atlas begins with two maps. A map of the world and a map of the United States would overlap. The first would include a great deal of territory not included in the second. The second would include a great deal of detail not mentioned in the first. This is exactly the relation between the two creation accounts. Genesis 1 describes the creation of the universe as a whole. Genesis 2:4-25 gives a more detailed account of the creation of man and says nothing about the creation of matter, of light, of the heavenly bodies, or of plants and animals, except to refer to the creation of animals as having taken place at an earlier time.

It is sometimes said that the creation story of Genesis 1 begins with a watery chaos and that of Genesis 2 with a dry earth. There is no contradiction in this because the two begin at different places in the whole series of creative events.

It is sometimes alleged that Genesis 2 gives a different order of events of creation from Genesis 1. Actually, however, only two creative acts are involved in Genesis 2: the creation of man and that of woman. There is no contradiction between the order in which they are described and that of Genesis 1.

Genesis 2 does not describe the creation of vegetation, as some interpreters allege, but simply mentions that God planted a garden. Even this act took place before the creation of man. Only by reading extremely primitive concepts into Genesis 2 could one insist on interpreting it as meaning that God created man and then laid him on the shelf for a few years while the garden that He proceeded to plant should grow large enough to be a satisfactory place for man to live. The verbs in Genesis 2:8,9 must be interpreted, in normal fashion, as implying an English pluperfect.

The same is true of v.19 where creation of the animals is specifically referred to. God, looking for a companion for man, brought before him the animals that He had previously created, to show him the need of a different sort of helper. Genesis 2 does not contradict Gen. 1 in any way, but adds to our understanding of the details of an important portion of God's creative activity.   A.A.M.

CREATURE (Gr. *ktísis*), in the NT the word denotes that which has been created (Rom. 1:25;

8:39; Heb. 4:13). Sometimes used with adjective *kaine* in the sense of the new creation (II Cor. 5: 17) or in contrast to the old man versus the new man (Gal. 6:15).

CREATURE, LIVING (Heb. *hayyâh*, Gr. *zóon*) a symbolical figure presented first in Ezekiel's vision (Ezek. 1:5ff), and again in Revelation 4: 6-9; 5:6,8,11; 6:1,3,5-7. In Ezekiel's vision there are four living creatures. They had the general appearance of a man, but each had four faces and four wings, and the feet of an ox. Under their wings they had human hands. The front face was that of a man; to the right and left of this were the faces of a lion and of an ox, and in the back was the face of an eagle. Fire gleamed from their midst. Later they are called "cherubim" (Ezek. 10:1ff). The living creatures in Revelation are somewhat modified from those in Ezekiel's vision.

CREED (Lat. *credo,* "I believe"), a rule of faith, a symbol, a public confession or declaration of Christian doctrine or belief. The creeds of Christendom group themselves into five more or less distinct groups. First are the ecumenical or earlier creeds, which include the Apostles' Creed (n.d.), the Nicene Creed (A.D. 325), the Chalcedonian Creed (A.D. 451), the Athanasian Creed, commonly ascribed to Athanasius (d. A.D. 333). The second larger division deals with the creeds of the Greek Church, embracing the confessions of Gennadius (A.D. 1453), the "Orthodox Confession of Peter Mogilas" (A.D. 1643), the Decrees of the Synod of Jerusalem (A.D. 1672), etc. In addition, the Greek Church tenaciously holds to the above-mentioned ecumenical creeds. The third division is that of the Roman Catholic Church, which in addition to the basic ecumenical creeds, holds to the Canons and Decrees of the Council of Trent (A.D. 1563-64), the Profession of the Tridentine Faith (A.D. 1564), the Papal Definition of the Immaculate Conception of the Virgin Mary (A.D. 1854), the Vatican Decrees of 1870, upholding the dogma of Papal Infallibilty, the Ecumenical Council summoned by the late Pius XII, where the dogma of the bodily assumption of the Virgin Mary was adopted (A.D. 1950). Within the Councils of the Roman Catholic church in the 1960's some modifications of the more stringent laws of said church seem to be taking place, such as the abolition of the "Sacred Latin" tongue for the modern languages.

The fourth division contains the Lutheran Confessional Statements, which include the Augsburg Confession, (A.D. 1530) for which Luther himself produced the doctrinal sections, a mild conciliatory decree, the Articles of Smalcald (A.D. 1537), the Formula of Concord (A.D. 1577).

The fifth and final division embraces the Reformed and Evangelical Church Creeds. These include the Swiss or Zwinglian Confessions (A.D. 1536-66), the Belgic Confession (A.D. 1561), the Decrees of the Synod of Dort (A.D. 1604-1619), the Remonstrance (A.D. 1610), the Canons of Dort (A.D. 1619), the Westminster Confession (1643-48). This confession consisted at first of the revision of the thirty-nine Articles of the Church of England, which was followed by a strong affirmation of the Nicene Creed. The Westminster Confession was likewise given a strong Puritanical or Calvinistic orientation.

Baptistic groups and Quakers doubt the advisability of creeds, having as a motto: "No creed, but Christ." Nevertheless, despite rancor, abuses and excesses, it seems that the Holy Spirit has been pleased in general to use the various creeds as an instrument to insure the doctrinal purity of the Church at large.   J.F.G.

CREEK (Gr. *kólpos*). Modern translations utilize the word "bay" as a substitution for the KJV "creek," identified as the traditional "St. Paul's Bay" about eight miles NW of the town of Zaletta on the island of Malta (Melita) (Acts 27:39).

CREEPING THING (See Animals, Insects)

CRESCENS (Gr. *Kréskes, increasing*), the companion of the apostle Paul at Rome who had departed for Galatia (II Tim. 4:10).

CRETE, CRETAN (krēt, krē′tăn, Gr. *Kréte, Krétes*, Acts 2:11, Titus 1:12), an island in the Mediterranean Sea with Cythera on the NW and Rhodes on the NE, forming a natural bridge between Europe and Asia Minor. Crete is about 156 miles long and from seven to 30 miles wide. Despite its enviable geographical position, Crete has never attained a prominent place in history, partly because of internal dissensions and, in more modern times, because of its acceptance of Turkish rule and the Islamic faith. In mythology Mt. Ida is the legendary birthplace of Zeus, the head of the Greek Pantheon. King Minos, the half historical, half mythological character, alleged son of Zeus, was an early ruler. Both Thucydides and Aristotle accepted the existence of King Minos and claimed that he established maritime supremacy for Crete by putting down piracy. Aristotle compares the institutions of Crete to those of Sparta. Crete is said to have been colonized by the Dorians from Peloponnesus. The most important cities of Crete are Cnossos, excavated by Arthur Evans; Gortyna near the gulf of Messara; and Cydonia. Around 140 B.C. the Jews established a large enough colony on this island to be able to appeal successfully to the protection of Rome.

CRETE IN THE OT — The Cherethites (I Sam. 30:14; Ezek. 25:16) held to be a group of Philistines, are identified as Cretans.

CRETE IN THE NT — A number of Cretans are represented as being present upon the Day of Pentecost. Paul visited Crete and left his assistant Titus in charge. In the opinion of the Apostle Paul, even the Christians in Crete were not of high moral character: "Cretans are always liars . . ." (Titus 1:12). The first words of this quotation are to be found in the hymn to Zeus by Callimachus. The particular lie of which the Cretans were always guilty was that they said the tomb of Zeus, a non-existent personage, was located on their island. Laziness and gluttony also characterized them. Titus is charged sharply to rebuke them (Titus 1:13). A storm on his journew to Rome forced Paul's ship into the port of Cnidus (Acts 27:17). The narrative does not specifically indicate that Paul actually landed on the island.

CRIB (Job 39:9, Prov. 14:4, Isaiah 1:3), a rack constructed for the feeding of domestic livestock. A manger (Luke 2:7). Isaiah complains that "the ox knoweth his master and the ass his master's crib" (Isaiah 1.3).

CRIMSON (Heb. *karmîl, tôlā′*), refers to the brilliant red dye obtained from a bug. The word is applied to garments (II Chron. 2:7,14; Jer. 4:30 KJV). The best known citation is doubtless the prophet's assurance in Isaiah 1:18.

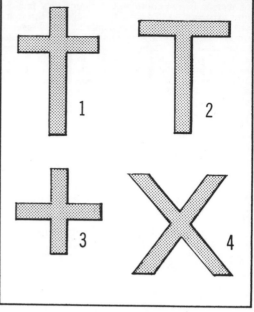

FOUR FORMS OF THE CROSS

CRISPING PIN (Heb. *hărîtîm*, Isaiah 3:22 KJV), pins for crisping or curling the hair. The term has also been translated as bags (II Kings 5:23), girdles, veils, and turbans. See DRESS.

CRISPUS (krĭs′pŭs, Gr. *Kríspos*, "curled," Acts 18,7, 8; I Cor. 1:14), formerly the ruler of the Jewish synagogue at Corinth; converted under the preaching of Paul and subsequently baptized by him.

CROP (Lev. 1:16), the enlargement of the gullet of a bird where food is partly macerated, removed by the priest for sacrificial purposes.

CROSS (Gr. *staurós*). There are three Biblical uses of the term: first, the cross in its literal aspect; secondly, the Cross as a symbolic representation of redemption; thirdly, death upon the cross, i.e., crucifixion. Our English word is derived from the Latin *Crux*. The cross existed in four different forms: 1, the *crux immissa*, the type usually presented in art in which the upright beam extends above the cross beam, traditionally held to be the cross upon which the Redeemer suffered and died; 2, the *crux commissa*, or "Saint Anthony's Cross" in the form of the letter "T"; 3, the Greek cross in which the cross beams are of equal length; 4, the *crux decussata*, or "Saint Andrew's Cross," in the shape of the letter "X."

(continued on page 461)

(continued on page 461)

THE FOLLOWING BIBLE ACCOUNT, *The Crucifixion*, was written by Curtis Mitchell. It is based upon the events related in the New Testament.

THE Crucifixion

IN all the tumultuous history of the world there had never been such a week.

Jerusalem lay under the springtime sun like a gigantic anthill, the hub of a half-dozen twisting caravans of Hebrews that came from all directions to keep the Passover in the Holy City. Within its thick walls Jews from all over the world jostled each other in good humor. They were residents of Greece and Damascus, Egypt and Phoenicia, Syria and Italy, and they packed the narrow streets like a crowd at a carnival.

Here also were the human leeches who prey on crowds of every age and civilization; beggars, peddlers, pickpockets, and cutthroats. This holiday was their harvest time. If we were to combine Christmas and the Fourth of July into one gigantic celebration, it might begin to compare with that Jerusalem holiday which commemorated the nation's escape from Egyptian slavery, when the Lord had struck down the first-born of each Egyptian family but had spared the Hebrews, and freed them. It was a most holy week for the faithful, but among the unholy it was a time for sin and thievery.

It was also a time, as we shall see, for betrayal and murder.

Earlier, at a last supper with his disciples, Jesus had stated the fact bluntly. "I say unto you," He asserted, "that one of you shall betray Me."

He had even indicated the traitor, adding, "It will be the one to whom I give a piece of bread dipped in gravy." He handed the bit to Judas Iscariot, saying, "What you are going to do, do quickly."

Judas, a man of great ability and the trusted treasurer of the group, ran from the room.

Now they entered the Garden of Gethsemane (geth-SEM-a-nee), on the lower slopes of the Mount of Olives, seeking a place of refuge from the tumult of the city. Actually, the spot was an enclosed olive grove that grew about an oil press, which is the meaning of the word "gethsemane." Did any of them, as they threw themselves onto the warm earth to rest, foresee the horror of the next twenty-four hours? Jesus certainly did, for He sank down in prayer, saying, "Father, all things are possible to You. If You will, take away this bitter cup. But if You decide otherwise, let it be according to Your will, not Mine."

Sleep Overcomes the Apostles

BEFORE going apart from His disciples to pray, Jesus had taken Peter, James, and John part of the way with Him and asked them to wait and watch for Him. But they had not watched. So great was their weariness that all of them sank into a hard slumber.

Finding them asleep, Jesus said, "Peter, could you not watch even one hour? Now watch and pray lest you be tempted again." And He withdrew.

Again the three fell asleep, and though Jesus roused them and ordered them to keep a watch, they failed anew as soon as He returned to His private prayers.

When He saw that they slept for the third time, He knew that His hour had come. Sorrowfully He asked, "Are you still sleeping and taking your rest? The Son of Man is betrayed into the hands of sinners. Rise, let us be going; see, My betrayer is at hand."

We know that Israel's high priests had already decided to kill Him. We know that Judas was already leading a band of Temple police and servants toward the garden. We believe that Jesus had already prophesied His own death. This situation had not happened by accident. He could have compromised with the Sadducees (SAD-yew-sees), the millionaire priests in charge of the Temple. He could have bowed to the scribes and Pharisees, who embroidered the Ten Commandments with such foolish requirements\ that they even proclaimed it wickedness to eat a hen's egg which was laid on the Sabbath.

As recently as last Monday (now it was Thursday night) there was time to submit to the authorities. They had allowed Him to enter the Temple and to speak without hindrance, but then His gorge rose and His temper flared with indignation at the sight of its outer court filled with bargain-driving merchants of lambs and doves. Stooping to gather a bundle of cords, He had twisted them swiftly into a whip. His eyes fell on the stalls of the money-changers and saw their cheating fingers counting out temple shekels.

His twelve disciples saw them too, but they did nothing except widen their eyes with fright as Jesus charged toward the tables.

"Beware! Here's a maniac," one merchant shouted.

Jesus's arm lashed out and His whip flicked a pudgy back. The cry of pain brought every eye in the vast court to bear on the powerful Man with the circling whip. They heard His lash and saw Him thrust money-burdened tables in all directions, scattering coins.

"What's got into You?" a banker demanded.

"It is written: My house shall be called a house of prayer for all the nations," Jesus said.

"Then leave us alone," the man cried. "We change the money of all nations into Temple money. We pay our booth rent regularly to the high priest."

Jesus ordered, "Begone! You have made this sanctuary into a den of thieves."

As he advanced, they broke before Him, a rabble fleeing from a single determined Man. Presently He, His disciples, and a host of worshipful pilgrims stood reverently in the cleansed Temple.

That act of Jesus was the last straw.

The Pharisees Act

OLD ANNAS, the wealthy head of the priestly family that ran the Temple, told the high priest, Caiaphas (KAY-ah-fus), "We must do something to silence that madman from Galilee." Annas, the most powerful Jew in Jerusalem, was wise in the ways of maintaining personal power. A secret ally of Pontius Pilate, he sensed how greatly the Roman governor feared the consequences of one more Judean riot. If the Roman permitted another disturbance, it might cost him his job.

"Pilate has come to Jerusalem in person to make sure our Passover is orderly," Annas explained. "This Jesus is obviously a revolutionary and these people from the country districts are like tinder."

Caiaphas said, "The Man from Galilee has support among the lower classes. If there is injustice, His friends will cause trouble."

"There will be no injustice, my son."

"You have a plan?"

"I have an excellent plan," Annas said. "It began some time ago with a discontented disciple. He calls himself Judas."

At the Garden of Gethsemane, Jesus was the first to hear the scuffling steps and muted voices of the Temple police. "Whom do you seek?" He called.

A voice answered, "We seek Jesus of Nazareth."

"I am He!"

Judas stepped out of the night and embraced his Lord, kissing Him on the cheek in the customary greeting between master and follower; but now it was a secret sign to the Temple officers. Two guards leaped forward and pinned Jesus's arms to His side. Big Simon Peter lunged to his feet, temper rising. Drawing a blade from his belt, he chose an opponent. His weapon bounced off the head of Malthus, servant of the high priest, severing his right ear.

Jesus' voice rang out. "Simon, put up your sword."

"But Master . . ."

"Put it back in its sheath. For all who take the sword will perish by the sword."

441

"But we're outnumbered, Master."

Jesus said, "Don't you know that I can appeal to My Father? If I call, He will send an army of angels. But no, it is prophesied that this must happen."

Already the police were searching the grove for His followers, but they had vanished, including one young man whose robe was clutched by a guard. That youth merely doubled himself up so that the robe pulled off over his head and he ran away naked.

Jesus reached out swiftly, touched the injured Malthus's wound, and it was healed. His voice rang out, "Have you come out as against a robber? Do you need swords and clubs to arrest Me when I sat day after day in the Temple and you did not seize Me?"

Captured!

T HEN the guards, seeing that He did not resist, bound Him. At last, He was a prisoner and at the mercy of His enemies.

It is remarkable that a Man so peaceful could have been feared so greatly. It becomes understandable only when we learn the urgent pressures involved.

On one hand there was Rome's insistence on the submission of its captive colony and every citizen in it. Any Roman soldier had the right to compel a Hebrew to carry his cloak and weapons for one mile. Individually, Jews were taxed without mercy. They had no political privileges. Their loyalty to the Caesars was the price they were required to pay in exchange for the right to worship their own God without interference.

Yet many of them recalled the history of the reign of King David and his far-flung Hebrew empire, and they yearned for its return. They were a people too proud to submit wholly to conquerers, so, while some plotted against the invaders, most of them prayed for the day when God would hear their prayers and send a Messiah (meh-SI-uh) to lead them to victory and freedom, as was promised by His prophets.

But what kind of Messiah?

All agreed that He would be a descendant of the house of King David. Some expected a warrior prince who would lead an Israelite army to victory. Others looked for a spiritual Messiah, a prophet perhaps, like Elijah, who would so cleanse the people that a just God would make them the first nation of the earth.

Members of both parties, observing Jesus of Nazareth and the crowds who followed Him, wondered if He was the Promised One.

But now Jesus was a prisoner, betrayed for thirty pieces of silver.

Thirty pieces! It is a ridiculously small sum in relation to the enormity of the crime, and scholars have long wondered why Judas did it. One theory holds that he was a member of a secret society that plotted against Rome.

He betrayed Jesus, it is argued, when He made it clear that He opposed a military rebellion. Or perhaps he reasoned that Jesus, when cornered, would employ His power to smite His enemies and then would be forced to declare Himself King of the Jews. It is all conjecture.

But this is fact: the Temple priests who ruled Judea would accept no Messiah except one of their own choosing; the Roman governor, Pontius Pilate, would execute any man who gave his loyalty to any king other than Caesar.

So the issues were set for the trials of Jesus on that Friday morning.

The First Trial

JESUS was arrested after dark on Friday, a day that started at sundown of the previous afternoon instead of at midnight, as is our custom. Immediately He was taken to the home of eighty-year-old Annas, string-puller, political boss, and ex-high priest extraordinary.

"Tell me what you teach," Annas demanded.

Jesus reminded him that He had always taught openly in the Temple and in the synagogues where the people gathered. He had taught nothing secretly. "Why do you ask Me what I preach?" He said. "Why not ask those who have heard what I've spoken. They know everything I've said."

An officer snarled, "That's no way to answer." He struck Jesus with all his strength. It was the first blow of many.

After a while, when the priest saw that he could not trick Jesus into a confession, he sent Him on to Caiaphas, whom he had named as the high priest for that year and who was also his son-in-law. Caiaphas had called an emergency meeting of the Hebrew council of state, which was called the Sanhedrin (SAN-heh-drin).

Guards jostled and pushed Jesus through the black streets, beating Him when He lagged, mocking Him when He stumbled. Finally, at the great hall of hewn stones they thrust Him before the sleepy-eyed council. Jesus gazed about the semicircle of bearded patriarchs. They were the most respected men of the city, His nation's supreme court, and His own last defense. In full attendance they numbered seventy-one, plus the vacant seat reserved for their ancient prophet Elijah, who, tradition said, had never died and might be expected to appear again at any time.

Caiaphas took the floor, in accordance with his high position, and attempted to prove, through questioning various witnesses, that Jesus had claimed divine powers.

One man testified that Jesus said, "I will destroy this Temple that is made with hands and in three days I will build another made without hands."

But another claimed that the exact words were, "I am able to destroy the Temple of God, and to build it in three days."

"Are You the Christ?"

A REQUIREMENT for the death penalty was total agreement of at least two witnesses. But no two could be found who agreed, even after being coached. So Caiaphas resolved to risk a direct question. With his robes swirling about him and the seal of his high office glittering against his forehead, he raised a fat finger and thrust it into the face of his Prisoner.

"By the living God, I solemnly charge You to answer," he said. "Tell us, are You the Christ? Are You the Son of the Blessed?"

Stone walls echoed his query. The assemblage held its breath. Some of them were secret followers of the Prisoner, and their minds cried, "It is a trap. Do not reply!"

Jesus gathered His strength to answer, fully aware of the awful consequence.

"I am," He said clearly.

A harsh cry exploded from a score of throats, and loudest of all was Caiaphas. But Jesus had not finished. He told them, with terrible earnestness, "And you will see Me sitting at the right hand of the Power of God and coming in the clouds of Heaven."

The council rose, their robes flapping like the wings of avenging angels. "Blasphemy!" they screamed.

Caiaphas tore his vestments, ripping the cloth as required by ritual, shouting, "What need have we of witnesses now? You have heard His blasphemy. What think you, members of the council?"

They answered, "Let Him die."

A few murmured against the decision, but their voices were weak.

The chant swelled "Death! Death! Death!" And some of the holy men of Jerusalem so far forgot themselves that they rushed at Jesus and struck Him with whatever came to hand, and spat on Him until their spittle dripped off His face.

"Before the Cock Shall Crow ..."

I N THE MEANTIME Simon Peter sat in the courtyard among the guards and others who had captured Jesus. He had come to be near his Lord, hoping to remain unrecognized. After a while a servant girl took a hard look and said, "You were with Jesus of Nazareth, weren't you?"

Peter walked away, saying, "I don't know what you're talking about."

After a while a second maid accused him by telling a guard, "This man is one of them."

Again Peter denied that he knew Jesus.

Finally, as he stood in a group, the man to whom he was speaking said abruptly, "Your speech gives you away. Your accent is that of Galilee. Certainly you are one of Jesus' followers."

The Crucifixion.

CARL BLOCH

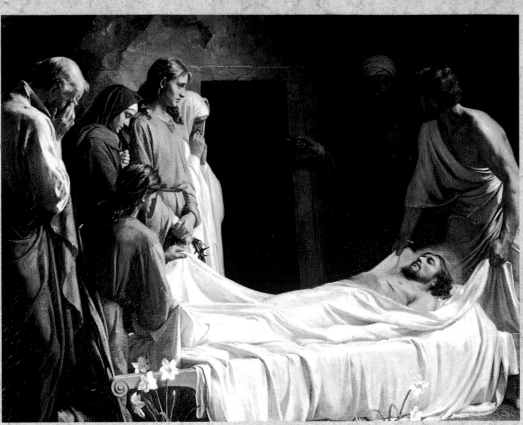

CARL BLOCH

The Entombment.

Ecce Homo (Behold the man).
ANTONIO CISERI

Christ captured in the garden.
GIUSEPPE CESARI

CARL BLOCH

Christ in Gethsemane.

Mourning over the dead Christ.

VAN DYCK

Christ at the column.

FABRES

GIOVANNI BARBIERI

The suffering Saviour.

PETER PAUL RUBENS

The elevation of the Cross.

Golgotha.

PAOLO VERONESE

Fearing what might happen, Peter roared a profane denial, cursing and swearing, "I do not know the Man of whom you speak," he cried.

In the distance a cock began to crow. Suddenly Peter recalled that Jesus had told him earlier that night, "Before the cock shall crow twice, you shall deny Me three times." He bent his head and rushed away sobbing, ashamed of his disloyalty.

At the door of the judgment hall there was a sudden commotion. A guard shouted, "Stay back. You're not wanted here."

Caiaphas called, "Who is that troublemaker?"

"You know me well," a hoarse voice replied. "I am Judas Iscariot." The intruder threw off the arms of a Temple guard and rushed before the startled Sanhedrin. His face was black with distress and his hands stuck out before him holding a pile of silver coins.

Caiaphas demanded, "What is this to us?"

Judas's shoulders shook with the violence of his emotions. "I have sinned in that I have betrayed the innocent blood of Jesus." His fists suddenly swung about him and the blood money he had taken from the priests crashed at their feet and rolled noisily along the floor. Guards dragged him away, but his sobs could be heard for a long time. Later, word came back that he had gone into a field and hanged himself.

In Judea, under Roman rule, only a Roman official could issue the order that would send a man to his death. Caiaphas sent a messenger racing ahead to Pontius Pilate to say that a traitor would soon arrive. "Run! There's no time to lose," he ordered.

He had good reason for haste. Friday morning was dawning. The Passover would commence with that afternoon's sunset. The Mosaic Law commanded that the corpse of a crucified Jew should not remain all night upon "the tree," as the cross was called in the Old Testament Book of Deuteronomy. If Jesus were to be executed, it would have to be prior to sunset.

He weighed the odds. Why not hold Jesus in prison until after the Passover and then crucify Him without haste and in good legal order? But if that were done, His followers might rally to His support. They might even desecrate the Passover with a mutiny. It was an awful thought. No, this way was best. The Sanhedrin had spoken, even though they had acted with illegal haste. Now, if Pilate could be persuaded to act, Jesus would be dead before the news spread. He would be dead by sundown.

Off to the Tower

So THE GUARDS hustled Jesus from the hall of hewn stones across the bridge over the Valley of the Cheese Merchants and thence northward to Pilate's dwelling in the Tower of Antonia. Behind them spectators marveled at the strange procession.

"He's that fellow from Galilee who's been preaching in the Temple," one explained. He pointed to the fetters. "They've stopped Him now for sure."

"Why've they done it?"

"Called Himself the Son of God, they say."

Another added, "He claimed to be King of us Jews, too."

"Old Pilate won't stand for that!"

A thin man looked swiftly to the right, to the left, and then whispered, "But maybe he will."

"He won't, I don't think."

"The Nazarene has friends. Some say one of them is Pilate's own wife."

"Impossible!"

"I've a cousin who works in the palace. It's whispered that Claudia Procula is a secret follower."

A messenger had raced ahead to alert the governor. Pilate met them at the entrance, blinking his large eyes in the new brightness of the day. "What accusation do you bring against this Man?" he asked.

A Temple priest said, "Sir, we found Him forbidding our people to pay tribute to Caesar and saying that He Himself is Christ, a king."

Pilate shrugged with annoyance, knowing from experience how often Hebrew politicians tried to get rid of their opponents by charging them with crimes against Rome. So he answered, "Have you tried Him by your own laws?"

The ranking member of the committee of priests said, "It is not lawful for us to put a man to death."

Pilate thought, "They want death for Jesus. This may be serious." He retired to a chair within the hall, saying to Jesus, "Follow me." Studying his man, noting the untroubled eyes and the unbowed head, he seemed to come to a judgment. "Your own nation and Your chief priests have delivered You to me and made serious charges," he said. "Are You the King of the Jews?"

"You have said so," replied Jesus with quiet dignity. And He added, "But My kingdom is not of this world. If My kingdom were of this world, then My servants would fight so that I would not be handed over to these people who are seeking to destroy Me."

Pilate gazed fixedly at the Prisoner.

"Then you *are* a king?" he asked, slowly.

"You say that I am a king," came Jesus' quiet response. "For this I was born, and for this I have come into the world, to bear witness to the truth. Everyone who is of the truth hears My voice."

Pilate thought that over for a long time and then he rose, saying "What is truth?" He walked rapidly to where the priests and their henchmen waited.

"I find no fault in this Man at all," he told them, and turned away, the matter settled.

Priestly lips curled and their howls were like those of coyotes. "No! No! He has stirred up all our people, teaching the Jews everywhere, from here even to Galilee, which is His home."

Galilee! Herod Antipas, the ruler of Galilee, had just arrived in Jerusalem and was quartered in the castle of his father, Herod the Great. As Jesus was

446

from the northern province, He ought to be judged by Antipas. Besides it would let Pilate off the hook.

"Show this Man to the tetrarch, Herod Antipas," he ordered. "He alone should judge Him."

Herod the Depraved

SO THE PRIESTS and their weary captive again trudged across Jerusalem to the court of the northern monarch. Now Herod Antipas was a true son of his infamous father. No royal scion of ancient history was more debauched or unprincipled. When he received the priests, they tore into Jesus, using lies and venom.

Herod stopped them. "I know this Jesus. He's a wonder-worker from Capernaum." Scratching his great stomach and belching the wine he had been drinking all night, he burst into a roar of laughter. "And I find Him here in Jerusalem just when I need entertainment. Good! Servants, awaken our guests! This Man is a magician. He shall perform for us."

A priest persisted, "But He violated our religious laws, Sire."

"Silence! I will speak to you later."

The tetrarch faced Jesus, peering at Him with yellow eyes. Cunningly he began to ask questions, but Jesus stood as tall and silent as a Lebanon cedar, saying nothing.

"Answer me, Jesus of Nazareth!"

Jesus said nothing. Herod's temper rose, swelling his neck and flushing his face. The priests saw their advantage. Herod was the man who had already beheaded Jesus' cousin, John the Baptist. They leaped to the attack.

"Sire, you witness His insolence. Surely, you believe now that He claims to be a king?"

Herod was suddenly convulsed by the ridiculous claim. "A king, is He? Ha! Then dress Him like a king."

His royal hand flung a purple robe around Jesus' shoulders. It was too small and hugged His frame with a ridiculous effect. A courtier bowed low in mock humility. Herod's men roared. One after another they performed every humiliating antic they could devise. Finally Herod shouted, "I weary of this. Take Him back to your Pilate. I shall pass no judgment in Rome's jurisdiction."

"But, Sire, Pilate expects you to sentence Him."

"Go away. I am ready for sleep!" Herod grunted, and closed his wrinkled lids.

As the priests retraced their steps, they were angry and vexed. An older man, bearded and wearing the long tassels of holiness on his robe, said, "This Roman is stubborn and I foresee that he intends to go easy with the Nazarene."

"We'll fill his ears with new lies."

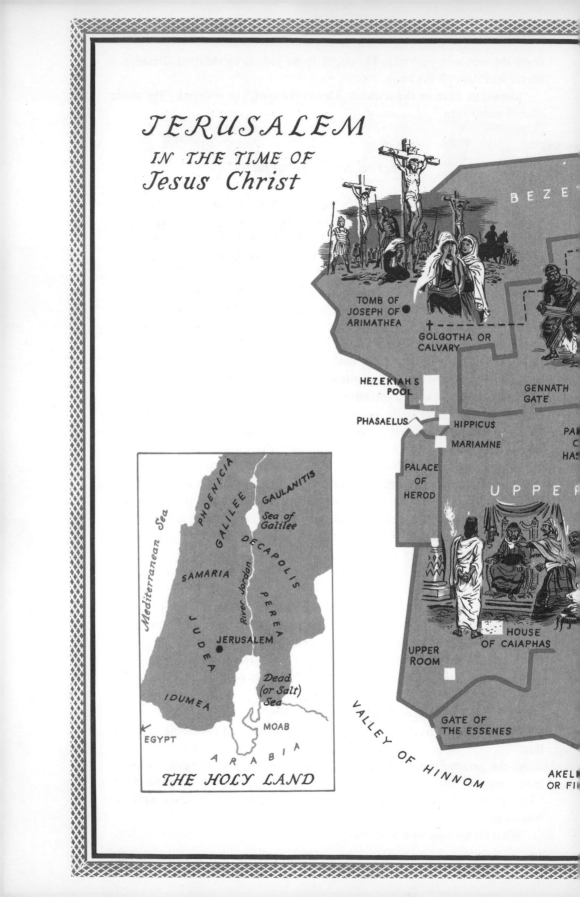

JERUSALEM
IN THE TIME OF
Jesus Christ

BEZET

TOMB OF
JOSEPH OF
ARIMATHEA

GOLGOTHA OR
CALVARY

HEZEKIAH'S
POOL

GENNATH
GATE

PHASAELUS

HIPPICUS

MARIAMNE

PA
C
HAS

PALACE
OF
HEROD

UPPER

HOUSE
OF CAIAPHAS

UPPER
ROOM

GATE OF
THE ESSENES

VALLEY OF HINNOM

AKEL
OR FI

THE HOLY LAND

PHOENICIA

GALILEE

GAULANITIS

Sea of
Galilee

Mediterranean Sea

DECAPOLIS

SAMARIA

River Jordan

PEREA

JUDEA

JERUSALEM

Dead
(or Salt)
Sea

IDUMEA

MOAB

EGYPT

ARABIA

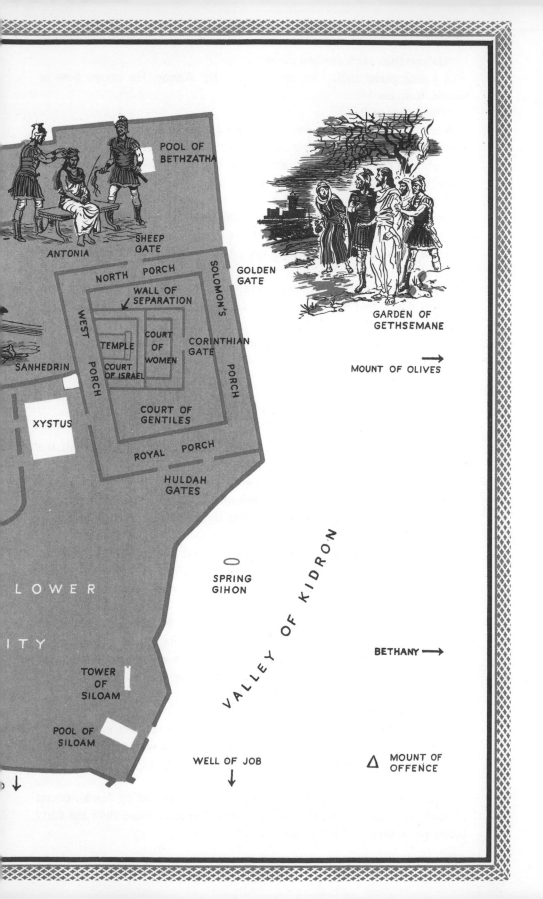

POOL OF
BETHZATHA

ANTONIA

SHEEP
GATE

GARDEN OF
GETHSEMANE

NORTH   PORCH

SOLOMON'S

GOLDEN
GATE

MOUNT OF OLIVES

WALL OF
SEPARATION

WEST

TEMPLE

COURT
OF
WOMEN

CORINTHIAN
GATE

PORCH

SANHEDRIN

COURT
OF ISRAEL

PORCH

XYSTUS

COURT OF
GENTILES

ROYAL   PORCH

HULDAH
GATES

LOWER

ITY

SPRING
GIHON

VALLEY OF KIDRON

BETHANY →

TOWER
OF
SILOAM

POOL OF
SILOAM

↓

WELL OF JOB
↓

△ MOUNT OF
OFFENCE

"He's no fool. He'll demand proof."

A young priest said, "We should send for Annas. He knows how to handle Romans."

"That may be."

When Pilate saw them enter his paved court, he noted that the crowd behind them had swelled until it almost filled the parade grounds. "Why have you returned?" he demanded. They told him of Herod Antipas and his refusal to pass judgment.

Pilate was a good soldier but a poor strategist. He could never decide when to take a stand. Now was the time, if ever; now was the moment to tell the priests that he would never approve their trumped-up charge. Instead he chose a half-measure. Standing on a low balcony, he addressed all the Hebrews:

"You have a custom that I should release a prisoner at Passover. I have told you that I find no wrong in this Jesus. Why, therefore, should I not release Him to you?"

A betasseled priest turned to younger associates. "Go among the people and call for the release of Barabbas instead. He is a thief but he is popular. Do this quickly."

The Mob Makes a Choice

A ROMAN OFFICER BELLOWED, "Well, what do you want? Shall the gracious Pilate release your king?"

A voice sang out, "No, not Jesus, but Barabbas." Other cries were an echo. "Give us Barabbas. Barabbas! Barabbas!" In a moment it was a roar.

Pilate thought, "What connivers, what frauds! They are determined to execute this innocent Man."

A servant handed him a slip of paper scented with his wife's perfume. Unfolding it, he read her note. "I've had a terrible dream about this Man called Jesus of Nazareth," Claudia wrote. "If you would please me greatly, have nothing to do with the plot against Him."

Behind masked eyes Pilate studied his problem. He wanted to grant her request. She had a fine intuition about these colonials. On the other hand, if he opposed the priests too openly, they would lodge complaints in Rome as they had done before. That would be bad, now that Tiberius Caesar was so suspicious. He decided upon a compromise.

"What shall I do, my lord?" his officer asked.

"Release Barabbas the robber," Pilate said, "and turn Jesus over to the soldiers to be whipped." Scourging with whips tipped with metal and sharp bones was a rugged punishment. Perhaps it would satisfy.

"How many stripes, sire?"

"Thirty-nine." That number was universally employed by Jewish courts in order to make certain that no one should receive more than the forty lashes prescribed by Mosaic law.

They hustled Jesus into the soldiers' quarters of the Praetorium. Six hundred legionnaires were in that Jerusalem cohort, near-savages from the distant outposts of the Empire. First they bound Jesus into a stooped position so that His back was arched like a drawn bow. Then they swung the scourge. Each blow was calculated, each stripe was delivered with the schooled cruelty of experience, planting every leather thong with its sharpened weights of metal and bone where they would torture the most.

A drunken soldier slashed a branch from a thorn bush and twisted it into a prickly circle. He held it up, eyes bright with malice. "A royal crown!" he cried. "Here's a crown for the Jew king." He squashed its terrible thorns into Jesus' scalp.

"The king needs a robe." A soldier stripped off his own scarlet garment and hurled it at Jesus. "And a scepter! Give the king a scepter." They found a willow staff and forced it into His hand.

Roman soldiers made a small ring, chanting, "All hail! All hail!"

Pilate heard them and gave a curt order. "Bring the king to me on the balcony."

When the governor strode onto his porch, the mob cried out excitedly. Below, the youngest priest leaned against the wall, still panting from the long run he had made to warn Annas. "My hunch was right," he thought. "This Roman fox is up to something."

Pilate, hearing Jesus' unsteady footsteps behind him, turned to face the mob. He had punished the Man they sent to him, not as vigorously as they demanded; but maybe it would be enough. Most Hebrews had never seen a man newly scourged. A scourge strips away flesh, exposing bone and sinew. If there were any mercy in those breasts, the sight of their countryman would surely arouse it. Suddenly Jesus was thrust before the crowd, a bloody figure in agony. Pilate shouted, "I bring Him forth that you may know I find no fault. Behold this Man!"

A gasp of horror ran through the crowd. Pilate knew a single moment of satisfaction, thinking he had won. Imagine his mentality, his twisted conscience, which could stomach the beating of an innocent victim and still say, "I find no fault." Yet he did hope to save Jesus, if doing so did not jeopardize his own position. And he might have done it except for the distant shrill voice that suddenly cut through the air, crying over and over, "Crucify Him!"

Annas Turns the Tide

I T CAME from a tiny old man who was forcing his way toward the front. With every step he screamed, and Pilate recognized the rasping tone. Old Annas! Swiftly the mob took up his cry, ever ready to follow the bloodiest leader.

Annas limped toward Pilate. Suddenly his manners changed to those of a fawning dog. He came close, eyes lowered, steps hesitant. His voice scarcely louder than a whisper, he said, "If you let this Man go, you are not Caesar's friend."

The old schemer had allies on Caesar's staff in Rome and he was threatening to tattle. Pilate said, "Annas, where is there harm in Jesus?"

"Whoever makes himself into a king, that man speaks against Caesar," Annas replied. "You know that as well as I do."

Despite everything, despite Claudia Procula's dream, Pilate saw now that he must give way. The boss of Jerusalem did not come without reason to the Roman seat of judgment on so great a day as the last one before Passover. The watching crowd was silent.

Pilate said, "Bring me a basin and water." When it came, he washed his hands slowly, proclaiming in a loud voice, "Behold what I do. I am innocent of the blood of this just Person. See to it!"

The priests sang out, "His blood shall be on us, and on our children."

Pilate faced them, admitting defeat. "What now? Shall I crucify your king?"

Like a well-rehearsed chorus, the priests proclaimed, "We have no king but Caesar."

"So be it. Let this Man be crucified!"

Roman soldiers led Jesus away again. Old Annas watched, eyes bright with triumph. "It is better that one Man should die," he said, "than a whole nation."

"So they took Jesus, and He went out, bearing His own cross, to the place called the Place of the Skull, which is called in Hebrew Golgotha . . ." There they crucified Him.

So says the Gospel of John, but surely it was not quite so simple.

What of the threat of Jesus' vanished disciples? Did the centurion in charge of the crucifixion party place guards around Jesus and the two thieves who were also to be crucified? Did he suspect, as many scholars have suspected since, that a rebellion, nipped only by Jesus' arrest, had been scheduled for that day by Jewish nationalists? Would a fanatical band charge suddenly from some dark alley to rescue their leader? During the night a man alleged to be a disciple had been seen sitting among Roman soldiers. He could have been a spy except for his denial. Three times, with violent oaths, he had denied that he knew Jesus of Galilee, yet from his dialect it was obvious that he himself was a Galilean. This happened before sunrise, and as he cursed, a distant cock could be heard crowing.

All this and more must have been in the centurion's mind as he assembled his party and marched it off to Golgotha.

The Road to Calvary

MODERN Jerusalem designates the route taken by Jesus with a street named the Via Dolorosa, or Way of Sorrow. It is a narrow, steep thoroughfare running below frequent arches from Pilate's judgment hall to the Church of the Holy Sepulchre. Nobody knows whether the route is authentic, and most Protestant scholars doubt it. If it is genuine, the pavement that Jesus actually trod lies beneath a layer of rubble thirty feet thick, the accumulation of almost two thousand years. Nevertheless, pilgrims from all over the world follow it annually, hoping to gain spiritual profit by mentally re-enacting the tortuous scene of the death march of the Savior of the world — as He trod that last lonely way before finally receiving the punishment due all men for their sin.

Whatever the route, its fame results only from its use by Jesus. But not by such a Jesus as has been depicted by the world's painters. Not the Man of vigor in the wilderness or the dynamic Preacher delivering the Sermon on the Mount. This was a human body that had been abused in the Hebrew council chamber, denied sleep through long hours, and flayed by Roman soldiers.

A bystander, Simon of Cyrene, is forced to help Jesus with the cross

Now it was commanded that a cross should be laid upon His lacerated shoulders. Jesus staggered with it only a short distance before its weight and His pain engulfed Him.

The efficient officer in charge ran his eye over the crowd of bystanders and picked a rugged outdoorsman named Simon from Cyrene in North Africa. "You! Lend a hand with that cross." Simon of Cyrene balanced the weight so that only a fraction of it fell on the suffering Jesus. Together they trudged up the relentless slope, through the city gate, and along the road toward the Hill of the Skull, Mount Calvary. Alert guards with flattened swords beat back those who pressed too closely.

Some of those in the crowd were women who had followed Jesus and His disciples in Galilee. Jesus saw them and said, "Women of Jerusalem, don't weep over Me, but weep over yourselves and your children. For days are coming when men will say, 'Blessed are those without children and those who have never borne children.' "

Finally they reached Golgotha. The centurion went about his work methodically. No raiders had threatened. No rioters had challenged them. Jesus and two other condemned men were laid on the ground, their shoulders on crossbars, arms outstretched. Two soldiers bound their wrists in place. A third opened their clenched fingers and drove a single spike so that it fastened

A soldier stands ready to whip the Prisoner if He lags

flesh to wood. Next he went to their feet. Step by step the horrible mechanics of crucifixion were completed, and then, under a darkening sky, three nearly naked bodies were raised aloft. Only one of them spoke during that excruciating moment. It was Jesus, saying, "Father, forgive them, for they know not what they do."

Dividing the Spoils

Now the guards turned to their next task, which was the division of Jesus' clothing. In a dice-throwers' huddle they took turns tossing marked stones for the best prize of all, Jesus' tunic. It was woven from the top without a single seam in it. Rather than cut it up they cast lots for it.

A solitary priest came striding up the hill wearing the air of a man having unfinished business. "I come to protest in behalf of the high priest," he declared.

The Roman officer said, "What now?"

"That sign on the cross. It's wrong. I protest its use!"

The centurion read the placard above Jesus' head, a sign required by

Roman law to describe the prisoner's crime. Its red letters spelled out: "Jesus of Nazareth, King of the Jews."

The priest argued. "It should read: 'This man said, I am King of the Jews.' "

"Pilate himself wrote that placard, Pharisee. Go to him."

The chief priests hurriedly sent an agent to Pilate's residence. Carefully he explained their objection: "You see, your excellency, this Man is not our king. He merely *claimed* to be our king—"

Pilate waved him away, saying, "What I have written, I have written."

Back at the cross the body of Jesus moved in agony. One of the religious leaders peered up at Him with hate in his eyes. His lips framed a taunt: "You saved others — why don't You save Yourself?"

A soldier, too, mocked the suffering Christ.

Scribes and elders added their jeers: "If He's the King of Israel, let Him come down off that cross and we'll believe Him!"

Jesus begins the agonizing climb to the Hill of Crucifixion

One of the thieves turned his head, railing at Jesus with the others. "Aren't You the Christ? Then save Yourself — and us."

The second thief remonstrated. "Be quiet and fear God," he told his companion. "We are receiving just punishment for our deeds, but this Man has done nothing wrong." Then, turning his face toward Jesus, the penitent criminal in one brief sentence revealed how his observation of the Lord had transformed his heart in these last moments: "Lord," he pleaded, "remember me in Your kingdom." Jesus had become his Savior and King.

As the crowd suddenly fell silent, Jesus replied to the man: "Truly, I say to you, *today you will be with Me in Paradise!*"

Darkness at Noon

SUDDENLY the daylight failed. Though it was just past noon and a blazing sun should have stood overhead, the earth lay under a smothering blanket of darkness. In the deepening gloom several women and a young man made their way close to the three crosses. One of the women was Jesus' mother. The young man was the disciple named John.

Jesus, stirring in His pain, caught a glimpse of them and His voice called out with its old authority. "Woman, behold your son!" He told Mary. "Behold your mother," He said to John. And from that moment on John took Mary into his own home and honored her as his blood parent.

The day wore on and the crowds on the slopes of Golgotha were silent. When the water clocks of Jerusalem registered near the hour of three, the darkness was stirred by four urgent words. In a loud voice Jesus cried:

"Eloi, Eloi, lama sabachthani."

Jesus crumples to the ground

An ancient white-robed Hebrew had worked his way in the darkness to a place close to the cross. The centurion demanded of him. "What did He say, wise one?"

The patriarch replied, "My God, My God, why have You forsaken Me?" When the Roman asked no more questions, he added, "It's the beginning of a Psalm written by our King David hundreds of years ago. In it he prophesied all the things that have happened to the Messiah this day: the times they spat on Him, the scourging, the casting of lots for His garments."

A call came from the central cross. It was Jesus saying, "I thirst." A soldier tied a sponge onto a javelin and poured sour wine over it. Mercifully he pressed it against Jesus' lips.

The ancient Hebrew spoke again. "And that was also prophesied by David when he said,

> 'My strength is dried up like a potsherd,
> and my tongue cleaves to my jaws;
> and thou dost lay me in the dust of death.' "

He paused, punctuating the prophecy with silence.

> " 'And they have pierced my hands and feet.' "

Roman soldiers strip Jesus of His clothing

Jesus turned His face from the sponge. Because of the darkness only those closest to the cross could see the shudder that convulsed His body. At the same instant He cried in a loud voice, "It is finished! Father, into Thy hands I commit My spirit."

With those words the mortal life of Jesus of Nazareth ended.

The Soldier's Judgment

THE ROMAN GUARDS shuffled nervously as they leaned on their spears, and their commander spoke thoughts that must have been in all their minds. "Truly, this was a just Man," he said.

Gently the earth began to move, rippling at first like the skin of a mastodon aroused from sleep, then stretching and wrinkling with the force of violent convulsions so that cliffs collapsed and boulders rolled into the valleys. Earthquakes were not unknown in Judea. They had come at half-century intervals for as long as Judeans could remember, and now the shuddering earth split into fissures so deep that burial vaults in a nearby cemetery were opened, revealing the bodies of many who had been dead for generations.

Jesus is nailed to the cross

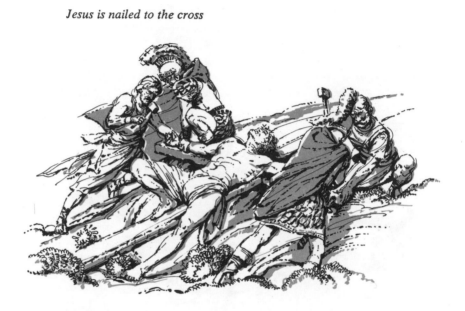

As abruptly as they came, the tremors ceased and daylight returned. The centurion checked the crosses set in their sockets. They were all erect, each holding a sagging body. The sound of hurrying footsteps drew his eyes to a young man who had just stopped before the bearded patriarch who was standing below the body of Jesus. For a long moment the old man asked questions and the youth answered. Then the young man departed and it seemed to the centurion that the old man stood straighter than before. Wondering, the Roman asked, "Do you get good news at a time like this?"

"The boy says that the curtain before our Holy of Holies is torn from hem to hem though no human hand has touched it."

"Maybe it's an omen," the centurion said, thinking of the auguries and portents of Roman gods.

"In truth, so it could be."

"What do you make of it, then?"

The patriarch said, "It was also written in our Scriptures: 'All the ends of the world shall remember and turn to the Lord and all the races of the earth shall worship Him.' "

"Even us Romans?"

"Romans and all other Gentiles, yes. For by rending our sacred curtain God has opened a way to Himself for all peoples of all races, through His Son, Jesus Christ."

He smiled gently at the officer. "My Lord is dead now and I own a new grave in yonder garden. May I take His body for burial if I obtain Pilate's permission?"

The centurion barked an order. "See to it that they are dead." His soldiers went to the thieves and broke their legs, which was both an added degree of punishment and a precaution adopted long ago to insure that a criminal pretending to be dead would not run away after being taken from the cross. Then one of the guards did a very odd thing. When he perceived that Jesus was already dead, instead of breaking His legs, he thrust his spear into His side and "at once there came out blood and water."

The Son of God — crucified between thieves

Now the centurion had done his duty. He spoke to the Jewish patriarch and his voice was different, more brotherly and less official. "Come, we'll see Pilate together," he said. "He'll want a report." A strange thought was stirring his mind, beneath heavy layers of habit and indifference, repeating itself insistently. With each step, each breath, each heartbeat it came again, growing louder, crying for utterance.

The judgment hall of Pontius Pilate loomed straight ahead, and their sandals made brisk sounds on the pavement. The old man said, "Centurion, why this long silence? What are your thoughts?"

"I was thinking," the Roman replied slowly, "that truly, the Man I crucified was the Son of God."

Mary, the mother of Jesus, and "the disciple whom He loved" watch heartbroken as the Lord's dead body is taken down from the cross

(continued from page 438)

Because of the sacrificial death of the Saviour upon the cross, the cross rapidly became interwoven into the theological construction of religious thinking, especially Paul's. In I Corinthians 1:17, the "preaching" (*kerugma*) of the Cross is set forth as the "divine folly" in sharp contrast to earthly wisdom. In Ephesians 2:16, it is presented as the medium of reconciliation. In Colossians 1:20, peace has been effected through the Cross. In Colossians 2:14, the penalties of the law have been removed from the believer by the Cross. How Paul as a pious Hebrew, to whom one hanged was accursed, and as a Roman to whom one crucified was an object of scorn (Gal. 3:13), came to glory in the Cross would be one of the absurdities of history, were it not for the fact that the apostle held the Crucified as the Christ of God. (Gal. 2:20). Crucifixion was one of the most cruel and barbarous forms of death known to man. It was practiced, especially in times of war, by the Phoenicians, Carthaginians, Egyptians, and later by the Romans. So dreaded was it that even in the pre-Christian era, the cares and troubles of life were often compared to a cross.

The details of the crucifixion of Christ are passed over, the evangelists resting content with the simple statement "They crucified him" (Matt. 27:35; Mark 15:24). Following His trial before the Jewish and Roman authorities, He was led forth for crucifixion. Preparatory to the actual ordeal itself, He was scourged. The prisoner was bent over, tied to a post, while the Roman lictor applied blow upon blow upon His bared back with a lash intertwined with pieces of bone or steel. This in itself was frequently sufficient to cause death.

The agony of the crucified victim was brought about by a number of factors. First, the painful but non-serious character of the wounds inflicted. Although there were two distinctive methods of affixing a living victim to a cross, tying or nailing, it is well established that Christ underwent the horror of the latter, or possibly both. The second factor causing great suffering was the abnormal position of the body. The slightest movement would be accompanied with additional torture. The third factor would be the traumatic fever induced by hanging for such a long period of time.

What was the physical reason for Christ's death? Recent medical studies have sought an answer to the question. When a person is suspended by his two hands, the blood sinks rapidly into the lower extremities of the body. Within six to twelve minutes blood pressure has dropped to 50 per cent, while the rate of the pulse has doubled. The heart is deprived of blood and fainting follows. This leads to an orthorastic collapse through insufficient circulation. Death by crucifixion is due to heart failure. Victims of crucifixion did not generally succumb for two or three days. Death was hastened by the "crucifragium" or the breaking of the legs. "When they came to Jesus and saw that He was dead already, they brake not his legs" (John 19:33). Sometimes, a fire was built beneath the cross that its fumes might suffocate the sufferer.

Among the Jews, a stupefying potion was prepared by the merciful women of Jerusalem, a drink which Christ refused (Mark 15:23). To such a death, the one who was co-equal with God descended (Phil. 2:5).   J.F.G.

CROW (See Birds)

CROWN, a band encircling the head to designate honor; there are three principal types of crowns: the royal crown, the priestly crown, and the crown of the victor. Some of the terms employed for "crown" in the OT are: Heb. *qodhqôth,* a part of the human anatomy, the *"crown" of the head, the pate* (Deut. 28:35, II Sam. 14:25, etc.); Heb. *zēr, that which encircles the head,* viz. *a garland of flowers* (Exod. 25:11); Heb. *nezer, that which is a symbol of dedication to the priesthood, the priestly crown;* Heb. *'ătārâh,* the customary term (I Chron. 20:2, Prov. 4:9). In the NT (Gr., *stéphanos* and *diádema* are used. The first refers to a garland or chaplet such as was worn by a victorious athlete. This type of crown is employed figuratively by Paul and John as a symbol of Christian triumph (II Tim. 4:8, Rev. 2:10). The diadem was a symbol of the power to rule.

Of particular interest is the crown of thorns which Jesus wore (Gr. *akánthinos stéphanos,* Matt. 27:29, Mark 15:17, John 19:2). The particular variety of thorns from which this crown was woven is impossible to determine, as there are about 22 words in the Bible used for the thorny plants, and the Greek word is a generic, not a specific term.   J.F.G.

CROWN OF THORNS (See Crown)

CRUCIFIXION (See Cross)

CRUSE (*krōos*), a small, porous, earthen vessel for the purpose of holding liquids (I Sam. 26:11, 12, 16; I Kings 19:6). In the NT *alabástron* as the alabaster cruse or flask for holding ointment — not a box as in KJV (Matt. 26:7, Mark 14:3, Luke 7:37).

CRYSTAL. Both Hebrew and Greek terms can be rendered "ice"; more likely it means rock crystal or crystallized quartz. The reason for the selection of the word "ice" is that the ancients believed that crystal was formed by the process of intense cold (Job 28:17; Rev. 4:6, 21:11, 22:1). See METALS and MINERALS.

CUBIT (See Weights and Measures)

CUCKOO (See Birds)

CUCKOW (See Birds)

CUCUMBER (See Plants)

CUMMIN (See Plants)

CUNEIFORM (*kū-nē'i-fôrm*), a system of writing by symbolic characters used chiefly in the Mesopotamian area in ancient times. The system is regarded as the forerunner of the alphabet. The cuneiform characters were developed by the Sumerians, who recorded them upon clay tablets which they baked firm in the oven. The term refers to the wedge-shaped characters of the script. At the time of the discovery of the personal library of Ashurbanipal of Nineveh (ruled 668-626 B.C.) by Layard and Rassam (1850-1854) literally multitudes of these clay tablets were unearthed, among them the Babylonian versions of creation and of the flood, which show striking similarities with the accounts in the OT. According to Olmsted of the Oriental Institute of the University of Chicago, more than half a million of these tablets are yet to be deciphered.

The Tel-El-Amarna Letters (1400-1350 B.C.), found in Egypt in 1887, consisting of 300 clay tablets are written in the Akkadian form of the cuneiform script. The Akkadian was the "Lingua Franca" of that day, i.e., the language of trade

⊢	'a	⫼	l
⩘	'e	⊥	m
⫼	'u	⇥	n
⫼	b	⩒	s
⎮	g	⧻	ṣ
⫼	d	⟨	ṣ̣
⩓	h	⟝	p
⊬	u (w)	⫼	ṣ
⟊	z	⋈	ṣ̣
⊹	ḥ	⊢	q
⊹	ḫ	⫻	r
⊬	ṭ	⩒	š
⫻	i (y)	✳	š̌
⊻	k	⊢	t
⟍	ġ		

CUNEIFORM ALPHABET from Ras Shamra.

and diplomacy used between Syria and Egypt. (See AMARNA, TELL-EL).Of still greater importance was the discovery between 1929 and 1939 at Ras Shamra in the NW of Syria of the Ugaritic literature. This was written in a Canaanite dialect closely related to proto-Hebrew. The Ras Shamra literature, dating closely c. 1400 B.C., gives us much information on Canaanite religion and presents many parallels to the OT in vocabulary and poetic style.   J.F.G.

CUP (Heb. *kôs*, Gr. *potérion*), a term used in a literal and figurative sense. Cups were of various forms and designs, and made of a variety of materials: gold, silver, earthenware, copper, bronze, etc. The cups of the Hebrews, whether metal or porcelain, often carried designs borrowed from Phoenicia and Egypt. All of Solomon's drinking vessels were of gold (I Kings 10:21). The cups mentioned in the NT were, beyond much doubt, of Roman style.

The word *cup* may also signify a laver (Exod. 24:6) or goblet (S. of Sol. 7:2; I Chron. 28:17). The cup is used as a symbol of prosperity or of Jehovah's blessing and, in reverse, of Jehovah's malediction upon the wicked (Ps. 11:6; 16:5; 23:5). The cup also represents drunkenness and other illicit pleasures (Prov. 23:31; 51:7; Rev. 17:4; 18:6). "Cup of consolation" (Jer. 16:7) stems from the oriental custom of sending to bereaved friends food and drink for their mourning feast. "Cup of salvation" (Ps. 116:13), "Cup of blessing" (I Cor. 10:16), or "Cup of the Lord" (verse 21). Paul here refers to the communion cup, over which the blessing is said prior to the feast which commemorates the Lord's death and burial. The cup from ancient times signifies fellowship. Thus, when the believer takes the cup of the Lord, he enters into fellowship with Him. The "cup of demons" (I Cor. 10:21) mentioned in opposition to the cup of the Lord can best be understood in this context. The apostle is saying in a figurative way that we cannot have fellowship with Christ and with the forces of darkness at one and the same time. At heathen feasts the cup was sacred to the name of the god in whose name the feast was being held. Thus at the communion service, the cup is sacred to the name of the Redeemer who instituted its practice (Matt. 26:27; Mark 14:23, 24; Luke 22:20). The "cup of trembling" literally, cup of intoxication (Isa. 51:17, 22; Zach. 12:2); "Cup of astonishment, desolation" (Ezek. 23:33); "Cup of fury" (Isa. 51:17-22); "Cup of indignation" (Rev. 14:10).

CUPBEARER (Heb. *mashqeh, one giving drink*), a palace official who served wine at a king's table. Cupbearers were men of confidence and trust. They are mentioned in Genesis 40:1ff; I Kings 10:5; II Chronicles 9:4; Nehemiah 1:11.

CURSE (Heb. *'ālāh, me'ērâh, qelālâh*; Gr. katápa), the reverse of "to bless." On the human level, to wish harm or catastrophe. On the divine, to impose judgment. In the oriental mind the curse carried with it its own power of execution. A curse was imposed upon the serpent (Gen. 3:14). Noah cursed Ham (Gen. 9:25). The curse of Balaam, the pseudo-prophet, turned to a blessing. (Num. 24:10). A curse was placed upon Mount Ebal for disobedience to the law of Moses (Deut. 27:1-9). The cursing of one's parents is sternly prohibited by Mosaic regulations. Christ commanded those who would be His disciples to bless and curse not (Luke 6:28). When Peter, at Christ's trial, denied that he knew Him, he invited a curse upon himself (Matt. 26:74). This passage is often misunderstood by Western readers. Paul represents the curse of the law as borne by Christ upon the cross for the believer (Gal. 3:13). The modern Western practice of cursing, i.e., using profane language, is never referred to in the Scriptures. See BLASPHEMY.

CURTAINS (Heb. *yerî'âh*). 1. The curtains of fine linen and goats' hair which covered the tabernacle (Exod. 26:1ff; 38:9ff). Gradually, the "curtains" gave their name to the entire structure.

2. Employed figuratively by Isaiah (40:22), referring to the heavens. He uses the word *dōq*, lit. "gauze."

CUSH (kūsh, Heb. *kûsh*). 1. The oldest son of Ham, one of the three sons of Noah. (Gen. 10:6-8, I Chron. 1:8-10). Among the descendants were Seba, Havilah, Sabta, Raamah, and Sabtecha. They were mostly located in Arabia. Nimrod is likewise said to be the son of Cush, but the word "son" probably means "descendant."

2. "Cush, the Benjamite," the title for Psalm 7, viewed as referring to King Saul, the Benjamite. Since Cush and Kish are similar in sound, they are held to be one. Saul's father's name was Kish.

3. Cush, the country. The name of the territory through which the Gihon flowed (Gen. 2:13); translated Ethiopia by KJV, but in view of the distance of Ethiopia in relation to the Red Sea, the site is probably in SE Babylon or Chaldea. The wife of Moses is referred to as a Cushite, making her a target of criticism by Miriam and Aaron (Num. 12:1). If this be Zipporah, the wife of Moses, mentioned earlier, her origin was that of the land of Midian. The earlier passages seem to indicate Cush as African, the latter as Asian. The precise identification of either the woman or the country constitutes an unsolved problem.

CUSHI (kū'shī), a member of the Cushite people.
1. The man sent by Joab to inform David that Absalom's rebellion was quelled and that the time was ripe for him to return to his throne. (II Sam. 18:21-32).

2. A contemporary of Jeremiah, the great-grandfather of Jehudi (Jer. 36:14).

3. The father of the Prophet Zephaniah (Zeph. 1:1).

CUSTOM, when not referring to a tax, usually means "manner," "way," or "statute" (Gen. 31:35; Judg. 11:39; Jer. 32:11). Heathen religious practice is referred to in Leviticus 18:30 and Jeremiah 10:3. In the NT it means "manner," "usage" (Luke 1:9; Acts 6:14) and "religious practices."

CUSTOM, RECEIPT OF (RV "place of toll"), from which Matthew (Levi) was called to follow Christ (Matt. 9:9). In post-exilic days the tribute was usually in terms of a road toll. The Romans imposed tribute or tax upon the Jews as upon all their subjects for the maintenance of their provincial government. Tax collectors or publicans were despised because of their notorious dishonesty and willingness to work for a foreign power.

CUTHA or **CUTH** (kū'thȧ, kŭth), the longer form preferable, one of the cities from which Sargon, king of Assyria, brought immigrants to repopulate the area of Samaria which he had sacked in 720 B.C. (II Kings 17:24-30). Because of their numerical predominance, the inhabitants of Samaria were henceforth referred to as Cutheans. As a result of mixture, a synthesis between Mosaism and heathenism arose. This is one of the explanations for the deep antipathy existing between the Jews and the Samaritans down into the days of the NT (John 4:9). *The ruins and temples of Cutha.* From the contract tablets found by Rassam at Tel-Ibrahim it now appears that the ancient name of Cutha was Gudua or Kuta. This city of high culture and commerce lay NE of Babylon and was one of its most important centers. Rassam describes its almost perfect ruins as being about 3,000 feet in circumference and 280 feet high. In it was a sanctuary dedicated to Ibrahim (Abraham). Both city and its great temple, the latter dedicated to Nergal, appear to date back to Sumerian times.

CUTTINGS (cuttings in the flesh), a heathen practice, usually done in mourning for the dead, which was forbidden to the children of Israel (Lev. 19:28). This cruel practice, extending from the cutting of the hair or beard to self-mutilation, was widespread among the heathen nations. Homer re-

fers to it in the *Iliad* where, in place of human sacrifice, the people cut themselves in mourning for the deceased Achilles. Besides being indicative of excessive grief, these cuttings were supposed to propitiate the idols of the heathen. They included tattooings, gashes, castrations, etc. In Elijah's day, the priests of Baal cut themselves till the blood ran in a vain attempt to make Baal answer (I Kings 18:28). Tattooing as a mark of allegiance to a deity, or as soldiers to their commander was also explicitly forbidden (Lev. 19:28). This practice was forbidden on humanitarian grounds and because most of it was performed as a religious rite to some local heathen deity. Solon forbade the women of Athens of his day to beat themselves till the blood ran. The holiness code of Israel reads, "Ye are the children of the Lord your God: ye shall not cut yourselves" (Deut. 14:1). The LXX adds the phrase, "in your flesh for the dead." The only cutting in the flesh allowed in Israel is that of circumcision at the command of God (Gen. 21:4).

CYLINDER SEALS, a cylindrical disc measuring from 1½ to 3 inches long — sometimes made of terra cotta, other times of precious stones. On it were printed for publication insignia of different descriptions.

CYPRUS (sī'prŭs, Gr. *kúpros, "copper"*), an island in the eastern part of the Mediterranean directly off the coast of Syria and Cilicia, 148 miles long and about 40 miles across. In mythology, it is famous as the birthplace of Zeus. Historically, its roots are deep in the past. The OT refers to it as the "Isles of Chittim" (*Kittim,* RSV, Ezek. 27:6).

The island is rich in copper deposits, hence, its name. In the pre-Christian era, a large colony of Jews settled there, who later formed the nucleus of the Christian church ministered to by Paul and company. During the Roman rule, the Jews were expelled from Cyprus in the days of Hadrian.

Barnabas, who accompanied Paul on his first missionary journey, was a native of the island (Acts 4:36), and with John Mark returned to evangelize Cyprus after they had left Paul's company (Acts 15:36-39). The Apostolic party passed through the island from Salamis to Paphos. At Paphos, Sergius Paulus, the imperial deputy of the island believed in Christ (Acts 13:12).

Cyprus has known various conquerors, in addition to the Assyrians who had been attracted by its rich resources. The Egyptians, the Hittites, the Phoenicians, the Greeks, Romans, Turks, and British have all taken advantage of its attractive character.

The aboriginal inhabitants of Cyprus seem to have been of Minoan stock. After the breakup of the Minoan civilization, the dark ages settled down upon the island. The curtain rose again when Hellenistic settlers from the Greek mainland reached it. Sargon in 709 B.C., made himself ruler of Cyprus and it paid tribute to Assyria until the days of Esarhaddon. The demise of the Assyrian Empire appears to have brought it relative freedom, until it was annexed to Egypt in 540 B.C. With the rise of Cambyses (526 B.C.), Cyprus passed under Persian rule until the time of Alexander the Great, to whom it surrendered voluntarily and helped with the siege of Tyre. During the late inter-testamental period it fell into the hands of the Romans (cf. I Macc. 10:13). A

ISLE OF CYPRUS. Barnabas, who joined Paul's first missionary journey, came from Cyprus. A Jewish settlement which existed on Cyprus before the Christian era was the nucleus of the Christian church ministered to by Paul. The island's name comes from its rich copper deposits.

number of the ill-famed guard of Antiochus Epiphanes were Cypriots. In 58 B.C. Cyprus was accorded provincial status by the Romans. In 22 B.C. it was made the direct charge of the Senate.

It was at Paphos in Cyprus that Elymas, the sorcerer, attempted to dissuade the deputy from becoming a Christian, and was punished by being deprived of his sight (Acts 3:11).   J.F.G.

CYPRUS, an island in the eastern Mediterranean, is referred to in the Old Testament as the "Isles of Chittim." Cyprus was famous for its copper, and its forests were cut down for smelting purposes. In the time of Hadrian, the Jews were expelled from Cyprus. This photograph shows Famagusta.

CYRENE, CYRENIAN (sīrē'nĭ, Gr. *Kyréne, wall*), a Libyan city in N. Africa, W of Egypt from which it was separated by a part of the Libyan Desert. It was situated some 2,000 feet above the Mediterranean from which it was ten miles distant. The coastline afforded a natural shelter from the heat of the Sahara. It is protected by steps of descending ranges about 80 miles to the S. The fertility and climate of the city are delightful and productive.

Cyrene, originally a Greek colony, was founded by Battus in 603 B.C. This veritable "oasis in the desert" attracted travelers and commerce from early times. Among its distinguished citizens was Carneacles, the founder of the new Academy at

renowned Persian Empire which was to continue until the coming of Alexander the Great. Seven years subsequent to the demise of Nebuchadnezzar, Nabonidus ascended the throne of Babylon, in 555 B.C. He was destined to be the last ruling sovereign of the neo-Babylonian Empire, for in the highlands of Iran another kingdom was forging out of its own program of conquest. With the defeat of the Medes, when Astyages, king of the Medes, was vanquished by Cyrus, the realm of Persia commenced to assume threatening proportions. Cyrus himself announced his genealogy: "I am Cyrus, king of the hosts, the great king, king of Babylon, king of Sumer and Akkad . . . son of Cambyses, the king, king of Anshan; the grand-

KING CYRUS OF PERSIA gave orders for the destruction of Babylon and for the division of the kingdom between the Medes and Persians—according to the prophecy written on the wall.

Athens. Aristippus, the Epicurean philosopher and friend of Socrates, also came from this city. Ptolemy Euregetes I incorporated Cyrene as a part of Egypt in 231 B.C. It later passed into the hands of the Romans, being willed to them by the last Ptolemy.

Cyrene is not mentioned in the OT but becomes important in the NT. A native of Cyrene, Simon by name, was impressed by the Roman soldiers into carrying the cross of Jesus (Luke 23:26). Thus Simon immortalized his city. There were also representatives of this city present in Jerusalem upon the day of Pentecost (Acts 2:10). Its Jewish population warranted a synagogue (Acts 6:9). Lucius of Cyrene receives mention in Acts 11:19, 20. Archaeology has shown that it was the Greek plan to make Cyrene the "Athens of Africa." The most interesting remains are a great system of tombs cut out of solid rock into the cliff. Architecture and paintings adorn these tombs.

CYRUS (sī'rŭs, Heb. *Kôresh*), the son of Cambyses, king of Anshan. With the rise of Cyrus began the

son of Cyrus . . . the great-grandson of Teispes . . . king of Anshan . . ." In this same inscription, Cyrus proceeds to relate how the city of Babylon opened its gates to him without resistance, thus confirming the Biblical account recorded in Daniel 5 when Darius, acting as vice-regent for Cyrus, took the city of Babylon in the name of Cyrus the Great. The neo-Babylonian empire was in no condition to resist the advance of Cyrus, and fell easy prey into the hands of the Persians. The OT sets the framework of reference against the backdrop of Belshazzar's impious feast (Daniel 5:1-30).

Cyrus entered Babylon on October 29, 539 B.C. and presented himself in the role of the liberator of the people. He allowed the images of the gods to be transported back to their original cities, and instituted a kindly policy of repatriation for captive peoples. His policies of moderation naturally extended to the Hebrews, whom he encouraged to return to Judea to rebuild their temple (II Chron. 36:22, 23; Ezra 1:1-6; etc.). Isaiah refers to Cyrus as the "Anointed One" (Isa. 44:27, 28; 45:1-5).   J.F.G.

Here are the ruins of the now famous monastery of Qumran. It was here that the Dead Sea Scrolls were found in 1947 by a Bedouin shepherd. The Dead Sea Scrolls have shed new light on the "silent" years between the Old Testament and the New Testament.

The photograph above is of the Tomb of David on Mount Zion. David brought the Ark to Zion, which thereafter became sacred.

This is the famous Tomb of Cyrus II, the Persian king who conquered Babylon and released the captive Hebrews.

*"My God, my God, why hast thou
forsaken me? why art thou so
far from helping me, and from the
words of my roaring?"*
(PSALMS 22:1)

We can almost hear the Israelites, during their captivity in
Assyria, chanting David's psalm. The relief shown depicts slaves
at work building the city of Nineveh.

D

DABAREH (dăb'à-rĕ), erroneous spelling of Daberath (Josh. 21:28).

DABBASHETH (dăb'à-shĕth), hill town of uncertain location, but adjoining the heritage of Zebulun (Josh. 19:10).

DABERATH (dăb'ĕ-răth), an ancient town near the western side of Mt. Tabor; part of the heritage of Issachar given to the Levites (Josh. 19:12; I Chron. 6:72). A strategic location, the probable site of the defeat of Sisera by Barak. (Judg. 4:14-22).

DAGON (dā'gŏn, Heb. *dāghôn*, probably *fish*), chief god of the Philistines. Originally worshiped by Canaanites before Philistine invasion of Canaan, as indicated by place names such as Bethdagon in Judah (Josh. 15:14), and in Asher (Josh. 19:27). Either a fish god or the god of agriculture, from *Dag,* "fish," or *Dagan,* "grain." On a wall of a palace in Babylon he is shown as half fish. That he was god of agriculture is supported by the tribute which priests and diviners bade the rulers to send when the ark was returned to Israel. Five golden mice and five golden emerods (*tumors,* ASV) were votive offerings expressing gratitude for Dagon's freeing their fields of mice and their bodies of tumors. Saul's head was placed in a temple of Dagon (I Chron. 10:10). Samson destroyed the temple of Dagon in Gaza (Judg. 16:30).   J.D.F.

DALAIAH (dăl'à-ī'à). 1. Descendant of David (I Chron. 3:1-24).

2. A priest of Aaron's line (I Chron. 24:18).

3. A prince who pleaded with King Jehoiakim not to destroy the roll containing the prophecies of Jeremiah (Jer. 36:12,25).

4. The founder of a post-exilic family whose genealogy was lost (Ezra 2:60; Neh. 7:62).

5. The father of Shemaiah (Nah. 6:10).

DALE, THE KINGS. 1. Where Abram met Melchizedek (Gen. 14:17).

2. Absalom's memorial (II Sam. 18:18).

WHEN THE PHILISTINES placed the Ark in their temple, the image of their god Dagon fell crashing to the floor. The Philistines had rejoiced at their capture of the Ark, thinking that this holy symbol of the Jews would be a good omen for them too. Now great fear came over the Philistines. They wanted to be rid of the Ark as hurriedly as possible.

CITY OF DAMASCUS, viewed from the east. Paul, then called Saul, was converted on his way to Damascus to arrest Christians. He continued on to Damascus and preached in the synogogues, which aroused the anger of the priests. He escaped by being let down from a wall in a basket.

DALMANUTHA (dăl-mȧ-nū'thȧ), a village on the W coast of the Sea of Galilee, adjoining Magdala (Matt. 15:39). Landing place of Jesus after feeding the multitude (Mark 8:10). It is mentioned only in the NT. Considerable ruins near modern Mejdel (Magdala) are considered the location.

DALMATIA (dăl-mā'shȧ, Gr. *Dalmatía, deceitful*), a mountainous province on the E shore of the Adriatic Sea. Christianity, implanted under Titus, (II Tim. 4:10), continues until today. It was ruled by Rome as early as 160 A.D. Paul may have visited in the province (Rom. 15:19); in his time it was regarded as part of Illyricum.

DALPHON (dăl'fŏn), one of Haman's sons who were slain and hanged after Esther became queen (Esth. 9:6-13).

DAMARIS (dăm'ȧ-rĭs, Gr. *dámaris*), a convert of Paul at Mars Hill (Acts 17:34).

DAMASCUS (dȧ-măs'kŭs, Gr. *Damaskós*), for more than four thousand years the capital of one government after another, a prize for which nation after nation went to war, a city whose boast for centuries has been, "The world began at Damascus, and the world will end there." It is a modern focal point between the Christian and the Mohammedan worlds, center of tourist interest and of international unrest.

It was founded some 2,200 years before Christ by Uz, a grandson of Shem (Josh. 1:6; 4). It is the capital of Syria, a small region of unique geological formation, lying between Mt. Hermon and the Syrian Desert. It is watered by the Barada and the Wady Awaj, Abana and Pharpar of the OT (II Kings 5:12). A 2,000 foot elevation gives it a delightful climate. Its gardens and olive groves still flourish after millennia of cultivation. By the time of Abraham it was well-enough known to be a landmark (Gen. 14:15). Caravan routes from the E, W, and S crossed in the city, carrying treasures of silks, perfumes, carpets, and foods.

Damascus and Syria played an important part in Biblical history. En route from Ur, Abraham found in Syria a steward, Eliezer, who was his heir presumptive until Isaac came (Gen. 15:2,3). From the days when Abram liberated Lot (Gen. 14:13-16), there were repeated periods of peace and war among his descendants, many of them involving Damascus. Abraham secured a wife for Isaac from Syria, hence Israel is of Syrian ancestry (Gen. 24; Deut. 26:5). Jacob labored long in Syria for Rachel (Gen. 29). Damascus was once a rich city whose fairs were far-famed (Ezek. 27:16). According to Josephus, Hadad was the first king (*Ant.* VII:5; 2). David subjugated and ruled the city for a season (II Sam. 8:5,6; I Chron. 18:3-6). Rezon, a deserter, slew King Hadadezer whom David had defeated, and made himself king. He hated Israel and harassed Solomon "during all the days of his life" (I Kings 11:23-25). Solomon had made extensive purchases from Syria (I Kings 10:29). Asa, king of Judah, bribed Ben-hadad, grandson of Rezon of Syria, to aid him against Israel, paying him with temple treasures (I Kings 15:16-21). Elijah, acting upon instructions from God, anointed Hazael to be king of Syria and Jehu to rule Israel, to the end that Judah might be punished (I Kings 19:15-17). Elah succeeded Baasha in Israel (I Kings 16:6) and while drunk was slain by Zimri who usurped the throne and destroyed the house of Baasha (I Kings 16:10-14). Zimri killed himself (I Kings 16:18); his son Omri succeeded him, and was followed by Ahab (I Kings 16:29). Ben-hadad attacked Ahab with a great force, but during a drunken orgy was overwhelmed. Ahab foolishly allowed him to return to his throne (I Kings 20:1-34). Later, becoming ill, he sent Hazael to consult Elisha who made a prophecy that led Hazael to assassinate Ben-hadad and usurp the throne for which Elijah had anointed him (I Kings 19:15; II Kings 8:7-15). Hazael overcame Ahaziah and Joram (II Kings 8:28), ravaged Reuben and Manasseh, and Israel (II Kings 10:32-33; 13:3).

A strong kingdom was developed under Ahab, with merchants in Samaria (I Kings 20:34). Syrians defeated Joash after he failed in a test before Elisha (II Kings 13:14-22). Ben-hadad II' succeeded Hazael, and Israel recovered her lost possessions (II Kings 13:24,25). Under Jeroboam Damascus was retaken by Israel (II Kings 14:28). Ahaz, in order to save his kingdom from Syria, made an alliance with Tiglath-Pileser (Pul) who destroyed Damascus and ended Syria's power for many decades (II Kings 16:7-9). The city remained of little importance until 333 B.C. when an army of Alexander the Great captured it. Then followed two centuries of rise and fall. In 63 B.C. Syria became a province of the Roman Empire (Jos. *Wars* 1:6;2).

During New Testament days Damascus was an important center, ruled by Arabia under Aretas (II Cor. 11:32). A strong Christian community had developed by Paul's day. While en route there to arrest the believers, Saul was converted (Acts 9:1-18). He escaped his Jewish enemies of the city by being let down from a wall in a basket (Acts 9:25; II Cor. 11:33). After a checkered history under Rome, Damascus was captured by Moslems in 635 A.D. and made the seat of the Mohammedan world. It remained the center of the Moslem faith until 1918 when it was put under French mandate after World War I. In 1946 it became a free state.   J.D.F.

DAMNATION (Heb. *rasha, to hold guilty*, Deut. 25:1; Isa. 50:9; 54:17, etc.; Gr. *kríno, to put under condemnation*, John 3:17,18; Rom. 14:22; *katakríno, to hold to be unpardonable*, Matt. 12:41; 20:18; Rom. 8:1,3,34; Heb. 11:7; *kríma* and *krísis, judgment, eternal punishment*, Matt. 23:33; Mark 12:40; John 5:29; Rom. 3:8; 5:16; 13:2; I Cor. 11:29,34; *apóleia, destruction, damnation*, II Pet. 2:3). The penalty for unbelief (II Thess. 2:12); for adulterous relations (I Tim. 5:11,12); for hypocrisy (Matt. 23:14); for treason (Rom. 13:2). When referring to the future, the words mean primarily eternal separation from God with accompanying awful punishment (see Ps. 88:10-12; Isa. 38:18); being cast into Gehenna (Matt. 5:29; 10:28; 23:33; 24:51; Mark 9:43, etc.). The severity of the punishment is determined by the degree of sin (Luke 12:36-48), and it is eternal (Mark 3:29; II Thess. 1:9; Isa. 33:14; 66:24; Jude 6,7)   J.D.F.

DAN (CITY), northernmost city of Palestine. Originally Leshem (Josh. 19:47; Judg. 18:29). Captured by Danites and renamed Dan (Judg. 18). It was a commercial center at one time (Ezek. 27:19). Here Jeroboam I set up the golden calf (I Kings 12). The city marked the northern limit of Israel in the common phrase "from Dan to Beersheba" (Judg. 20:1; I Sam. 3:20, etc.).

DAN (TRIBE OF), the tribe to which Dan the fifth son of Jacob gave origin, and, the territory allotted it in Canaan. One son is mentioned among those who migrated to Egypt (Gen. 46:8,23). By the time of the Exodus his offspring had increased to a total of 62,700 men (Num. 1:39). The tribe acted as rear guard during the Exodus (Num. 10:25). They were given a fertile area lying between Judah and the Mediterranean Sea, occupied by the Philistines whose lands extended from Egypt to the coast W of Shechem (Josh. 13:3). Failure to conquer Philistia made the Danites move northward where, by a bit of strategy, they conquered Leshem (Laish of Judg. 18:29), and renamed it Dan (Josh. 19:47; Judg. 18:1-29).

REGION OF DAN (Tell El-Kabi), one of the sources of the Jordan River, near Caesarea Philippi.

The heritage of Dan, though small, was productive and, with the acquisition of extra lands, provided for growth. Aholiab and Samson were Danites (Exod. 31:6; Judg. 13:2, 24). Jeroboam, Solomon's servant, set up a golden calf in Dan and put high places throughout Israel (I Kings 12:25-33). Menahem stayed Pul (Tiglath-Pileser) by bribery (II Kings 15:14-20), but eventually Pul returned, overran Israel and took many Danites into captivity (I Chron. 5:26). Little is known of the tribe from that time.   J.D.F.

DANCING has formed a part of religious rites and has been associated with war and hunting, with marriage, birth, and other occasions since the records of man began to be written. It grew out of three basic human reactions: 1, the desire to imitate movements of beasts, birds, even the sun and moon; 2, the desire to express emotions by gestures; 3, gregarious impulses.

Throughout past ages dancing has been associated with worship. Closely related to religious praises was the sacramental dance in which worshipers sought to express through bodily movements praise or penitence, worship or prayer. Out of the primitive dances the esthetic dance of civilized ancient nations slowly developed. In these the primary concern of the dancers was to reveal grace, speed, and rhythm, often to appeal to the carnal nature of both participants and spectators. Vashti refused to expose herself to this end (Esth. 1:12). Priests of all pagan religions cultivated dancing, but at times found it the source of dissipation and harm. For ages it has been accompanied by clapping of the hands. Percussion and other noise-making instruments seem to be native to the dance (Judg. 11:34; Ps. 68:25).

The Hebrew people developed their own type of dancing, associated in the main with worship. Basically, it was more like modern religious shout-

LION MONUMENT in the ruins of Babylon, supposedly marking the site of the lions' den where Daniel walked unharmed when he had been cast in by Darius the Mede.

ing by individuals, or processions of exuberant groups. Three things characterized it: 1, the sexes never intermingled in it, except where pagan influences had crept in (cf. Exod. 32:19); 2, usually dancing was done by women, with one leading, as in the case of Miriam (Exod. 15:20,21). In this incident, as well as on other occasions, a form of antiphonal singing was used. 3. Dancing usually took place out of doors. For women dancers, see Exodus 15:20; Judges 21:19ff; I Samuel 18:6; Psalm 68:25. Men danced solo, as in the case of David before the Ark (II Sam. 6:14-16), and in groups, as when Israel celebrated the victory over the Amalekites (I Sam. 30:16). The time for dancing was recognized by the writer of Ecclesiastes (3:4). Job complained against the rich because of their ability to dance (Job 21:11). Jeremiah bemoaned the tragedy that made singing and dancing out of place (Lam. 5:15). The redemption of Israel was to be celebrated by dancing, both virgins, and men and boys having part (Jer. 31:13). The Romans introduced the Greek dance to Palestine. Primitive Christian churches allowed the dance, but it soon caused degeneracy and was banned, as is indicated by many of the early Christian writers.   J.D.F.

DANIEL (dănyĕl, Heb. *dānîyē'l* or *dāni'ēl, God is my judge).* 1. David's second son (I Chron. 3: 1;—Chileab, II Sam. 3:3).

2. A post-exilic priest (Ezra 8:2; Neh. 10:6).

3. The exilic seer of the book of Daniel. The prophet was born into an unidentified family of Judean nobility at the time of Josiah's reformation (621 B.C.); for he was among the select, youthful hostages of the first Jewish deportation,

taken to Babylon by Nebuchadnezzar in 605 B.C., the third year of king Jehoiakim (Dan. 1:1,3). The reliability of this date and, indeed, of the whole account has been consistently attacked by hostile criticism. Daniel's dating, however, simply follows the customary Babylonian practice of numbering the years of a king's reign *after* his accession-year (contrast Jer. 46:2 which speaks of this date as Jehoiakim's fourth year). The publication, moreover, of D. J. Wiseman's Nebuchadnezzar tablets demonstrates that after the Babylonian defeat of Egypt at Carchemish in 605 B.C. Nebuchadnezzar did "conquer the whole area of Hatti" (Syria and Palestine) and "take away the heavy tribute of Hatti to Babylon" (*Chronicles of Chaldean Kings* (626-556 B.C., London: Trustees of the British Museum, 1956, pp. 26,29), just as claimed in Daniel 1:2 (cf. II Chron. 36:6-7 and J. B. Payne, "The Uneasy Conscience of Modern Liberal Exegesis," *Bulletin of the Evangelical Theological Society,* I:1 (Winter, 1958), pp. 14-18).

For three years Daniel was trained in all the wisdom of the Chaldeans (Dan. 1:4-5) and was assigned the Babylonian name Belteshazzar, "Protect his life!", thereby invoking a pagan deity (4:8). Daniel and his companions, however, remained true to their ancestral faith, courteously refusing "the king's dainties" (1:8, tainted with idolatry and contrary to the Levitical purity-laws). God rewarded them with unsurpassed learning (1:20), qualifying them as official "wise-men" (cf. 2:13). Upon Daniel, moreover, He bestowed the gift of visions and of interpreting dreams (1:17; cf. Daniel's wisdom in the Apocryphal stories of *Susanna* and *Bel and the Dragon*).

Near the close of his second year (602 B.C.) Nebuchadnezzar required his fellow-Chaldeans, who as the ruling strata in society had assumed the position of priestly diviners (2:2; cf. Herodotus, I:191), to identify and interpret an undisclosed dream that had troubled him the preceding evening (2:5,8, ASVmg). The hoax of spiritism and astrology was duly exposed, but when judgment was pronounced upon the enchanters Daniel and his companions were included under the death-sentence. But the "God in heaven that revealeth secrets" (2:28, cf. 2:11) answered Daniel's prayer for illumination (2:18-19). Daniel revealed both the dream, depicting a fourfold image, and its import of four world empires (Babylon, Persia, Greece, and Rome) that should introduce God's Messianic kingdom (2:44; see DANIEL, BOOK OF). Nebuchadnezzar forthwith elevated him to be chief over the wise-men (2:48 does not, however, state that he became a pagan priest, as inferred by those who would discredit Daniel's historicity). He further offered him the governorship of the province of Babylon, though Daniel committed this latter appointment to his three friends (2:49; see SHADRACH, FURNACE).

In the latter years of Nebuchadnezzar's reign (604-562 B.C.), Daniel's courage was demonstrated (4:19, cf. 4:7) when he interpreted the king's dream of the fallen tree. Tactfully informing his despotic master that for seven "times" (months? cf. 4:33) pride would reduce him to beast-like madness, he reiterated "that the Most High ruleth in the kingdom of men" (4:24-25; cf. its historical fulfillment twelve months later, 4: 28-33).

In 552 B.C., after the retirement of king Nabonidus to Arabian Teima and the accession of his son Belshazzar to the royal dignity (ICC, p.

67), Daniel was granted his vision of the four great beasts (Dan. 7), which parallels Nebuchadnezzar's earlier dream of the composite image. Then in 550, at the time of Cyrus' amalgamation of the Median and Persian states and of the growing eclipse of Babylon, Daniel received the prophecy of the ram and the he-goat, concerning Persia and Greece (8:20-21) down to Antiochus IV (8:25). On Oct. 12, 539 B.C., Cyrus' general Gobryas, after having routed the Chaldean armies, occupied the city of Babylon. During the profane revelries of Belshazzar's court that immediately preceded the end, Daniel was summoned to interpret God's "handwriting on the wall"; and the prophet fearlessly condemned the desperate prince (5:22-23). He predicted Medo-Persian victory (v. 28), and that very night the citadel fell and Belshazzar was slain.

When Darius the Mede (presumably Gobryas, or another official of similar name, cf. John C. Whitcomb, *Darius the Mede,* Grand Rapids: Eerdmans, 1959, pp. 17-24) was made king of Babylon by Cyrus (5:31; 9:1), he at once sought out Daniel as one of his three "presidents" (6:2; cf. Whitcomb, *op. cit.,* p. 17, on the established historicity of such appointments), because of his excellency, and was considering him for the post of chief administrator (6:3). Daniel's jealous colleagues, failing to uncover valid charges of corruption (6:4), proceeded to contrive his downfall through a royal edict prohibiting for thirty days all prayers or petitions, save to Darius himself. Daniel was promptly apprehended in prayer to God; and Darius had no recourse but to cast him into a den of lions, as had been prescribed. God, however, intervened on behalf of His faithful servant (cf. 6:16) and shut the lions' mouths, though they subsequently devoured his accusers, when condemned to a similar fate. It was in this same first year of Darius, as the seventy years of Babylonian exile drew to a close, that the angel Gabriel answered Daniel's prayers and confessions with a revelation of the "seventy weeks" of years (490 yrs., Dan. 9:24-27), from the decree for rebuilding Jerusalem (under Ezra (?), 7:18,25; cf. 4:12-16) to the Messiah, His death, and the confirming of the Gospel to Israel (458 B.C. through A.D. 33). "So Daniel prospered into the reign of Cyrus the Persian" (Dan. 6:28; 1:21).

The last known event in the life of Daniel took place in the third year of Cyrus (536 B.C.), when he was granted an overpowering vision of the archangel Michael contending with the demonic powers of pagan society (10:10-11:1); of the

THE FOUR COMPANIONS—Daniel, Shadrach, Meshach and Abednego—spent the night on their knees, praying for God's mercy and for signs that would help them to find out and interpret Nebuchadnezzar's dream. At sunrise Daniel called the captain of the guard to take him to the king.

THERE WAS NO SOUND of growls from the lions. Not one lion bared his claws nor opened his mouth. The lions sniffed Daniel's presence and nudged his body, then went off to lie down and sleep. Daniel spent the rest of the night in thanksgiving and praise. Next morning, King Darius found Daniel unharmed, untouched, singing praises to his God.

course of world history, through the persecutions of Antiochus IV (11:2-39); and of the eschatological antichrist, the resurrections, and God's final judgment (11:40-12:4). The vision concluded with the assurance that though Daniel would come to his grave prior to these events he would yet receive his appointed reward in the consummation (12:13). Thus in his mid-eighties, after completing his inspired autobiography and apocalyptic oracles, he finished his honored course.

The historicity of Daniel the prophet is confirmed, both by the words of Christ (Matt. 24:15) and by references to his righteousness and wisdom, as witnessed by his prophetic contemporary Ezekiel (14:14,20 and 28:3, in 591 and 586 B.C., respectively), though modern critics have attempted to relate the latter passages to a mythological Daniel of Ugaritic legend. Those, however, who stand committed to the truth of Scripture, find in Daniel a timeless demonstration of separation from impurity, or courage against compromise, of efficaciousness in prayer, and of dedication to Him whose "kingdom is from generation to generation" (Dan. 4:34).   J.B.P.

THE FOLLOWING BIBLE STORY, *Daniel the Prophet,* was written by Curtis Mitchell. It is based upon the events related in the Book of Daniel.

Daniel the Prophet

HE THREE young princes of Judah, prisoners of the great King Nebuchadnezzar (neb-yeu-kud-NEZ-er) of Babylonia, sat tensely in their quarters. Their faces were set and their jaws clenched so that hard ridges rose above the swarthy planes of their sharp young faces.

Shadrach (SHAD-rack), always impatient, flung out his hands. His voice was harsh with anxiety. "Why doesn't he return? Surely Daniel has failed."

"Don't underestimate Daniel," said Abednego (uh-BED-nee-go), the thoughtful one. "He's the favorite of the king's chief officer, remember."

Sounds of the busy city filtered through the slotted windows in the stone walls, reflecting the commerce and power of this capital of the civilized world six centuries before the birth of Jesus Christ. But no tramp of feet or chatter of voices proclaimed the return of their friend and leader.

Since their capture in Jerusalem several years earlier, they had often wondered what might be in store for them. Other Jews had been scattered by the thousands throughout the empire's villages, but members of the Hebrew royal family had been held in palace quarters and given many liberties. Now, however, some definite plan seemed to be afoot.

Meshach (ME-shack), smallest of the three princes, said, "Let's go over it again. What did the king's order say? What will be required of us?" He liked to organize a problem and then tackle it.

"We're to be trained for service in the king's court," said Abednego. "The Babylonians want to avail themselves of the skills of our people. That won't be too bad—provided they allow us to worship God, to observe the laws of Moses, and to eat food that is ceremonially clean."

Meshach snorted. "It's hardly likely that the king will concern himself with such matters as the law of Moses. Did he honor Moses when he allowed his soldiers to steal the sacred dishes from our Temple in Jerusalem and to bring them to Babylonia?"

Abednego tapped his nose reflectively. "If we can once get into the court, we may find a way of persuading the king to return those vessels."

"Now you're parroting Daniel," little Meshach said, "but it may still be a good idea." His eyes fell on the clay tablet that bore the king's order. "Let's see what we're in for."

They gathered about the strange writing. Abednego read, "It calls for youths without blemish."

"With quick minds," Meshach added.

"And endowed with an understanding of learning."

Suddenly they broke apart and faced the doorway, hearing the swift, unmistakable footsteps of their friend Daniel. As he entered, Abednego cried, "What happened? Start at the beginning."

Breathing deeply, Daniel sat down. "First, I told the king's chief officer that we could not defile ourself with the king's food."

"He didn't like that, I'll bet," said Meshach.

"He explained that his job was to get us into top physical condition. If he fails, the king will have his head. So I proposed a test. Give us ten days, I said. Give the four of us vegetables and water for ten days but give all the others the king's own rich food and wine. Then examine us. I promised we'd be healthier than any other candidates."

"Did he agree?"

"He is a good friend of mine," replied Daniel, "and he is willing to risk his life for us. Are we willing to do *our* part to keep our bodies and our minds stronger and keener than those of the others...?"

Meshach hesitated. 'What happens if we fail?"

Daniel arose slowly. "We cannot fail if we place our faith in the living God. Has He not sustained our people in the past? If they are suffering now, it is because they disobeyed Him. But if we obey Him and do His will, He will preserve us. Do you agree?"

Impulsively the three crowded around Daniel, clasping his arms. "We do —the Lord God of Israel being our helper!" murmured Abednego, fervently. The others nodded, their eyes glowing.

Babylonia and the World

THOSE FOUR teen-agers from Jerusalem were typical of the cream of their nation, now dispersed over the ancient world by a series of conquerors. Yet courageous voices continued to proclaim the Hebrew faith despite all calamities. Ancient Jeremiah, too old or too troublesome to be taken into exile, remained with a ragtag remnant in the homeland to promise seventy years of fire and brimstone to breakers of the Law. There was also young Ezekiel, who had walked the endless miles from the Jordan to the Tigris (TY-griss) and Euphrates (yew-FRATE-ease). Now, from a synagogue that he had established on foreign soil, he spoke constantly of the one God who could reprieve his Chosen People, in due course, when they deserved it.

476

Such were the sober teachings that had sent Daniel scurrying that critical day to his friend, the king's chief officer, to protest the order requiring the eating of forbidden foods.

Ten days was the agreed length of the test. After ten days the chief officer called Daniel, Shadrach, Meshach, and Abednego. His wise eyes swept over their young bodies, comparing their muscles with those of the boys who had eaten the king's food.

"I see fat," he challenged.

Daniel replied, "Good friend, you see flesh that is hard as rock."

The officer poked their ribs, their stomachs, their biceps. A twinkle came into his eyes. "Good for you! It is muscle indeed." He turned to the food steward. "This is an order. For three years, until this training ends, these boys will eat nothing but vegetables. No rich foods, no wine!"

"Thank you, friend," Daniel said.

At last the day came for the final inspection of the young trainees. One by one the class of nobles, including Daniel, Shadrach, Meshach, and Abednego, was given tough mental and physical tests. King Nebuchadnezzar himself asked the final questions. Then they were dismissed.

Consulting their scores, the king mused, "I find here a most remarkable situation."

"You are pleased with the class?" the chief officer asked.

"I am particularly pleased with the young princes of Judah," Nebuchad-nezzar said. He consulted the records again. "In body, they are superb. But in matters of wisdom and understanding, they are ten times better than any of the enchanters or magicians in my kingdom. And that's not all. According to his tests, one of these remarkable youths far outstrips even his brilliant companions."

"Who is that, Sire?"

"His name is Daniel," said the king.

Dreams and the Mystery of the Future

As THE YOUNG EXILES grew into manhood, they considered among themselves what to do with their lives. Their world was vastly different from ours.

The minds of the men of that day, although sharpened by conflict and commerce, were clouded by superstition. Magicians and soothsayers flourished. Each nation had its own battalion of gods and each god had his battalion of priests. Kings and conquerors sought constantly to see into the future. Some of their methods now seem remarkably stupid. They dropped oil into a vessel of water and read the future by the shape of floating droplets. At night they studied the stars and became the first civilized humans in history to assume that each person on earth had his own personal star-god in the sky. Thus the hocus-pocus of astrology became the mother of astronomy. Or they forecast the future by reading signs in a sheep's liver. Young Daniel, now a member of the king's court, heard these matters discussed and carried them back to his friends.

"I've seen a sheep's liver," said Abednego. "It's covered with a thousand tiny wrinkles, like the neck of the oldest woman in the world."

"Like a million worms," added Meshach.

Daniel said, "The priests say they can read the future from them. It takes a long apprenticeship. Each twist has a special meaning."

"I don't believe a liver can tell a thing," said Shadrach.

"You believe in dreams, don't you?"

"I believe that God sent dreams to our forefathers," Shadrach replied thoughtfully. "I know He spoke to Abimelech (uh-BIM-eh-leck) and Jacob and Joseph and Solomon. But dreams are not sheep livers."

"You are right," Daniel said. "A dream that speaks to a man in his bed comes from God, and only He can reveal its meaning," he added, expressing the common belief of his time that all dreams were messages from God.

Sometimes the young men talked of another subject dear to them — their escape from Babylon. Camel trains moved up the valley to Damascus daily and then around the fertile crescent of the Mediterranean coast and on to Egypt. "I say we ought to go," Shadrach argued. "What can we accomplish in this soft-living country?"

"Most of our people are here," Daniel said. "Because we sinned, we're under God's punishment, as the great prophets warned."

"But how long will it last?"

"God will tell us." Daniel looked across the roofs of the city to the soaring tower of Babel. On its peak stood a temple dedicated to Marduk (MAR-dook), Babylon's highest god. Some of Marduk's priests were the king's close friends, and their jealousy of the power of the God worshiped by the Jews was well known.

Abednego read his mind. "You're thinking you can outsmart the Marduk priests, aren't you, Daniel? You're thinking you might some day bring King Nebuchadnezzar to worship our God. Am I right?"

"I'll certainly try."

"I'd much rather be in Jerusalem right now," mused Abednego.

Daniel faced him squarely. "Abednego, our people are scattered through a thousand villages, but at least we're permitted to worship our God. Ezekiel and the others are even reading the Law in public buildings. Are the ruins of Jerusalem better than this? No, we need to grow strong here. Then, when our time is come, we'll return to our holy city and rebuild our Temple."

Meshach stepped to a window. His slow speech compelled attention. "Look at that, Daniel." He gestured toward the avenue that ran to a massive gate named after the goddess Ishtar.

A commotion on the distant avenue caught their eyes. The sound of wailing came through their window. They saw men dressed as soothsayers and magicians stumbling along as if suddenly taken sick.

"Something's happened," Shadrach said. "I'll find out what."

When he returned his eyes were bright. *"Now* will you listen to me?" he demanded of Daniel. "There's no time to lose if we want to live through this night."

"Have you lost your mind?" Daniel asked.

Shadrach called toward the hallway. "Friend, come and tell us the truth."

An old man entered slowly, his body sagging, his face ashen. They recognized him as the king's favorite magician. He began to mumble, "The king called us together, all of his magicians and soothsayers. He told us of a terrible dream that had come during his sleep, and he required us to give him its meaning."

Daniel said, "That's your business, wise one. Is this a problem?"

The old man braced himself visibly. "He promised us honors if we gave an interpretation. If we failed, we were condemned to be torn limb from limb. Already he has signed the decree. It condemns every one of our profession in the whole kingdom — including you, Daniel, and Shadrach, Meshach, and Abednego!"

"But why?" Daniel demanded. "Why?"

The magician said, "There was no dream to interpret. The king cannot remember. He knows only that he *had* a dream. Yet, he required us to say what he dreamed and to explain its meaning."

The chamber lay suddenly silent. Unless the king could recall his vision, there could be no interpretation.

Heavy steps resounded from the corridor and a burly officer thrust himself into the room. "I'm on the king's business," he said. "All of you, follow me."

Daniel spoke calmly. "Welcome, good Arioch (AR-ee-ock). As captain of the king's guard and our old friend, you are welcome."

The captain's eyes dropped. "I've got my orders, Daniel. Don't make it hard for me."

Daniel asked, "You've been told to slay us? Why is the king's decree so severe?"

"You know the fakers around him. I think he wants to get rid of them."

"But is their death and ours, too, really necessary?"

"He signed the decree, Daniel."

Daniel took a deep breath, saying, "I do not lie to you, Arioch. Go to the king and make an appointment for me to speak with him. Say that I'll recall his dream *and* its meaning."

Arioch stepped close and looked searchingly into the young Hebrew's eyes. His big fist rested on his sword hilt, his fingers fidgeting. Daniel stepped up to him, put a hand on each of his shoulders, and spun him about. "Trust me, good friend, and avoid the sin of murder. Give me only one night and your king shall hear all about his dream."

The big captain walked away slowly. "I have not seen you or talked with you this day — understand?" he said. "But when the sun rises, I'll know where you are and I'll carry out the decree of Nebuchadnezzar."

As he vanished, the old palace magician whispered, "A tunnel goes through the city walls. A merchant lives nearby whose camels are the swiftest in Babylon."

"No, thanks. I intend to see the king tomorrow," Daniel replied.

The old man sucked his teeth in disbelief. "But no magic can reveal a forgotten dream."

"Not magic, but God," Daniel said.

The Princes Pray for a Revelation

THAT NIGHT, Daniel joined Shadrach, Meshach, and Abednego in reviewing their problem. "Let's spend this night on our knees," he said. "God's mercy will show us how to save our lives."

The night hours passed as they prayed and finally the blackness began to lighten. Suddenly Shadrach called to Meshach and Abednego, "Listen to Daniel. Listen hard!"

Daniel had drawn a little apart but his voice was clear and jubilant, almost like a hymn: "Blessed be the name of God forever and ever, to whom belong wisdom and might. He changes times and seasons; He removes kings and sets up kings; He gives wisdom to the wise and knowledge to those who have understanding."

Daniel cried, "To You, O God of my fathers, I give thanks and praise, for You have given me wisdom and strength, and have now made known to me what we asked of You, for You have made known to us the king's matter."

At sunrise Daniel's fist hammered against the door of Arioch, captain of the king's guard. "Get up. Take me to your king. I know his dream!"

Hastily the captain led the way to the throne room. Columned with marble, carpeted with silk, it echoed with Nebuchadnezzar's heavy voice as he demanded, "If you have news, let me hear it."

Daniel answered, "No *man* can solve this mystery, but there is a God in Heaven who reveals mysteries, and He has made known to you through your dream, O Sire, many things that will take place in the future."

The king shifted his huge bulk impatiently. "Show me this future."

Daniel said, "O King, as you lay in bed, thoughts came to you of what would happen hereafter. But in order that you may know the meaning as well as the thoughts that were in your mind, He who reveals mysteries has revealed them to me."

"Get on with it," snapped Nebuchadnezzar.

"You saw a great image, mighty and bold, and shining so bright that it was frightening. The head of this image was of fine gold."

"So it was." The king leaned forward with parted lips.

"Its breasts and arms were made of silver."

"Indeed!"

"Its belly and thighs were of bronze. Its legs were of iron and its feet were partly of iron and partly of clay. As you looked, a huge stone struck the clay feet and they crumbled at once into rubble."

The king pressed his hands against his eyes. "In truth, I did dream of such a stone."

"When the feet collapsed, the whole image fell down and broke apart and turned into dust, and then a wind rose and carried away every grain until not one trace of gold, silver, bronze, iron, or clay could be found."

The king licked his lips like a man who is afraid of the next step. Breathing deeply, he said, "Young Daniel, that in truth was my dream. Now tell me its interpretation."

Daniel urging Nebuchadnezzar not to bow
before him, a mere man

Daniel lowered his voice. Without hesitating, he made the dream's meaning clear. The gold head represented King Nebuchadnezzar himself. After his death, another but lesser king would arise, then a third kingdom, represented by bronze, and finally one of iron, which would collapse into several parts, some of which would be strong as iron and some as weak as clay. Ultimately, over all these pieces, the God of Heaven would set up a kingdom so mighty that it would never be destroyed but would stand forever.

At the end of the recital, Captain Arioch growled, "Our king will never fall, Daniel."

Daniel's voice became a biting reprimand. "The dream is certain, its interpretation sure!"

Suddenly, the king lurched from his throne and fell on his knees, his hands spread wide in homage to Daniel's God, who could reveal such things. Aghast, members of the court stood transfixed at the spectacle of the world's mightiest man on his knees. Quickly, Nebuchadnezzar gave orders:

"Let an offering and incense be given to this able fellow." He turned to Daniel. "Truly, your God is the God of gods and Lord of kings and a revealer of mysteries, for you have told exactly what I dreamed."

Thus young Daniel, the exiled prince of Judah, won the king's favor and received, within a short time, an appointment to be ruler over the whole province of Babylon. In turn, Daniel appointed Shadrach, Meshach, and Abednego as his chief assistants so he could take time from his duties and remain close to Nebuchadnezzar at court.

Condemned to Death

SOME OF the king's advisors resented the young Hebrew's rise in favor. Their first blow to unseat him was struck, not at Daniel, but at his three friends.

The occasion was the unveiling and dedication of a gigantic statue, an image that the king had built on the plain near Babylon. On the appointed day every ranking official of the empire, as well as thousands of spectators, assembled about the statue's base. The king's heralds warned the crowds, shouting last-minute instructions. "When you hear the sound of the horn, pipe, lyre, harp, and bagpipe, you are commanded to fall down and worship this golden image," they cried. "And whoever does not fall down and worship shall be cast into the fiery furnace!"

Shadrach, Meshach, and Abednego before the king

Then the music sounded and all present prostrated themselves save Shadrach, Meshach, and Abednego, who, by the Law of Moses, could not worship any image.

Immediately the incident was reported to the king. He called the young Jews into the royal presence and gave them a grim warning. "I'm told that you refuse to worship my god or my golden image," he said. "If this is true, I'll give you one more chance. Bow down to my image and all will be well and good. Refuse, and you'll be cast into a fiery furnace, and no god shall deliver you from my hands."

Shadrach, Meshach, and Abednego stood straight and defiant, replying, "O Nebuchadnezzar, we have no need to answer you in this matter. The God whom we serve can deliver us from your fiery furnace and out of your hands, if it is His will; but even if it is not His will to save us, O King, we will not serve your gods or worship the golden image you have set up."

No man had ever defied Nebuchadnezzar so bluntly. His face flushed until it was almost purple. "Fire up the furnace until it is seven times hotter than usual, and bind these insolent wretches and throw them at once into the fire," he told his strongest warriors. So soldiers tied up the young nobles, rushed them to the pit where the flames roared, and flung them in.

The heat was so great that the guards nearest to the flame were burned alive before they could take a backward step.

Watching at a distance, Nebuchadnezzar shielded his eyes and peered into the heart of the furnace. Suddenly, a stricken look twisting his features, he strode closer to the furnace. The sight before him was unbelievable. *Four men were sauntering through the flames, their arms and legs free!*

"I see four men — unharmed!" the king cried. "And the fourth looks like a son of the gods!"

Counselors and officers watched in disbelief. Nebuchadnezzar called, "Shadrach, Meshach, Abednego! Come forth, come forth!" The young men obeyed, walking out of the fiery pit unscorched, uninjured. There was not even the smell of fire about them.

Nebuchadnezzar held out his hands to the Jews, saying, "Blessed be your God who sent His angel and delivered you who trusted in Him, who set at nought my command, who yielded up your bodies rather than worship any god except your own."

Hushing the crowd, he announced, "I make a new decree. Any people, nation, or language that speaks anything against the God of Shadrach, Meshach, or Abednego shall be torn limb from limb, and their houses shall be laid in ruins, for there is no other god who is able to deliver in this way."

Then he promoted the three young men to new positions in the government, and soon they were able to employ their offices in making more bearable the plight of their exiled countrymen.

Daniel in the lions' den.

COLOR ILLUSTRATIONS BY MAURICE BOWER

The king stares in amazement as the hand begins writing on the wall.

Nebuchadnezzar's first vision.

Daniel's friends emerge from the fire.

At the sound of the music all but three men bow before the statue.

King Darius stares in disbelief as Daniel emerges from the lions' den.

Daniel's vision of the angel Gabriel.

*Daniel interprets the handwriting
on the wall.*

*Daniel's enemies discover him
praying to the true God.*

The angel joins the three youths inside the blazing furnace.

The King's New Dream

As Babylonia fattened on captured nations, Nebuchadnezzar came to feel that he was superior to any monarch who ever lived. In proof of his own greatness, Nebuchadnezzar poured Babylon's resources into his capital city, completing immense irrigated parks and canals, repairing the Tower of Babel, which could be seen for miles, and cultivating hundreds of exotic herbs and plants in his Hanging Gardens. He made Babylon so beautiful that no matter where he looked or walked nothing could offend his eye.

Nevertheless, one area remained in which he was not supreme.

It became known the morning a manservant burst from the king's bed-chamber and ran to the captain of the guard. "The king's in a fit," he cried. "Go to him."

"It cannot be," Arioch protested.

"Go see for yourself. He trembles like one with palsy. His teeth chatter. His legs won't support him."

"Call the soothsayers," Arioch ordered. Striding into the bedchamber, he found his emperor clutching the bedclothes, eyes wide with terror.

"It came in the night," Nebuchadnezzar bleated.

"What came, Sire? No man, surely. Your guard has been doubled."

"Idiot, it was a dream that I can't drive away." The king fell back on his bed-cushions. "Call my wise ones. They'll help me."

Presently soothsayers, enchanters, and magicians began to arrive in groups, combing their beards and adjusting their garments. When they were assembled the king said, "I command you to listen to my dream and give me its meaning."

The dream was remarkable indeed.

The king said, "A mighty tree grew out of the earth. It grew so tall that it reached to Heaven, and it grew so broad that all the birds of the air lived in its branches, and its fruit was so numerous that all the world's animals fed from it, and its shade was so dense that all beasts of the field found comfort under it.

"Then I saw a holy one come down from Heaven and he spoke, saying, 'Cut down this tree, cut off its branches, and scatter its fruit. Chase away the beasts and the birds. Leave only the stump, which shall be bound with a band of iron and bronze; let it stand amid the tender grass. Let him be wet with the dew of the heavens; let his lot be with the beasts; let a beast's mind be given to him; and let seven times pass over him.'"

An ancient priest held up a withered hand. "You spoke first of a tree. Now you speak of *him* whose lot will be with the beasts, as if the tree were a man. Was this a tree or a man, Sire?"

The king's face reddened with rage. "Imbecile! Idiot! I tell you what I dreamt. How do I know?"

"I'm trying to understand . . ."

The king screamed across the room, "I, King Nebuchadnezzar, dreamed this thing. A holy one, a heavenly watcher, gave orders for the destruction of the tree and its flocks and none protested or could stop its destruction. What is the meaning?"

The wise men closed their ranks and the swift hum of their voices filled the vast bedchamber. Finally, they fell silent and the old man who had spoken earlier now said softly: "O great and mighty one, O magnificent Sire who shall live forever . . ."

The king jumped to his feet, exasperated. "What does my dream mean?"

"We do not know," the old man said.

"How dare you *not* know?"

The king tottered on his paralyzed feet. His eyes searched their ranks. "I perceive that the Hebrew Daniel is not among you. Where is he? Where is

*Wise men advising
the aged king*

my governor, the man I named Belteshazzar (bell-teh-SHAZZ-ur) in honor of my god Bel?"

"He has just arrived," the captain responded.

"Sire, I am here," Daniel said, entering.

The king dismissed his unhappy sages and turned to the foreign princeling. He repeated the details of his dream, watching Daniel's eyes as he spoke, watching the play of Daniel's fingers upon the counterpane. Finally he said, "I suspect the worst, Daniel. Now, don't be easy on me. Don't let my dream or its meaning alarm you or soften your words."

A Grave Problem for Daniel

DANIEL thought to himself, "I see a horrible fate for this man. I foresee him cast out, broken, and driven mad. But he won't want to know such things even if they are true. No, I can't tell him."

"Help me, Belteshazzar," the king urged.

Suddenly Daniel saw that he was dealing with a different man from the emperor of yesterday. This was no tyrant, but a tired leader whose searching, fumbling mind had suddenly grown sick. Daniel wondered, "If he could learn to follow the true God, he could stand the truth. Do I dare hope?"

Daniel spoke slowly, almost as if reading. "O Sire! I wish that this dream and this interpretation were for your enemies."

"It is bad, then?"

Daniel explained that the great tree reaching to Heaven was a symbol of the king, whose might had already spread over the world.

"What of the holy one who came from Heaven and ordered it cut down?"

Daniel said, "The holy one spoke for God to say that you will be driven from Babylon to live like an animal, and that you shall go mad and think like an animal, and know no friends for seven years."

"Rubbish!"

Daniel continued, "But at the end of that time, you will have come to recognize that the Most High One rules the kingdom of men and gives to whom He will. You shall be restored to power only when you admit that God rules." Daniel's voice deepened suddenly and he moved as close as he dared. "O King, hear my counsel! Practice righteousness. Show mercy to the oppressed. Break off your sins, that you may be saved. . . ."

"Enough, good Daniel!" the king ordered. "If there is more, continue. If not, I believe you have other duties."

Daniel went back to his office, wondering if he had said too little or too much. For some months, work took up his time. Then one day the king took him to the roof of the royal palace. It looked out across a sea of housetops, over groves and fields, over immense fortress walls. Nebuchadnezzar said,

"Behold the greatest city on the earth, this great Babylon which I've built by my own might as a royal residence, for the glory of my majesty."

An uneasiness filled Daniel's mind. He wondered why the king had chosen this day to make such a boast. Had another dream reminded him of that earlier warning? Did he seek reassurance?

Suddenly, there was a sound like thunder in the sky, and the sound turned into words uttered with enormous solemnity. "O King Nebuchadnezzar, to you this is spoken." They searched the spacious dome of blue, finding nothing but empty sky, but the voice thundered on. "Your kingdom is to be taken away. You shall be driven from among men. You shall live with the beasts of the field. You shall eat grass like an ox until you have learned that the Most High rules the kingdom of men and gives it to whom He will."

The king turned abruptly from Daniel, listening intently. "Did you hear that?" he said softly.

"I heard only thunder, Sire."

Suddenly a distant babble rose above the rooftops. The cries were harsh and foreign, unlike the soft accents of the valley people. Nebuchadnezzar walked away, his shoulders hunched as if against an expected blow. Presently he broke into a trot, then into a run. The yells grew loud and a squad of hairy soldiers sprinted abruptly onto the rooftop. The king saw them and raced away, fleeing from their naked swords.

After a time, when the sounds of pursuit had faded, Daniel descended the long stairs to confront the new ruler of Babylon, marveling at God's way of carrying out his judgment.

So seven years passed during which time Nebuchadnezzar lived like an animal, a fugitive madman. One day, when his time was finished, he returned to his capital and met some of those who had once been his supporters. Now his hair was as long as eagle feathers and his nails were like bird claws. His mind, however, was clear. Beyond question, he was again a king in ability and intellect.

"We must restore him to his throne," the lords said.

"It will be as God foretold," Daniel agreed.

So Nebuchadnezzar became king again, prosperity continued in Babylonia, and everywhere God was honored. A royal edict left no doubt of the king's personal conversion. "Now I, Nebuchadnezzar, praise and extol the honor of the King of Heaven," he decreed. "All His works are right and all His ways are just. And those who walk in pride, He is able to abase."

All that Daniel had predicted had come to pass.

The Busy Governor

DANIEL of Judah must have been a busy man. Nebuchadnezzar had made him governor and utilized his ability as an administrator. Even under King Belshazzar (bel-SHAZ-er), he apparently won the privilege of being left alone to do his job. It was a good arrangement for both. Belshazzar gave riotous parties in his palace, where the walls were so thick — eighteen feet — that no sound of revelry could be heard by the public. And the king's minister, Daniel, gave his attention to the knotty problems of government.

"Your brow is creased," an aide told him. "Are things so bad?"

"Our troubles increase by the minute."

"You need to relax, Daniel. Why not tonight at the king's feast? He's asked a thousand guests."

"I don't attend the king's parties."

"But just this once."

Daniel pointed to a list of the day's affairs. "How can I take time from these matters?" he asked. His fingers ticked off the list: swamp drainage to provide more land for cultivation . . . military preparations to hold the Medes to their seven mountain ranges . . . investigation of the rumor that a soldier named Cyrus was winning a reputation as a military genius in those mountains . . . support for his countrymen who were making studies of the writings of Joshua, Samuel, and the Hebrew Judges and Kings . . . a report on several reckless countrymen who were urging a Jewish rebellion. He thought, "Despite all the teaching of Jeremiah (jer-e-MY-ah) and Hezekiah (hez-e-KY-ah), they are unwilling to bide their time. What can I do with such lunatics? Unless I can stop them . . ." Remembering, he saw in his mind's eye the two Jews, Zedekiah (zed-e-KY-ah) and Ahab (AY-hab), who had already been roasted alive by Nebuchadnezzar for sedition.

The Handwriting on the Wall

A N OFFICER stalked into the room, sword at side, and beckoned to Daniel. "The king, may he live forever, wants you in the great banquet hall."

"You must be mistaken. He does not require me to attend his feasts."

"Come with me, Daniel. Take my word that you must."

"But I'm already about the king's business."

"The king's mother spoke your name. That's all I know. Now come!"

Daniel thought, "The king's mother is my friend. When Nebuchadnezzar appointed me, she was very kind. Young Belshazzar has been a trial to her. So I'll go."

At the palace, Daniel walked througn a great columnęd court, past sculptured bulls and lions that stared from jewelled eyes as he went by. Then he entered the vast banquet hall, with its high ceiling. A thousand men and women were assembled there before long tables heaped with meats, wines, and every luxurious delicacy.

Moments earlier, Daniel felt sure, care-free revelry must have reigned among these hard-faced, dissolute banqueters. But now an ominous hush had come over them. They sat motionless, staring toward the far end of the hall. It was as if an icy wind of doom had blown through the vast, echoing chamber and had penetrated their very hearts. Daniel himself could not avoid a slight shiver. The king, high on the royal dais, was plainly stricken with terror, while his courtiers and wise men cowered about him, helpless to comfort their trembling monarch.

Suddenly the king spied Daniel. Frantically he beckoned him to the dais. As Daniel approached, the king moistened his lips with his tongue and whispered hoarsely, "Daniel—what does it mean? What do these strange writings mean? My wise men and sorcerers are not able to tell me!"

Daniel looked to the place where the king was pointing. High on the wall, gleaming above the flickering torches, huge letters spelled out four words: *Mene, mene, tekel, parsin.*

Daniel's glance fell on the wise men who obviously had already failed to satisfy their king's demand, then returned to the words of mystery. Studying them, he became aware of their significance. "Who wrote those words, Sire?" asked Daniel.

Belshazzar sputtered, "We were drinking and eating. A hand appeared, all of a sudden, holding in its fingers a writing instrument. As we watched, it wrote what you see. We were causing no harm, Daniel. I have sacrificed to all my gods."

Daniel interrupted, his eyes flashing across the sea of tables. "Do I see here the sacred gold and silver vessels that King Nebuchadnezzar brought from our holy Temple in Jerusalem? O King, did you and your dancing girls and your lords and their wives drink wine from those holy vessels? Did you toast the idols of your gods of gold, silver, iron, wood, and stone? Did you do that with the holy vessels, O King?"

The king's eyes became cunning. "We meant no disrespect, Daniel. But tell me the meaning of those words and I will put a chain of gold around your neck, give you purple robes, and make you third in command of my kingdom. Unlock this secret to me, Daniel, and these honors shall be yours."

An old woman stirred on a nearby cushion and Daniel recognized the former queen, the wife of Nebuchadnezzar. Her lips formed a warning, as they had often done before. They said: *"Give the king an answer. Give it quickly."*

"You will be the third ruler," Belshazzar said again. The words on the wall were suddenly illuminated by a light that flooded Daniel's mind, a light that revealed God's awful judgment. That judgment was terrible beyond imagining. Daniel wondered how one should face a king while telling him that he stood condemned to death. Could this be done without feeling the royal sword?

Slowly he began to speak: "Let your gifts be for yourself. Give your rewards to another." The king's hand fell to the hilt of his dagger but Daniel now knew his course, knew that this king was a sinner, an idolater, a living violation of every law of God. His voice took on an edge.

"O King, the Most High God gave your father glory and majesty, and when Nebuchadnezzar hardened his heart, the Most High turned him into a beast until he knew that God ruled the kingdom of men. But you, his son, have not humbled yourself. Instead, you have fought the Lord. You have brought the utensils from God's Temple and defiled them with toasts to your own gods. The true God, who puts breath into you, who gives you life itself, you have not honored. So He sent a living hand to write His judgment on you."

Every eye in the room was fastened on the wall with its crimson letters. Daniel read the inscription, *Mene, mene, tekel, parsin*. Those words had formerly been used to designate several small coins. Now they possessed an ominous significance.

The king's command was a scream. "What do they mean, Daniel?"

"This is the interpretation," Daniel said. "This word *mene* means that God has numbered the days of your kingdom and brought it to an end."

Belshazzar gulped and then he whispered. *"Tekel?"*

"Tekel means that you have been weighed in the balance *and found wanting."*

"Parsin?"

"Parsin means that your kingdom is to be divided. It will be given by God to the Medes and Persians."

The great king rose swiftly to his feet. His legs were no longer shaking. Filling the hall with his regal bulk, he was a grim man who had heard a grim message.

A priest babbled, "Mighty One, our god Bel is of a different mind. There's no cause for . . ."

"Silence!" The words of Daniel lay like coals of fire in Belshazzar's mind. He knew that they were true, for he had heard often from his mother of Daniel's supernatural skill. Knowing the truth, he did what he had to do.

First, he made good his promises. Commanding that Daniel be clothed in the purple robes of Babylonian royalty, he placed a heavy chain of gold about his neck. Then a proclamation was ordered for all to read. By royal edict, Daniel became the third ruler of the kingdom.

Then immediately, that very night, the rule of King Belshazzar ended. Daniel's own brief account in the Bible gives no further details, merely saying, "That very night Belshazzar, the Chaldean king, was slain, and Darius the Mede received the kingdom."

A Trap Is Set

THE POWER of man waxes and wanes and so does the power of empires. Daniel's life, which began at a time when the Assyrian Empire was the world's greatest power, continued through the Babylonian reign and into the days of the Medes and the Persians.

Like all conquerors, Darius the Mede required treasure with which to pay

his armies. So he taxed his subjects, charging harshly for the peace his rule
brought and for the order he established. Under him, Babylonia was divided
into one hundred and twenty provinces, called satrapies, each ruled by a
royally appointed satrap. Over these satraps sat three presidents. Under
Darius the Great, Daniel became one of those presidents.

When his appointment was announced, the bazaars of Babylon buzzed
with gossip. Old Daniel had done it again, they said; he had captured the
favor of this new king. Daniel, a Jew in exile, a man without a country,
wielding only the power of his integrity — Daniel was still in the saddle.

Camel-drivers on distant caravan routes asked, "What's it like under the
Mede? Is Daniel still on top?"

"On top for now," some replied. "A few think he won't last long."

"He'll bring luck to King Darius," supporters argued. "He's got the head
for it."

Daniel's court enemies plotting against him

"He'll have no head at all from what we hear," detractors blurted, and then fell silent. And not another word would they utter, for they were talking about one of the three greatest men of the kingdom of the Medes, and spies might report their words.

In Babylon, the jealous lords who hated Daniel sat one day in a secret room behind a guarded door and pledged, "We are jointly resolved that Daniel, exile of Judah, must die." Among them were the two other presidents. This oath was their answer to King Darius's announced intention to make Daniel the first man of the kingdom.

The presidents discussed their plan. "The Jew is protected by his honesty. How do we get around that?"

"I believe I can trip him," one said. "I've been studying the laws of his God and his religion."

He explained his plan, step by step, leading to the trap which would be triggered by the tradition among Medes that a law, once established by the king, was forever in force and could not be changed.

Next day, they took an odd proposal to their king: "Your many subjects should know your greatness, your generosity, and your divine nature," they said. "Therefore, let there be ordained by royal decree a period of thirty days during which no man shall make a prayer or a supplication to any god or any man except you."

Darius was flattered. "Would this notion give pleasure to my subjects?" he demanded.

"The governors of the kingdom, the prefects, the satraps, and the counselors are wholly agreed."

"You have already discussed this?"

"We have, and we further agree, Sire, that whoever breaks your ordinance and makes petition to anyone but you shall be cast into the royal den of lions." One of the plotters stepped forward bearing an official document. "Now, O King, sign the decree and establish the law so it cannot be changed."

Smiling smugly, Darius the Great put his signature to the document.

When Daniel heard of the new law, he went to his own house, where the windows of an upper chamber were always open toward Jerusalem, and he got down on his knees as usual, praying and giving thanks to God. He did this three times that first day and each day thereafter, as he always did, because it was an obligation of his faith.

The jealous presidents, watching from a nearby roof, made certain of his actions, then ran immediately to the palace. "We've got him now," they crowed. "The royal lions will tear him to bits."

Before Darius they charged, "Daniel defies you and your law, O King, for he continues to make his petition to his God three times each day."

At last, the king saw the trap they had set for Daniel. The presidents

pressed him for action. "Isn't it the law of the Medes and Persians that no
edict of a king can be changed?"

"True."

"Then should not this Daniel be placed in the royal den of lions, according to your edict?"

Darius could find no way out. He had no choice but to send soldiers to
conduct Daniel to the lions' den. "I'll meet you there," he told them. "Bring
him right away."

Standing above the pit, the king looked into yellow, hating eyes. His lions
were as fierce as could be trapped and assembled for the sport of nobles.
Starved enough to be savage, they padded about the den, their tails twitch-
ing at the scent of humans. Daniel came up behind the king, escorted by
guards. Already the sun had set.

The sorrowing king said, "Daniel, may your God, whom you serve con-
tinually, deliver you." But Daniel made no answer.

In the Lions' Den

T HE ATTENDANTS knew what to do. When Daniel had been pushed into
the den, a great stone was laid on the entrance and sealed with the
king's own signet ring. Then Darius retired to his palace.

King Darius peering at Daniel in the lions' den

But he could not sleep. Instead, he fasted through the hours of darkness, refusing entertainment in order to meditate. Daniel had been so calm, he recalled. He had allowed himself to be thrown into the den showing no fear, almost with the air of a man entering a temple. A strange person, this Hebrew, who worshiped a strange, strict God called the Most High.

After a while, the dawn came down the eastern hills. Darius fastened on his robes and sandals, called his escort, and rushed back to the den of lions. "Daniel," he called in anguish, "Daniel, has your God delivered you?"

*Officials being tossed to the lions
after their plot against Daniel is exposed*

A bird was singing in the distance, and a farmer could be heard scolding his camel. Then Daniel's clear voice answered with the respectful greeting due his monarch. "O King, live forever," he said. "My God has sent an angel who shut the lions' mouths. They have not hurt me because I have done no wrong."

Rejoicing, Darius broke the seal on the gateway and removed Daniel from the den, feeling his hands and arms in disbelief. "There's not a mark on you!" he marvelled.

"I trusted my God," Daniel said.

The king thrust his friend down the path. "Go home and rest. Sleep, eat, and come back to me rested. In the meantime, I must do a needed thing."

When Daniel had departed, the monarch spoke to his captain. "Find the other two presidents, the two who conspired against Daniel. Bring them back here at once. Bring also their wives and their children. This is my order."

The captain and a squad of soldiers dashed away toward the city. Calling his secretary to his side, King Darius said, "Write these words into a decree and send it to all the people. Put it into every language used in my dominion, so that men may tremble and fear before the God of Daniel, for He is the living God. His kingdom shall never be destroyed and His dominion shall last to the end of time. This God delivers and rescues. He works wonders in Heaven and on earth, for He is the One who saved Daniel from the power of my lions."

Striding to the pit's edge, the king glared down at his kingly beasts. He was a man as absolute and ruthless in his way as the lions were in theirs. But he was not at ease any longer, because the thing he had seen that morning had revealed to him another Power that was greater than his own.

The secretary said, "Anything more, Sire?"

"You will see to this," Darius ordered. "When the guards bring back those who plotted against Daniel, and when they are gathered with their wives and their children, drive them all into the den of lions."

The sun was rising. Darius looked angrily across the flat fields, but nothing stirred, nothing moved. In the distance, his palace caught the sun and sent back a thousand golden reflections. The king began to walk into the city, his feet crushing the clods and weeds. "The God of Daniel is the living God," he said, keeping time with his steps. "His dominion shall be to the end of time." Walking and talking to himself, he returned to his capital city, where Daniel already lay asleep.

Daniel's Visions

As THE DAYS went by, and grew into months, and the months into years, the Jews in Babylonia began to wonder how much longer their exile in Babylon would last.

When would God finally hearken to their cries of repentance...when would He grant them the privilege of returning to their beloved homeland and of rebuilding the broken walls and the ruined buildings of Jerusalem, and of erecting once more the holy Temple?

They were not left without an answer. To men who were sensitive to the leadings of God, the future was about to be revealed. Daniel was one of these men. As a prophet who knew the Lord and strove to live in His holy will, Daniel was to be shown the shape of things to come in a series of visions that were as marvelous as they were frightening. It was as if the hand of the Lord were painting on a vast canvas, stretching across all eternity, a preview of mighty happenings that were to commence in the not too distant future and extend to the very end of time...

Perhaps Daniel's first inkling of these wonders came when he fell into a dream in which he saw four huge wild beasts come up out of the sea. The first was like a lion having eagle's wings, the second like a bear, the third like a leopard with four heads and great flapping wings...and finally there came a fourth beast, strong and dreadful to behold, with great iron teeth with which it devoured its enemies. This creature had ten horns and one smaller horn. The little horn made war upon God's saints, until at last the Ancient of Days —God Himself—came and sat in judgment upon the wicked beast, who was then destroyed.

The animals, Daniel learned, represented the mighty kingdoms of the Gentile world, which would wax strong and despotic, but which would at last be cast down and destroyed by the overruling hand of God.

Again, while staying in the capital city of Susa, Daniel had a vision as he stood at a river bank. A ram suddenly appeared, charging and snorting ferociously, and trampling down everyone who dared oppose it. Then a he-goat came out of the west and, defying the ram, finally overcame it. As if in answer to Daniel's puzzlement, the angel Gabriel appeared and explained the vision to Daniel. The ram represented the kingdoms of Media and Persia, the he-goat was Greece. All would become mighty nations, but would eventually fall in defeat. Daniel was so overcome by the dramatic prophecy which he had seen that he lay disturbed and ill for some days.

Then one day, while his mind was brooding over the sad condition of Jerusalem, he drew forth from his precious possessions a copy of the writings of the prophet Jeremiah. Years earlier, Jeremiah had predicted the captivity of the Jews, their exile to Babylonia. He had likewise prophesied the happy day when they would return to Jerusalem. As Daniel read these ancient Scriptures, he was seized with the feeling that he must pray to God on behalf of his fellow Jews. Clothing himself in the rough garments of mourning, and sprinkling himself with the ashes which signified penitence, Daniel bowed in prayer. Humbling himself before the Lord, he acknowledged his own sins and those of his people.

"We beg your help," he cried, "not on the grounds of our righteousness, but on the ground of Your great mercy. Hear us, O Lord, forgive us, and heed our petition! These are Your people, and Jerusalem is Your city—do not delay in bringing our deliverance from this land and our return to Jerusalem!"

As Daniel agonized in prayer, the angel Gabriel again appeared and spoke to him. In solemn words, the messenger recounted the things which were to happen to the Israelites and to their enemies. Later Daniel wrote these things down, and they are to be found in the ninth chapter of the book which bears his name, *The Book of Daniel* in our Bible.

The Final Vision

IN THE THIRD YEAR of the reign of Cyrus, ruler of Persia, Daniel was privileged to behold still another vision—and this is the last one which the prophet sets down in his book.

Daniel was standing on the banks of the Tigris river when suddenly he looked up and saw a man clothed in fine linen garments, with a belt of gleaming gold about his waist. He was a heavenly messenger, and his face shone with the brightness of lightning. His voice, when he spoke, sounded like the voices of a great multitude of men. In awesome reverence, Daniel fell prostrate; but the messenger spoke gently, urging him to stand up. Trembling, Daniel arose.

"Do not fear, Daniel," said the angelic visitor. "From the first day you humbled yourself before God and tried to understand these marvelous visions which He sent you, your words have been heard. Be strong and of good courage. I have come to tell you what is written in the book of truth."

Then begins one of the most graphic recitals of future events in all the Bible. Kings were to arise and become strong and make alliances. Wars would come like a whirlwind, cutting down thousands. There were to be mighty conquests, and plundering, plots and treachery. But in the end, the Lord God would triumph. And His kingdom—a kingdom of truth and righteousness—would reign forever and ever.

Daniel's mind reeled at this stupendous view of the future.

Finally he asked, "When will all these things be over?"

"Go your way, Daniel," he was told, "for the words are shut up and sealed until the time of the end. None of the wicked shall understand; but those who are wise shall understand."

SO ENDS DANIEL'S STORY as recorded in the Old Testament. The remainder of his career is unknown.

But whatever his end, no other Jew of the exile left a deeper imprint on his fellowmen, nor was any man of that era more loyal to his God.

He had gone through terrible testings in the realms of pagan kings. Never had his devotion wavered. In each testing he had remained faithful to God, and each time the Lord had honored his faith by delivering him from his troubles.

For Daniel, the curtain that veils the future from most men had been drawn aside, and he had been granted a glimpse of things to come. He was able to peer past the sorrow and desolation of the present and to behold the final triumph of the Kingdom of God.

DANIEL, BOOK OF, although standing as the last of the major prophets in the English Bible, it appears in the Hebrew OT (which consists of "the law, prophets, and writings") as one of the "writings." For though Christ spoke of Daniel's *function* as prophetic (Matt. 24:15), his *position* was that of governmental official and inspired writer, rather than ministering prophet (cf. Acts 2:29-30).

The first half of the book (chapters 1-6) consists of six narratives on the life of Daniel and his friends: their education (605-602 B.C.), Daniel's revelation of Nebuchadnezzar's dream-image, the trial by fiery furnace, his prediction of Nebuchadnezzar's madness, his interpretation of the handwriting on the wall (539 B.C., the fall of Babylon), and his ordeal in the lions' den (see DANIEL, SHADRACH). The second half consists of four apocalyptic visions, predicting the course of world history. Their scope may be outlined as follows:

cause of the more Jewish orientation of the remaining three visions. That of the ram and the he-goat depicts the coming victory of Greece (331 B.C.) over the amalgamated empire of Media and Persia (8:20-21) and the subsequent persecution of Judah by Antiochus IV (168-165 B.C., 8:9-14,23-26). Chapter 9, on the 70 weeks, then illuminates Christ's first coming, 69 "weeks" of years (= 483 yrs.) after the decree for Jerusalem's rebuilding, presumably to Ezra in 458 B.C. (Ezra 7:18,25; cf. his results, 4:12-16). With God-inspired accuracy, Daniel thus inaugurates the 70th week in A.D. 26, with the baptismal anointing of Christ (Dan. 9:25; Luke 3:21-22; 4:18). In the midst of this week the Anointed One is to be cut off (Dan. 9:26), thereby making reconciliation for iniquity (9:24) and causing Old Testament sacrifice to cease (9:27; see Matt. 27:51; Heb. 9:8-12). Yet for an additional three and one-half years, God's redemptive covenant will be con-

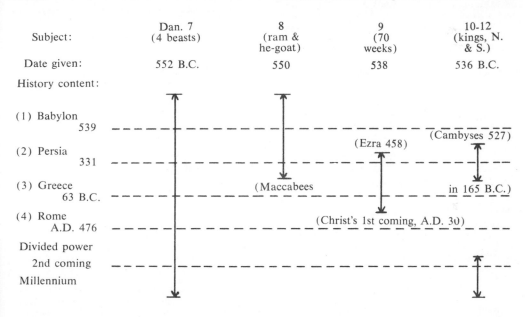

Subject:	Dan. 7 (4 beasts)	8 (ram & he-goat)	9 (70 weeks)	10-12 (kings, N. & S.)
Date given:	552 B.C.	550	538	536 B.C.

History content:

(1) Babylon 539

(2) Persia 331   (Ezra 458)   (Cambyses 527)

(3) Greece 63 B.C.   (Maccabees   in 165 B.C.)

(4) Rome A.D. 476   (Christ's 1st coming, A.D. 30)

Divided power

2nd coming

Millennium

Daniel 7 envisions the rise of four beasts, explained as representing successive kings (kingdoms, 7:23). The description parallels that of the image in chap. 2. The first empire must therefore be contemporary Babylon (2:38); and the fourth, Rome, in which God's Messianic kingdom was set up (2:44). Between lie Persia and Greece. The vision further describes the disintegration of Rome into a tenfold balance of power (2:42; 7:24; Rev. 17:12,16), the eventual rise of antichrist for an indefinite period of "times" (Dan. 7:8,25), and his destruction when a "Son of man" comes with the clouds of heaven (7:13). This last figure symbolizes the saints of the Most High (7:22), epitomized in Jesus Christ, the "last Adam" (Mark 14:62; I Cor. 15:45). For though His kingdom was "set up" at His first coming, it will "consume [earth's pagan] kingdoms" at His glorious second advent (Dan. 2:44) and millennial reign ("a season," 7:12).

Chapters 2:4b-7:28 are composed in the international language of Aramaic. But with chapter 8, Daniel resumes his use of Hebrew, probably be-

firmed to Israel (cf. Rev. 12:6,14), after which Jerusalem will be rendered desolate (A.D. 70, Dan. 9:26-27; Matt. 24:15). Other evangelical interpreters terminate the 69th week with Christ's death and commence the 70th week with a covenant of antichrist, before His second coming. Chaps 10-12, after elaborating on the succession of Persian and Greek rulers through Antiochus, then moves on to "the time of the end," foretelling Antichrist's tribulation (Dan. 11:40-12:1), the resurrections of the saved and the lost (12:2, cf. Rev. 20:4-6,12), and the final judgment (Dan. 12:2).

The authorship of the book of Daniel is nowhere expressly defined, but is indicated by the autobiographical, first-person composition from 7:2 onward. Unity of style and content (as admitted by Driver, Rowley, and Pfeiffer), plus God's commitment of "the book" to Daniel (Dan. 12:4), implies the latter's authorship, shortly after his last vision, in 536 B.C. (10:1).

Modern criticism, however, overwhelmingly denies the authenticity of Daniel as a product of the sixth century B.C. Indeed, as early as A.D. 275 the neo-Platonic philosopher Porphyry had categorically repudiated the possibility of Daniel's miraculous predictions. Anti-supernaturalism must bring the "prophecy" down to a time after the events described (especially after Antiochus' sacrilege of 168 B.C.); or, if the latest possible date has been reached, it must then reinterpret the predictions to apply to other, already-accomplished events. Consequently, since Daniel was extensively quoted (and misunderstood) as early as 140 B.C. (Sibylline Oracles 3:381-400), rationalists have no alternative but to apply the supposed coming of the Messiah and the fulfillment of the 70 weeks to Maccabean times, rather than Christ's, even though this requires "surmising a chronological miscalculation- on the part of the writer" (ICC, p.393). Dating Daniel in the second century is thus the result, fundamentally, of presuppositions of skepticism and is opposed to the actual evidence and testimony: for it makes the book's record of itself a deception and a fraud; and Jesus Christ, who believed that "Daniel the prophet" did predict Roman imperialism (Matt. 24:15), it charges with falsehood based on ignorance.

The surface arguments of current negative criticism may be classified as historical, literary, and theological. A number of specific censures have been advanced against Daniel's historical authenticity. These may, however, be dismissed, either as arguments from silence or as answered by recent archaeology (see DANIEL). More generally, it is asserted that Daniel conceived of a fictitious Median empire, existing as a separate kingdom between Babylon and Persia (thus allowing Daniel's fourth empire to be identified with Greece rather than Rome, as required by liberalism's presuppositions). But the very passage adduced (5: 31-6:1) speaks of unified Medo-Persia (6:8,12 cf. 5:28); and Daniel elsewhere identifies his second empire as the dual kingdom of Media *and* Persia (7:5, cf. 8:3,20) and his third, as the fourfold Greek (7:6, 8:8,22). Again, the fact that the apocryphal book of Ecclesiasticus, written about 180, omits Daniel from its survey of Scripture proves little other than the Sadducaic prejudice of its writer; for he likewise disregards the book of Ezra, whose high theology parallels that of Daniel. Fragments of Daniel have, moreover, been discovered among the Dead Sea scrolls of Qumran, datable to the very second century B.C., in which the book's fraudulent composition is commonly claimed.

On literary grounds Daniel has been questioned because of its utilization of certain terms of Persian or Greek origin. The book itself, however, was not written until the Persian period; and its Greek words are limited to the names of musical instruments, as "psaltery" (3:5), that may early have been imported into Babylon. Among the apocryphal literature from Qumran, there has been recovered a "Prayer of Nabonidus" (RB 63:3 July, 1956), pp. 507-415) that closely parallels Daniel's record of Nebuchadnezzar's madness (Dan. 4). Far, however, from proving Daniel to be a corruption of this third century work, the Qumranic legend, though garbled, serves to suggest the essential historicity of Daniel's account. As to the so-called "late" Aramaic and Hebrew languages of Daniel, Edward J. Young has concluded that "There is nothing in them which in itself necessarily precludes authorship by Daniel

in the sixth century B.C." (*An Introduction to the Old Testament,* rev. ed.; Grand Rapids: Eerdmans, 1958, p. 392).

Lastly, the theology of Daniel, with its apocalyptic eschatology, Biblicism, and developed angelology, is said to prohibit exilic origin. Yet Isaiah had composed an apocalypse, describing the resurrection in terms similar to Daniel's, as early as 711 B.C. (Isa. 26:19 — negative critics deny its authenticity, too!); when Daniel in 538 B.C. devoted himself to the inspired "books" (Dan. 9:2), the Old Testament canon was complete, except for three minor prophets, the last two books of Psalms and Chronicles — Esther (see CANON); and Daniel's angels, both in name and in function, stand naturally in the Hebraic religious development. His book was designed to inspire Jewish exiles with confidence in the Most High (4:34-37), and those of God's people today who will approach this book in faith believing will discover therein victorious supernaturalism that overcomes the world.   J.B.P.

DAN-JAAN (dăn′jā′ăn), a town covered by David's census (II Sam. 24:6). Hebrew *dān ya′an,* "Dan played a pipe," indicates it was a suburb of Dan. It was on the road to Ijon or Sidon (I Kings 15:20; II Chron. 16:4).

DANNAH (dăn′à), a mountain town given by Caleb as part of the heritage of Judah (Josh. 15: 49). Its location is uncertain but not far from Hebron. Some authorities make it modern Idnah.

DARA, DARDA (dăr′à, dăr′dă), a member of a noted family of wise men. He was either a son of Mahol (I Kings 4:31) or son of Zerah (I Chron. 2:6).

DARIC (dăr′ĭk), a Persian gold coin used in Palestine after the return from captivity (Ezra 2:69; Neh. 7:70-72 ASV). It was worth about $5.00. See MONEY.

DARIUS (dă-rī′ŭs, Heb. *dāryāwesh,* Gr. *Dareíos*), a common name for Medo-Persian rulers. Numerous cuneiform tablets contain references to them, especially to Darius Hystaspes. Darius, the Mede, seems to have been the same as Gubaru who was an officer in the army of Cyrus, probably governor of a Persian province N of Babylon. His name is possibly a translation of "Darius." He was the son of Ahasuerus, hence a Mede (Dan. 9:1). Belshazzar's notable feast (Dan. 5) ended in the destruction of the Chaldean Empire, and Darius the Mede (Gubaru) became ruler of the province by appointment of Cyrus at the age of 62. Daniel tells us that Darius the Mede was not heir to the throne, but nevertheless was made king (Dan. 5: 31). He seems to have exercised authority contemporaneously with Cyrus.

Cuneiform records list Nabonidus as the last king of the Medes; so Belshazzar, his son, was ruling in Babylon while his father was away at war. Darius reorganized the government and gave Daniel a high place (Dan. 6:1-3). Evil princes set out to destroy him (6:4-9). Jehovah rescued Daniel from the lions and thus advanced his cause before the king (6:10-23). Darius the Mede seems to have ruled for only a brief time (10:1; 11:1).

Darius Hystaspes was the greatest of the Persian rulers. Cambyses, the son of Cyrus, continued the conquests which his noted father had started.

He did not, however, recognize the claims of the Jews (Jos. *Ant.* XI:1:2). In one of his campaigns he was defeated by the Egyptians, and on his way home committed suicide. Taking advantage of the king's defeat, a pretender named Smerdis was made king by zealots of the Magian religious sect and he ruled one year (Jos. XI:3;1), until slain by Darius and other princes, Darius having had himself made king. He was a collateral descendant of Cyrus who, according to tradition, had selected Darius to succeed him. Between the reign of Cyrus and that of Darius, the Jews had been mistreated, and work on rebuilding Jerusalem and the temple stopped (Ezra 4:1-6). An appeal was made to Darius who made search and discovered the original decree of Cyrus favoring the Jews. Under his lenient reign, they restored the walls of the city and rebuilt the temple (Ezra 6:1-15). Darius was beset by rebellious subjects and spent much time in putting these down. He reorganized the government and extended its boundaries. He conducted many magnificent building enterprises and encouraged men of letters, especially the historians who extolled his prowess (Josephus, *Ant.* XI:1:3). The Greeks never yielded to him, however, and after some futile campaigns, his forces were overwhelmed in the battle at Marathon 490 B. C. Darius planned another campaign against the Greeks, but rebellion in Egypt interfered, and death in 486 B. C. ended his career. He was succeeded by Xerxes, a grandson of Cyrus the Great.

The beginning of the inscription of DARIUS, *King of Persia* (521 - 486 B.C.), *on the rock of Behistun*.

⟨ 𒀸 𒁹 𒉿 ⟨ 𒁹 𒈨 𒅗 𒁹 ⟨ 𒈨 𒌋 𒈨 𒅗 𒁹 𒊍
  ∫ A da m   ∫ da r ya wa u š   ∫ b š a ya th i ya
  I (AM)   DARIUS   THE KING

⟨ 𒈨 𒅗 𒁹 ⟨ 𒈨 𒌋 𒈨 𒅗 𒁹 ⟨ 𒈨 𒅗 𒁹 𒊍 𒉿 𒁹 ⟨
  ∫ wa zar ka   ∫ b š a ya th i ya   ∫ b š a ya th i ya na m
  THE GREAT (ONE). THE KING (OF)   KINGS,

⟨ 𒈨 𒌋 𒈨 𒅗 𒁹 𒊍 ⟨ 𒊑 𒈨 𒈨 𒅗 ⟨ 𒈨 𒌋 𒈨 𒅗 𒁹 𒊍 ⟨
  ∫ b š a ya th i ya   ∫ par s iy   ∫ b š a ya th i ya
  THE KING (OF)   PERSIA,   THE KING (OF)

𒁹 𒈨 𒅗 𒈨 𒅗 𒈨 𒁹 ⟨ 𒊍 𒈨 𒅗 𒈨 𒈨 𒁹 ⟨ 𒊑 𒈨 𒊑 ⟨
  ∫ dah yu na m   ∫ wi š ta s pa h y a   ∫ p u th ra
  COUNTRIES,   HYSTASPES'   SON,

𒊑 𒈨 𒅗 𒈨 𒅗 ⟨ 𒈨 𒊑 𒈨 𒅗 ⟨ 𒊍 𒈨 𒈨 𒅗 𒈨 𒅗 𒈨 𒈨
  ∫ ar ša ma h ya   ∫ n p a   ∫ ha ha m ni š i ya
  ARSAMES'   GRANDSON,   THE ACHAMENIDIAN.

TRANSLATION of part of an inscription of Darius in ancient Persian.

Darius, the Persian (Neh. 12:22). There is uncertainty among scholars as to whether this was Darius Nothus or Darius Codomannus, but evidence favors the claim that he was the latter, whose kingdom was destroyed by Alexander the Great in 330 B. C. Following a disastrous defeat near Arbela the Persian Empire crumbled, Darius the Persian being its last king.   J.D.F.

I N THE CONSPIRACY against Daniel, the signature of King Darius was obtained on a decree that was actually a trap to send Daniel to the lions' den.

"...Thus saith the Lord
God unto Jerusalem;
Thy birth and thy nativity
is of the land of Canaan;
thy father was an Amorite,
and thy mother an Hittite."
(EZEKIEL 16:3)

When Israel conquered
Canaan, intermarriage with
the Hittites became common,
even though it was forbidden
by Mosaic law. The prophet
Ezekiel's reference to the Hittites was actually a condemnation of his people for breaking
the marriage code. This relief
from the 9th century B.C. depicts a Hittite.

"And David put his hand in his bag, and took thence a stone, and slang it, and smote the Philistine in his forehead, that the stone sunk into his forehead; and he fell upon his face to the earth."
(I SAMUEL 17:49)

This relief of a warrior with a sling was sculptured in the time of David (10th century B.C.).

DARKNESS (Heb. *hōshekh, the dark*, Gr. *skótos, darkness*), used in the Old and the New Testaments both in a literal and in a figurative sense. For ages mankind has associated it with evil, danger, crime; it has also been the metaphor whereby mystery is described and the place of eternal punishment has been pictured. Several uses of the term are found in the Scriptures: 1. To denote the absence of light (Gen. 1:2,3; Isa. 45:7; Job 34:22).

2. To depict the mysterious (Exod. 20:21; I Kings 8:12; Ps. 97:2; Isa. 8:22; II Sam. 22:10; Matt. 10:27).

3. As ignorance, especially about God (Job 37:19; Prov. 2:13; Eccl. 2:14; John 12:35; I Thess. 5:1-8).

4. To describe the seat of evil (Prov. 4:19; Matt. 6:23; Luke 11:34; 22:53; John 8:12; Rom. 13:12; I Cor. 4:5; Eph. 5:11).

5. Presenting supernatural events (Gen. 15:12; Exod. 10:21; Matt. 27:45; Rev. 8:12; 16:10).

6. A sign of the Lord's return (Joel 2:2; Amos 5:8; Isa. 60:2; Matt. 24:29).

7. An agency of eternal punishment (Matt. 22:13; II Pet. 2:4,17; Jude 6,7; see also Job 2:1-5; 20:20).

8. It describes spiritual blindness (Isa. 9:2; John 1:5; I John 1:5; 2:8; Eph. 5:8), sorrow and distress (Isa. 8:22; 13:10; Ps. 23:4). It never holds sway where the Redeemer has come to shed His light (Col. 1:13).

DARKON (dár'kŏn), a descendant of Solomon's servant, Jaala, who returned with Zerubbabel from exile (Ezra 2:56).

DATHAN (dā'thăn), a great-grandson of Reuben (Num. 16:1). He, with his brothers, Abiram and Korah, rebelled against Moses (Num. 16:2-15), for which sin they were swallowed by the earth (Num. 16:31-35; see also Num. 26).

DAUGHTER (dô'têr), is a word of various uses in the Bible. It refers to both persons and things, often without regard to kinship or sex. There is the familiar usage of child to parent (Gen. 6:1; 20:12; 24:23; Judg. 11:34; Matt. 15:28). Not prized as highly as sons they were sometimes sold into slavery (Exod. 21:7). The word is used to indicate a remoter relationship, as when Rebekah is called "my master's brother's daughter" (Gen. 24:48) although she was the speaker's granddaughter (Gen. 24:15,24). It often refers, to any female descendant, regardless of the nearness of relations (Luke 1:5). Jacob's sons called their sister a daughter (Gen. 34:13-17; see Ps. 45:13; 144:12). It represents women in general (Gen. 28:6; Num. 25:1). It was often used in the figurative sense, referring to offspring (Isa. 22:4; Jer. 9:1; Lam. 4:10); to those who worshiped the true God (Ps. 45:10; S. of Sol. 1:5; 3:11; Isa. 62:11; Zech. 9:9; Matt. 21:5; John 12:15). Physical means of making music, the mouth, ears, etc., were called daughters of music (Eccl. 12:4).

DAVID (dā'vĭd, Heb. *Dāwîdh, beloved* or, as in ancient Mari, *chieftain,* BA 11 1948, p. 17), Israel's greatest king, described in I Samuel 16 through I Kings 2:11 (I Chron. 11-29), plus many of the Psalms, he ranks with Moses as one of the most commanding figures in the Old Testament.

David was born in 1040 B.C. (II Sam. 5:4), the youngest son of Jesse of Bethlehem (I Sam. 16:10-11), and developed in strength, courage, and attractiveness while caring for his father's sheep (16:12, 17:34-36). When God rejected Saul,

A "MODERN DAVID," a shepherd boy with a sling, the weapon with which David stunned the giant Goliath.

the prophet Samuel sought out David and secretly anointed him as Israel's next king; and the youth became correspondingly filled with God's Spirit (16:13). Saul, meanwhile, summoned David to periodic appearances at court, to soothe his own demon-possessed mind by skillful harp-playing (16:18, 17:15). While still in his teens, David gained national renown and the friendship of Saul's son Jonathan (18:1-3; cf. 20:12-16, 23: 16-17) through his faith-inspired victory over the Philistine champion Goliath (17:45-47). Saul's growing jealousy and four insidious attempts on David's life served only to increase the latter's popularity (cf. 18:13-16,27). At length, urged on

BETHLEHEM, the City of David, with a shepherd and his flock, illustrative of David's younger life.

by David's rivals (cf. Ps. 59:12), Saul openly sought his destruction; and, though frustrated by Samuel and the priests at Nob, he did succeed in driving David into a life of outlawry (I Sam. 19: 11, 21:9).

David fled to Philistine Gath, but his motives became suspect. Only by a stratagem and by God's grace (I Sam. 21:12, Ps. 56:3, 34:6-8) did he reach the wilderness cave of Adullam in Judah (Ps. 142:6). Here David was joined by the priest Abiathar, who had escaped Saul's retaliatory attack upon Nob (cf. Ps. 52:1), and by a variety of malcontents [I Sam. 22:2]. On three separate occasions Saul attempted to seize David: when fellow-Judeans from Ziph betrayed his presence, after his deliverance of Keilah (I Sam. 23, Ps. 54: 3); at the cave of En-gedi by the Dead Sea, where Saul was caught in his own trap (I Sam. 24, Ps. 7: 4, 57:6); and upon David's return to Ziphite territory, when he again spared his pursuer's life (I Sam. 26). Near the end of 1012 B. C., however (27:7), David in despair sought asylum in Gath, feigning vassalage (27:8-12; 28).

Upon the destruction of Saul at Mt. Gilboa in 1010 B.C. and the Philistine domination of Israel from Beth-shan (cf. the demonstrated aban-donment of Gibeah, Saul's capital, G. Ernest Wright, *Biblical Archaeology,* Philadelphia: Westminster, 1957, pp. 122-123), David composed his moving lament of "The Bow" (II Sam. 1:19-27), the authenticity of which is unquestionable (R. H. Pfeiffer, *Introduction to the Old Testament,* New York: Harper, 1941, p. 351). Shortly thereafter, David's forces advanced inland to Hebron, where he was declared king over Judah. His appeal, however, to the northern and eastern tribes elicited no response (II Sam. 2:7); and for five years most of Israel lay under Philistine control.

In 1005 B.C. Saul's general, Abner, enthroned Ish-bosheth, a son of the former monarch; but in the conflict that followed David's arms gained ascendancy. Abner himself eventually transferred his support to David, only to be treacherously slain by David's vengeful commander, Joab (II Sam. 3). But after the death of Ish-bosheth (II Sam. 4) all Israel acclaimed David king, 1003 B.C. (II Sam. 5:1-5; I Chron. 11:10, 12:38).

Realizing that their "vassal" had gotten out of hand, the Philistines undertook an all-out attack upon reunited Israel. David, however, after an initial retreat to Adullam (II Sam. 5:17, 23:13-17), expelled the enemy in two divinely-directed

TALES OF DAVID the shepherd boy's beautiful singing had reached King Saul, and now the king's messenger had come to escort David to the royal court.

DAVID'S TOWER, near the Joppa (Jaffa) Gate. The tower was restored by the Turks and used for a time as a prison. The Joppa Gate is one of the gates of the old walled city of Jerusalem. It once connected the Old City and the New City.

campaigns (5:18-25; cf. the archaeological confirmation of his reoccupation of Beth-shan, Wm. F. Albright, *The Archaeology of Palestine and the Bible,* New York: Revell, 1932, pp. 40-44). He next established a new capital by capturing the Jebusite stronghold of Jerusalem. This strategic site on the Benjamite border served not only as an incomparable fortress, vulnerable only to the "scaling hooks" of Joab (II Sam. 5:8; Merrill F. Unger, *Archaeology and the Old Testament,* Grand Rapids: Zondervan, 1954, pp. 206-208), but also as a neutral location between the rival tribes of N and S. David then constructed "Millo," a fortification (?) that "filled up" Jerusalem's breached northern wall (R. A. S. Macalister, *A Century of Excavation in Palestine,* New York: Revell, 1925, pp. 104-106). Actually, because of Maccabean demolitions on the hill Ophel (David's City of Zion), no ruins survive that may be assigned him with confidence, though Davidic fortifications have been uncovered at Debir and Beth-shemesh. Joab, for his bravery was confirmed as commander (I Chron. 11:6). Under him were organized twelve corps of militia, each with 24,000 men, on periods of one-month duty annually (I Chron. 27). David's military organization also included the professional Cherethites and Pelethites (Cretans and Philistines) and certain elite groups: "the 600" mighty men (II Sam. 15:18; cf. I Sam. 27:2), "the 30" heroes, and "the 3" most distinguished (II Sam. 23; I Chron. 11).

David also elevated Jerusalem into his religious capital by installing Moses' ark of the covenant in a tent on Zion (Ps. 24; II Sam. 6; cf. Num. 4:15 on the death of Uzzah). He honored it, both with a dedicatory psalm (I Chron. 16, from Pss. 96, 105, 106) and with a permanent ministry of Levitical singers under Asaph (I Chron. 25; 16:5,37, 42). Once criticized as post-exilic fiction, these

regular *sharim* have been authenticated by even earlier Canaanitish parallels from Ugarit (Unger, *op. cit.,* pp. 215-218; cf. BA 4 (1941), pp. 33-47). Eventually David organized 38,000 Levites under hereditary leaders, appointing them as doorkeepers, treasurers, or even district judges (I Chron. 23-26). The Aaronic priests he divided into 24 rotating courses, which were continued into NT times (I Chron. 24:10; Luke 1:5).

From 1002 to about 995 B.C., David expanded his kingdom on all sides: W against Philistia, taking Gath, one of its five ruling cities (II Sam. 8:1); E against Moab, (8:2); N against Syria, in two campaigns (10:13 and 18, cf. 8:3), to the Euphrates River; and S against stubborn Edom (I Kings 11:15; Ps. 60:10). An alliance with Hiram of Tyre enabled David to construct a palace in Jerusalem (II Sam. 5:11). David's political organization shows analogies with Egypt's, his "cabinet" (8:15-18) including such officers as the recorder (public relations official), the scribe (secretary of state; Albright, *Archaeology and the Religion of Israel,* Baltimore: Johns Hopkins, 1953, p. 120), and other later additions (20:23-26). Over all, however, whether tribal princes (I Chron. 27:16-24) or royal officials (27:25-31), David reigned supreme.

Rest ensued (II Sam. 7:1; 22:1-51 = Ps. 18), and David proposed a permanent temple for Jehovah in Jerusalem. But while the Prophet Nathan denied David the privilege of building God's house (because of excessive bloodshed, I Chron. 22:8; 28:3), he revealed that God would build David's "house," raising up his son to construct the temple (II Sam. 7:13a) and establishing his dynasty (7:13b), to culminate in the incarnation of God's eternal Son (7:14). This "Davidic covenant" (Ps. 89:3; 132:12) mediates Christian salvation for all (Isa. 55:3; Rev. 22:16), climaxing God's promises, begun in Genesis 3:15 and accomplished in the new testament of Jesus Christ. God's Spirit then inspired David to compose Messianic psalms, depicting the deity of Jehovah's anointed Son (Ps. 2), His eternal priesthood (Ps. 110), His atoning death (Ps. 22), and His resurrection, ascension, and coming kingdom (Pss. 2, 16, 68). Some of David's greatest achievements lie in this literary sphere. Of the 150 canonical psalms, 73 possess titles asserting Davidic authorship. These references, moreover, appear in the oldest MSS and warrant full acceptance (Robert Dick Wilson, PTR 24 (1926), pp. 353-395). David also composed some of the titleless psalms (cf. Pss. 2, 95; Acts 4:25; Heb. 4:7); he stimulated Asaph and his associates to the inscripturation of others; and the king personally compiled the first book of the Psalter (Pss. 1-41; cf. his closing doxology in 41:13). One of the world's best loved compositions is David's heart-affirmation, "The Lord is my shepherd . . ." (Ps. 23).

(continued on page 535)

THE FOLLOWING BIBLE STORY, *The Young David,* was written by Richard Dunlop. It is based upon the events related in the First Book of Samuel, Chapters 16 through 31, and in the Second Book of Samuel, Chapters 1 and 2. The appearance of Joab as the king's messenger is fictional.

THE
Young David

N THE MORNING of the boy's
exalted day, the hungry sheep of Jesse spread over the stony hills about
Bethlehem, nibbling at the parched tufts of grass. The sun mounted the sky
as usual, devouring the shadows cast by the rocks, until at noon it stood
high in the heavens, flooding the hot earth with its brilliant rays. A thirsty
lamb bleated in the heat.

On a hillside David, a shepherd boy, was idly picking stones for his sling
and flinging them with unfailing aim at the stump of a dead oak which had
withered by the side of a long, dry watercourse. He grinned with satisfaction
at the thump of stone on wood. But when the lamb bleated again, he got to
his feet and scrambled down the hill into a ravine, where he gathered the
animal into his arms. The boy knew each member of his flock by sight
and by name, and the lamb snuggled against him as if it knew him too.

"Be still, little one," he soothed in a voice which was as merry as it was
compassionate.

Laboriously the boy climbed the hill and descended into a cleft on the far
side until he came to the pool of still water. In this dry country only a few
springs bubbled from the rocks. In the season of the raging sun David knew
that he must keep his flocks close to one of them. He gently patted the lamb's
fleece as it drank. Only when it lifted its head did he thrust his own hands
into the cool water and drink thirstily.

The boy and the lamb stayed in the shadows of the cleft in the hill while
the afternoon passed over the land. Dark-haired, his eyes a deep brown and
his skin fair despite the browning sun, David was such a fine-looking boy
that in the house of Jesse he was a favored and often spoiled son.

But the truly remarkable thing about this lonely shepherd boy had little to
do with his face and lithe figure. It looked out of his eyes when he took his
musical instrument from his shoulders and began to play upon it. It was a
harp, and David played it often to charm away his loneliness.

Now in a sweet but clear voice David sang the old songs of his people, songs which told how Moses had brought the Israelites out of Egypt, songs which told of Ruth, who was his great-grandmother. But as the afternoon shadows crept down the hill, David plucked new melodies from his strings to go with the new words which came from his heart. Lost in his music, he paid no attention as the lamb wandered up the hillside away from the pond.

"The Lord is my shepherd, I shall not want," sang David. "He makes me lie down in green pastures. He leads me beside still waters . . ."

David felt the first chill of evening. He paused and looked thoughtfully into the clear pond. Surely, God restored the soul as the cool waters restored the thirsty lamb.

From the top of the hill the lamb bleated in fear. A coughing snarl brought David trembling to his feet, his slingshot in hand. The lamb sprang down the slope as the massive head of a lion appeared on the crest. The huge beast growled again and deliberately descended the hill, fixing the lamb and the boy with its evil yellow eyes.

"The Lord is my shepherd," prayed David in a terrified voice. He had always known that there were wolves, lions, and bears in the hills and that sometimes they came down upon flocks, but it had never happened to him. The lion snarled again and showed its jutting teeth.

"The Lord is my shepherd. I shall not want," repeated David.

His arm and his knees steadied. He faced the lion unflinchingly. Swiftly he fitted a stone to his sling and swung it mightily. The rock flew through the air and struck the lion a terrible blow in the eye. The animal sank down with a groan. David watched the beast warily, for he expected it to rise again. But soon he realized that he had killed the lion. He, a boy, had killed a lion!

In that very moment another fearful growl came from the darkening hill. A bear shambled over the crest on its way to the water. Once again David's sling whirled, and a stone sped through the air. It too struck home with terrible force. The bear faltered and slid lifeless down the hill to the pool. David shouted with triumph. He, a boy, had killed a lion and now a bear!

But even before the hills had thrown back the last echo of his triumph, the exaltation fled David and left him a frightened shepherd boy again. A wonderful power had caught him up and guided his stones. Now it left him. He ran up the hill, the shivering lamb beneath his arm. He did not stop until he came to the stone wall which protected the rude houses of Bethlehem from marauders. Once in the town, he slowed down, walking breathlessly to the flat-roofed house of stone and mud bricks which was the home of Jesse, his father.

The House of Jesse

THAT NIGHT the seven grown sons of Jesse were sitting with their father and mother on the skins of sheep and goats which were stretched on the earthen floor. A fire burned in the middle of the room in an open pit. Since there was no chimney, the smoke found its way to the rafters, where haunches of mutton were hanging. The mother had just gone to the cooking

508

pot to taste a simmering stew when David burst wild-eyed and frenzied into the room.

"Father!" he cried, "I have killed a lion and a bear!"

The brothers jumped to their feet. Always they had envied David because of his fine looks and his ability to spellbind strangers and friends alike with his songs and dancing. Now he came shouting an impossible story.

"You lie, little brother!" cried Abinadab (uh-BIN-uh-dab).

"You have made up a foolish boy's tale," said Eliab (ee-LYE-ub).

"I have told the truth," said David indignantly, his brown eyes blazing. Ignoring the dish of steaming meat set before him, he dashed to where Jesse was sitting on his black goatskin, gloomily studying his youngest son.

"Father, I did kill the lion and the bear," insisted David.

"Can a boy of twelve summers kill beasts such as those?" asked Jesse, tugging at his beard. "I have never reproved you, my son, for your stories, but I cannot tolerate a shepherd of mine leaving his flock and bringing falsehoods from the fields."

David looked desperately to his mother, but her eyes showed that as always she agreed with his father.

"Perhaps little David is afraid of the dark in the hills," suggested Eliab. "My brothers and I shall go with him and guard this little boy while he guards the sheep."

David flushed with shame, but the brothers snatched him up and carried him laughing as they marched off to the field.

But when they arrived, they stopped laughing. There on the hill by the still waters lay a dead bear and a dead lion. They were filled with wonder.

"How could anyone so small have done this?" they asked one another, staring uneasily at their young brother. For the first time their jealousy gave way to something close to dread. They had long known he was a strange child, a boy of moods, of gaiety and then reflective melancholy, a shepherd boy who knew so little of the world but who seemed to be able to understand human hearts. Mysteriously this young singer of songs had destroyed these great beasts.

"It is a sign," said Abinadab, "and I do not like it."

If the remarkable victory of David over the wild animals was a sign, the brothers in the months that followed could not find a clue as to what it meant. David was unchanged. They could bully him as freely as before. He only escaped their blows through his nimbleness. As before, when the shepherds gathered together to feast, it was David who sang the old songs and danced wild dances of delight, his dark brown hair burnished by the flaming torches, his limbs whirling and his eyes shining with inspired pleasure. Old Jesse tugged his beard with contentment when the villagers clapped David on the back and applauded.

But for the most part, David remained in the hills with his sheep, singing his songs, dreaming of things which he never told about, and practicing with his sling. When a sheep wandered too far, David would fire a stone just beyond him so that the sheep, hearing it fall, knew that he should return to his shepherd.

David had an uncanny control over the stones from his sling.

Another Strange Sign

THROUGH THE LAND of Israel word went from shepherd to shepherd of this golden boy who had killed a lion and a bear and who could so move the heart with the sweetness of his songs and the joyous abandon of his dances. One day, in the proud city of Ramah (RAY-muh), word of the boy came to an old man with a gray beard who sat pondering bitterly about the king. Long ago this man had anointed Saul king, but now Saul no longer did his bidding; nor, the old man was grimly certain, did he do the bidding of God.

For years the old man, Samuel, greatest of the prophets since Moses, had refused to look upon Saul, first of the kings. The mind of Saul, in his royal loneliness, brimmed full of evil thoughts which, it was whispered through the corridors of his palace, were driving him mad. Now Samuel sought for a boy whom he would anoint as he had once anointed Saul. Could this singer of songs be the boy he sought? Calling together his priests, the prophet told them that he would go to Bethlehem to make a sacrifice to God. After the services were over, he would spend the night with Jesse, the leading man of the village.

When word reached Bethlehem that Samuel, already a legend in his own lifetime, was going to visit the village, the simple people of the place were caught up in a frenzy of preparation. They baked breads, made fig cakes, and got out the best grape wine from their storerooms. There would be hundreds of important visitors, and all must be entertained. But it was in the household of Jesse that the most feverish preparations went forward, for Samuel had said he would stay there.

"It is a pity," said Abinadab to his brother Eliab, "that David will so disgrace us when Samuel presents himself before our father for the hospitality of our house."

Surely, all the brothers agreed, David would take advantage of the occasion to show off his singing or his ready tongue, from which amusing or moving words flowed so readily.

"We cannot win any favors from Samuel while David is in the house," said Eliab, who had a certain honesty about him.

So the brothers arranged that all the shepherds who otherwise might be able to take David's place in the fields would be away that night. David easily saw through their plot, and he was dismayed. He hungered for a glimpse of the great world of kings and prophets which a visit from Samuel brought close. But if he complained of his brothers to his father, it would only cause old Jesse pain at a time when he was already upset with the household's strenuous preparations.

"Do you come in peace?" asked the elders of Bethlehem when Samuel arrived at the village gates. They asked fearfully, for hundreds of followers accompanied the prophet, and in troubled Judah large bodies of men often meant plundering.

Samuel pierced them with his dark eyes. "Peacefully," he said. "I have come to sacrifice to the Lord. Sanctify yourselves and come with me to the sacrifice."

510

The people did as he said, their hearts filled with thanksgiving. After the services, Samuel and his attendants went to the house of Jesse, where their host's wife was just finishing cooking the evening meal. But the prophet had no eyes for the most tempting food that Jesse's household could provide. He looked instead upon the faces of the seven sons, who stood anxiously by.

Finally Samuel began to scowl, for he did not like what he saw. "Are these all your children?" he demanded sourly.

Jesse, anxious to please, answered, "There remains the youngest, and he is keeping the sheep."

The old prophet drew himself erect, and in a stern voice demanded, "Send and fetch him. We will not sit down till he comes here."

Jesse immediately despatched a servant, and the family and elders settled back to talk and wait. But Samuel stood alone, staring bitterly into the fire. Had he come all this way for nothing?

Suddenly the door burst open. David, out of breath from running, his hair mussed by the night wind, rushed in.

To Samuel he seemed as wild as the night out of which he had come. The boy's eyes sparkled with excitement. As the old man's dark eyes burned into his, David's heart was filled with a tumult of strange, only half-understood emotions. He knew that Samuel read his every thought. When the prophet rose from his seat, David fell on his knees before him and looked with now frightened eyes at the floor.

In a low voice Samuel chanted words which David could not understand. Then David felt a sticky oil being poured on his head. He smelled its sweet aroma as Samuel placed strong fingers on the boy's curly hair and spoke again in a mutter which David could not make out.

When he had finished, the prophet sat down to his dinner, and attention which had focused so sharply on David dissolved into the sounds of hungry men eating and talking about the events of the day. Nobody mentioned the strange thing Samuel had done. The boy crept from the lighted room out into the night, where the bright stars of God twinkled inscrutably. Was the hand of Samuel upon his head another sign of things yet to come? David wondered; but the friendly stars, beneath whose gaze he had watched his sheep for so many nights, had no answer.

A Royal Summons

ONCE AGAIN months crept over the hills of Judah. The rains greened the grass for the hungry sheep. The sun heated the rocks so that they split in the cold air of night. David tended the flocks of his father. Everything seemed normal, except that now his brothers kept a suspicious distance from him.

But while Bethlehem drowsed quietly, at the palace of Saul, courtiers smiled at the grim prophecies of Samuel, who had predicted that Saul would lose his kingdom. Surely the great king who had brought victory and power to Israel, who was the beloved of his people, would continue to reign gloriously. When the wheel of time had turned to the last day of Saul, his brave son Jonathan, who had shown his mettle in overcoming the Philistine (fih-LISS-tin) invaders, would surely follow him to the throne.

But amid all the glory of his court, the mind of Saul was giving way. His victories had been won, his government was popular, Samuel had carried his hatred to his grave, but Saul grew daily more melancholy. He would brood on the throne or in the privacy of his chambers until he fell into a trance from which it was hard to rouse him. Sometimes, springing from his trance, he would hurl his spear at the first man he spied. Even Jonathan, the crown prince, dared not disturb him for fear of his life. The court musicians alone seemed to be able to help him. Their sweet playing quieted the monarch when the sickness came upon his mind. But in time they too lost the power to soothe.

"I tire of the men who make music for me," said Saul in despair. "Is there no sweeter music in my kingdom?"

Men and women shook their heads, for now they believed that Saul was doomed by the prophecy of Samuel. But one courtier remembered the tales the shepherds told of a boy singer of Bethlehem who sang not only the songs of his people but songs of his own heart.

"He is the youngest son of Jesse," the courtier told Saul.

Somebody else remembered that Joab (JOE-ab), a young army officer stationed at the court, was the son of Zeruiah (zee-ROO-yuh), an elder daughter of Jesse. Why not send Joab to bring his youthful relative to court? A boy who sang so beautifully should sing for more than sheep or rude shepherds.

The young soldier Joab smarted at the idea of being sent to escort a boy to court, a boy singer at that. Was this a job for an officer of the army? Nonetheless, he hurried to Bethlehem with the king's orders and went directly to the house of Jesse, his grandfather.

The old man was overjoyed at the honor the king had bestowed upon his house. "David shall go with you, Joab. But guard the boy well, for he is my youngest son."

The aroma of baking bread filled the house. Jesse intended to send bread, a kid and a bottle of the finest wine in Judah, the wine made from his own grapes, as presents for the king.

"Why does the king invite an upstart boy to his court?" demanded Abinadab, his suppressed hatred for David blazing forth.

"He will disgrace our family," said Eliab. "We who should be famed for our prowess in battle must be known at the court as the family of the boy singer. Singing is a slave's business."

Joab agreed with the brothers, but he had the king's orders to carry out.

The Journey

THAT VERY EVENING Joab set out with David for Gibeah (GIB-ee-uh). As they rode down the road through the dusk, he could not keep his eyes off the strange harp which David carried upon his shoulders.

"It would be well with you," he said finally, "if your instrument of music proves an instrument of magic. If you fail to charm the king's temper, you may find the king's spear in your chest."

Joab expected the boy to be frightened, but David smiled and rode confidently at his side. The two riders went by a roundabout way to Gibeah in order to avoid the city of Jerusalem, which was then still held by the warlike Jebusites (JEB-yew-sytes). Their path took them close enough to the city so that they could make out its twinkling lights from the top of a high hill.

"Why don't the people of Israel drive out the enemies of the Lord?" David suddenly demanded.

There was a passion in his voice which astounded Joab. He took a sharp look at this boy uncle of his. David took no notice, for he was staring down at the sleeping city of his country's enemies. When he did turn to Joab, he wanted to know why Joab thought the city could not be captured. He questioned his relative about the defenses, and they rode away from the city talking excitedly of how they might some day storm Jerusalem.

By the time they cantered through the gates of Gibeah and clattered down the streets to the quarter of the city where the king had his palace, Joab knew that David, despite his youth, was no mere singer. Somehow the boy had come by a clear head for military strategy. Even so, Joab was happy to leave him at the dwelling of Abner, commander-in-chief of King Saul's armies. What David might be in the future was one thing, but on this sultry afternoon he was just a singer from the country. It was best that an ambitious officer not make a point of claiming him as his relative.

In the palace of Abner, David found himself for the first time in his life among the rich furnishings and tapestries which adorned the dwellings of the mighty. He studied the beautiful things with fascination as he waited in the anteroom. But still more interesting to David were the men who also waited to see Abner. He watched them without appearing to do so, for he could see that in this world of the court a boy did not gape open-mouthed at lords and captains as he might if they came upon him by surprise in the hills as he cared for his sheep. David's keen mind quickly learned the manners and the ways of the men about him.

As the day closed, David was ushered through a curtain which screened off the private apartment of the general. He had been taught how to bow before the noble officer, who was the king's cousin, but he was stricken with uncertainty as he entered his presence. Abner, with the simplicity which often goes with greatness, immediately walked over to the boy, lifted his chin with his hand and looked into his deep brown eyes. David, unwavering, returned his gaze.

"The king is even now suffering," said Abner after he had talked a while with the boy to put him at his ease. He explained the nature of the ruler's illness. "You must be watchful," he said. "Our good king would not ordinarily harm a hair of a child's head, but in his fits of madness an evil spirit guides his spear arm."

David blanched slightly but continued to look steadily into Abner's eyes. The general took him by the shoulder and walked by his side from the house. Commander-in-chief and shepherd boy went together down the street among the houses of officials and rich men to the palace of Saul, which was oddly quiet. Guards spoke in soft voices. The king's beautiful daughters, Merab (MEE-rab) and Michal (MY-kul), whom David glimpsed in a side chamber, were sitting back on their heels gently weeping.

The Mad King

ABNER gave David's shoulder a final reassuring squeeze and directed him to go on alone through a door. High on his throne sat Saul, the king. His noble frame was erect, but his gray hair hung over his forehead and his eyes stared with unblinking dread at some unseen specter. For a moment David quailed before the terrible sight of the mad king. Then he threw himself at the feet of the frozen figure which towered so dreadfully over him.

It was particularly terrifying that Saul did not seem to notice him at all. David rose slowly, clutching his harp to him, and softly began to draw from it the music of an old folk song. Now he sang of Moses, then of Abraham, his voice clear and liquid. Never in the long history of his people was there a singer such as David, and the songs he sang penetrated through the darkness of Saul's mind to the flickering reason within. Saul stirred. He put his hand to his chin and listened as he followed with his eyes the handsome boy before him. It was almost as if the Lord had sent an angel to sing away his pain and his terror.

Then the anguish welled up again, and Saul's eyes darted about the room as if he were a lion enmeshed by hideous unseen pygmies. David, the shepherd, who had known fear on the lonely hills when darkness lowered upon him, now saw that the sickness of the king was fear. What terrible thing the king feared was never to be known, but David, who had slain a lion and a bear, now sang one of his greatest songs, a psalm of such great faith that it has come undimmed through the years.

> The Lord is my shepherd, I shall not want;
> He makes me lie down in green pastures.
> He leads me beside still waters;
> He restores my soul.
> He leads me in paths of righteousness
> for His name's sake.
>
> Even though I walk through the valley of the shadow of death,
> I fear no evil;
> for Thou art with me;
> Thy rod and Thy staff,
> they comfort me.
>
> Thou preparest a table before me
> in the presence of my enemies; . . .

As David sang, the king's brow unknitted and his hands ceased their furious searching for a raveling on his tunic. His eyes grew calm.

> Thou anointest my head with oil,
> my cup overflows.
> Surely goodness and mercy shall follow me
> all the days of my life;
> and I shall dwell in the house of the Lord
> for ever.

Before the serenity of these inspired words, the king's madness fled. He called David to him in his deep voice. David knelt at his feet, his eyes drinking in the calm kindness of his king's face. As for Saul, looking down on the divinely gifted boy before him, he would have said more; but in his wonder at the peace which had come to him through this youth he could not break his silence. Finally he signaled for David to leave, and David passed from the presence of the king whose mind he had healed.

The Beautiful Sisters

IN THE DAYS that followed David stayed at court, expecting that the king would call him again to his presence. But Saul did not send for the singer. Cured of his melancholy, he had thrown himself back into the demanding task of governing his kingdom, taking care of pressing problems which had waited overly long for solutions. He sent royal presents to the boy; but David, who had looked upon the face of greatness, hungered now to be with the king again.

But there were other charms in the city for a shepherd boy who was at last seeing the world. Most marvelous of all were Merab and Michal, the exquisite daughters of Saul, who were about his age. David could not keep his eyes from the dark shining hair of Michal, and when she spoke to him in her gentle voice, he was bemused by the beauty of it. Michal was enough of a grown woman to see how the shepherd boy who had cured her father had fallen in love with her. She was also princess enough to assume a supreme indifference and to keep him at the distance which was appropriate for a singer of songs. David lay awake at night dreaming of Michal.

One morning, after another such sleepless night, Joab came to him. He brought presents from the king to take to Jesse, his father, and the king's bidding to be on his way to Bethlehem. Saul was confident in his new-found health that he would never need David again. Better that the boy should be returned to his birthplace than kept at the court, where it was said that his eyes saw little but the king's own daughter.

On the dusty road to Bethlehem, every step took David farther away from his dreams of the court and the beautiful princess. It had almost seemed as if the portents of the past were to be realized, but now he was on his way home to the loneliness and monotony of a shepherd's life. Only the presence of a guide kept the boy, whom events were shaping into a man, from weeping in his disappointment.

Jesse gave thanks to God that his youngest son had come home, and he listened eagerly to David's tales of Gibeah. Even David's brothers were for the moment overawed. Village elders sought to honor the boy who had brought fame to Bethlehem, but David spent little time within the walls of the town. He preferred to be with his sheep, where beneath the sparkling stars he could dream of the haughty princess who had awakened his love only to bring torment to his heart. "If only I could win great battles for the king," David mused as he watched his sheep, "then I might dare to hope for Michal's hand."

515

Angrily he fired a stone from his sling. There was scant chance that he would ever be asked to use his sling in the service of Saul; and, even if he could, what chance would there be for him to win battles?

Yet David's musings led him to action. If it would take greatness to win a princess, he must be prepared to seize greatness by the throat and make it his own, if ever the opportunity came his way. As he moved his flocks over the rugged hills from pasture to pasture, he peopled each valley and each thicket with make-believe enemy soldiers. He deployed his own troops in maneuvers designed to win the battles. While he was with Joab and Abner, David had questioned them about the battles of Saul. He knew how the king had won each victory. He knew, too, how he had suffered his defeats. Sometimes, when the moonlight played tricks with the shadows, he imagined that he saw hundreds of the dread Philistine chariots sweeping across the valley towards him. To avoid the chariots, David knew that his soldiers must always fight battles in the hills. And he was convinced that a nation of shepherds with their skill could turn the sling into a major military weapon, which might one day free their land of the menacing Philistines.

Strangely, on nights when the wind blew hard, he thought he heard a giant voice calling, and he knew not what it meant or why it called.

The King Goes to War

ONE DAY Joab came riding to Bethlehem, but not to call David to court. Up and down the land it was known that the Philistines were marshaling for an attack on Israel. Joab was recruiting officers for the army that Saul was even now forging into a mighty weapon for the defense of his kingdom.

David hoped ardently that Joab would pick him for the army, but the young officer ignored him pointedly and chose instead his three eldest brothers. The other four brothers were told that they should keep ready in arms; when the war flamed up, they would be called.

Only David was refused any place in the army of the king. "Singing is one thing," Joab sneered. "Fighting is another."

David was sent back crestfallen to the fields, while his fortunate brothers marched away to the army.

Soon the campaign began. The Philistines crossed the border into Judah in force and seized a strategic position from which they could strike into the heart of the country. Saul quickly led his army into the field and camped along the valley of Elah (EE-luh) to protect his cities from the invaders. Insolently the Philistines advanced until they occupied the mountain on the opposite side of the valley. There they paused and hurled taunts at Saul's men.

One morning a giant Philistine, better than nine feet in height, clanked forward in his impenetrable armor from the ranks of the army. His spear was as enormous as a weaver's beam, and his baleful eyes gleamed with the murder he hoped to do that day.

"Am I not a Philistine and you servants of Saul?" he cried. "Choose a man for yourselves, and let him come down to me. If he can fight with me and

David beheads Goliath.

COLOR ILLUSTRATIONS BY CARL MUELLER

David soothes Saul with his songs.

*A stone from David's sling
fells the lion.*

Goliath taunts the Israelites.

Samuel anoints David.

David's rendezvous with Jonathan.

Saul consults the witch of Endor.

The wedding of David and Michal.

David crowned king.

Goliath staggers under the impact of the stone.

kill me, then we will be your servants; but if I prevail against him and kill him, then you shall be our servants and serve us."

A silence born of fear settled upon the army of Israel. No champion stepped forward to meet this giant.

"I defy the armies of Israel this day. Send me a man, that we may fight together!" roared the giant, his voice rumbling across the narrow valley.

Daily the giant Goliath (go-LYE-uth) of Gath, as the quaking Israelites learned he was called, put in his appearance. Daily the morale of Saul's army sank further. Saul dared not send a champion against the huge bear of a man, because if the best man his army could find was easily killed, then defeat would be inevitable.

David Goes to the Front

N O WORD reached Bethlehem about Goliath and the dismay which he hurled into the camp of Israel. In fact, no word was reaching home at all. One morning Jesse, after a sleepless night of worry, called David to him. David was the last son remaining at home.

"I must have news of your brothers," he told the stripling. "You shall be my messenger."

He provided David with a bushel of parched corn and ten loaves of their mother's fresh bread to give to his brothers. To their battalion commander the father, hoping as a parent often will for favor for his sons, sent a dozen cheeses. The very next morning, before his father could change his mind, David left for the fighting front.

After a hard journey, he reached the camp of the army just as Goliath was roaring his daily torrent of abuse and blasphemies at the Israelites. Leaving the gifts he brought with the soldiers who guarded the camp, he hurried forward to where the outposts of Israel were ranged along the mountainside. He could look across the valley, through which flowed a gentle stream, to the opposite hill. There the Philistines had gathered to enjoy the discomfiture of their enemies.

Goliath strode in front of the ranks of his comrades. Before him marched a self-important shield-bearer. The giant lumbered about in his heavy armor, roaring at the skulking men of Israel.

"The man that kills him," said a white-faced soldier standing next to David, "deserves the king's daughter."

Already David had been studying the giant. He realized at a glance what havoc this Philistine was playing in the army of his king. Now he heard words that rekindled his hopes. If only he could destroy that wild-eyed giant strutting his armor before them, he would then deserve Michal! Instantly, he knew what he must do.

"Who is this Philistine," demanded David, his clear voice carrying through the ranks, "that he should defy the armies of the living God?"

He spoke with deep emotional conviction, and the soldiers, though seeing only a youth, listened. They did not laugh as he proclaimed that he was

517

ready to fight the giant. There was something arresting in the lad's gaze, and it almost seemed to the soldiers that this boy might deliver them from the monster who stalked before their lines.

Hearing a commotion, Eliab, an officer now, hurried to the spot. To his anger he found his young brother holding the soldiers with the power of his tongue.

"Why are you here?" he demanded of David. "With whom have you left those few sheep in the wilderness?" He spoke with the contempt that a man shows for a boy he dislikes. "I know your pride and the wilfulness of your heart. You have come down to watch the battle."

The youth that Eliab addressed so scornfully was not to be put in his place by an irate brother. Nor was he going to air a family quarrel before the soldiers. He put off his brother with a few words. "What have I done now? Was there not good reason for me to speak?"

He did not give Eliab a chance to answer, but turned his back on him and went on talking to the crowd. Soon officers and men alike were listening to David's brave words, and the brother had no choice but to stand aside. Saul, mindful of the disaster that might be triggered by a Goliath victory, had ordered that nobody should dare to fight the giant without his permission. So now the soldiers took David to him. Once more the shepherd boy from Bethlehem looked upon the face of the king.

"You will never be able to fight against this Philistine," said Saul, remembering only the boy who had come to sing him from his madness. Pitying him, Saul added, "You are only a boy, and he is a man of war from his youth."

Saul's pity was wasted on David, who was filled with a wild exaltation. "Your servant kept his father's sheep," he said staunchly, "and when a lion or a bear came and took a lamb out of the flock, I went out after him and smote him and rescued the lamb from his mouth. Your servant smote both the lion and the bear: and this Philistine shall be as one of them, since he has defied the armies of the living God."

Saul was impressed. It seemed to him now that this youth might well prevail where no grown man could. He looked at David and believed in him. "Go—and the Lord be with you," said the king.

David and Goliath

A TENT was given to David, and to it was sent a brass helmet, a coat of mail, and a sword, all made of the finest metal. Saul wanted his young champion to be as well protected as Israelite armorers could make him. Immediately David put on the magnificent armor and, boylike, preened himself on his fine appearance. But by the time he had walked to the tent of Saul he had determined that, beautiful as this armor might be, he would set it aside. In the fields of Bethlehem he had had no opportunity to learn how to use it.

"I cannot wear these pieces, for I am not trained to," David said to the king. He stripped off the armor and handed it to an attendant.

The king did not argue, for he was busy making plans for the battle that he knew would follow immediately after the struggle between the two champions. If David slew Goliath, he wanted his forces ready to charge the Philistines. They would, Saul reasoned, be stunned and thrown into confusion by the fall of their mightiest warrior.

In the valley, men on each side exchanged boastful shouts. The Israelites prayed for victory but scarcely expected it. Their ranks parted, and when they saw the slim figure of a teen-ager, wearing no armor, carrying no shield or sword or spear, even their prayers stopped.

David sheds the king's armor

The Philistines stared in equal silence at the sight: a brown-haired boy, walking gracefully and with unfrightened purpose toward their giant.

David paused only at the stream, where he carefully picked some stones from the bank and washed them off in the water. These he put into his shepherd's bag. The stillness grew more oppressive by the moment. At last Goliath could stand it no longer.

"Am I a dog, that you come to me with stones?" he shouted at the youth. "Come to me, and I will give your flesh to the fowls of the air and the beasts of the field."

519

David recognized the hot anger in Goliath and provoked him further. If the giant could be made to rage, he would lose the use of whatever good judgment he had.

"You come to me with a sword and a spear and a javelin," David shouted in his high, penetrating voice, "but I come to you in the name of the Lord, the God of the armies of Israel, whom you have defied. This day will the Lord deliver you into my hand. I will strike you and take your head from you, and I will give the carcasses of the Philistine soldiers this day to the fowls of the air and the wild beasts of the earth. . . ."

David paused, not simply to study the effect of his words, but because it seemed to him that the same great Voice that had sounded as a mighty wind through his psalms was about to speak through him again. When he resumed, his own voice had a deeper, strangely thrilling quality to it.

"I will crush you so that all the world may know that there is a God in Israel; and that all this assembly may know that the Lord saves not with sword and spear. For the battle is the Lord's, and He will deliver you into our hands."

David skipped from stone to stone across the stream while Goliath with a roar rushed toward him. David had no intention of being impaled on the enormous spear and jumped back across the water. Goliath, mindful of what jeopardy a spill from a slippery stone could plunge him into, stopped at the brink and bawled with rage.

David selects stones from the stream

David continued to tease the giant with the tantalizing prospect of spearing his quick figure. At last Goliath, hot and tired beneath the load of his armor and spear, charged furiously toward the brook, leaving his shield-bearer behind. He halted but an instant to push back his helmet and mop the sweat from his forehead.

In that instant, David saw his chance. He thrust his hand into his bag and put a stone to his sling. The stone whirred through the air and sank with a crunch into Goliath's forehead. The giant collapsed.

Catlike, David was on him. Standing on the prostrate Goliath, he drew the giant's enormous sword from its sheath and chopped the head from the body, shouting with triumph.

This was what the Israelites were waiting for. In full battle array they charged the terrified Philistines, who stared shocked at the fall of their champion. By evening the Israelites had routed the enemy, and David, the shepherd boy, was the nation's hero.

An Officer of the King

WHEN CALM SETTLED upon the valley with the setting of the sun, Saul sent for the young conqueror. David found the royal tent set up in a grove of oaks and the king waiting with his stalwart young son, Prince Jonathan, at his side. David, who had heard much about the battle prowess of Jonathan, could not help but glance with admiration at him even as he listened to a grateful king thanking him for his own brave exploit. Jonathan, for his part, plainly returned David's admiration.

This time Saul would not think of allowing David to return to Bethlehem. He insisted that the youth stay close to him, for he now cherished David as his own son. He gave David a command in the army, but made no mention of his daughters.

David left the tent of the king, scarcely believing the change in his circumstances that the day's events had brought. He started to walk away through the jubilant camp, but turned when he heard his name. It was Jonathan, who had followed him.

The prince held out his hands in friendship. The smile on his face was so frank and understanding that David felt deeply moved. In his boyhood he had had few friends. Now he was to have a friend of such unwavering affection as to make up for all the loneliness of the years past.

In the battles that followed, many around the king envied David his rapid promotion to high rank. They comforted themselves with the belief that certainly a mere youth would blunder in a position of command and would either meet death in the fighting or be demoted for his mistakes. But David had fought countless imaginary battles through the hills around Bethlehem, and now in real encounters with the Philistines he proved a master of reconnaisance, with an uncanny ability to turn the terrain to the advantage of his soldiers. Most important, his great bravery and his youth and charm won the hearts of his men. Hardened veterans, they followed anywhere that their leader took them, though he was still little more than a boy.

So it was that when the war came to a successful end, David marched to Gibeah at the head of a triumphant army. Women packed the streets of the cities he passed through to get a glimpse of the handsome young general. They sang:

> Saul has slain his thousands,
> And David his ten thousands.

The rout of the Philistines

The new song had a catchy tune to it, and soon all Israel was chanting it. Saul, who for months now had been growing increasingly moody again, resented bitterly the fame of the young man. Would Samuel's dire prophecies be fulfilled through this youth whom the king's favor had elevated to high office?

For the moment Saul kept his peace. Taking their cue from the king, the politicians and officers of Israel gave all honor to David and sought his friendship. Even the commander-in-chief, brave Abner, befriended him, and Ahithophel (uh-HITH-oh-fel), one of the wisest of the king's younger counselors, took David under his wing and painstakingly explained the ins and outs of governmental life. Joab too, now that David's promise had turned to reality, was proud to claim kinship with him. David's glory even seemed to melt the hatred in the hearts of his brothers.

David Wins a Wife

I F DAVID could have Michal as his wife, he believed that he would be completely happy. Yet there was despair in his heart, because his sharp eyes had noticed that Saul was no longer pleased with him. He saw no way to win Michal now.

But hope would flame anew each time he was with her. He became a young man intoxicated. Michal smiled at him beneath her dark lashes, but she knew that she was a princess born and that her hand must go to the man her father chose. Sometimes David would tell her brother Jonathan of his love for Michal, and Jonathan, true to his friend, did all he could to help him. He urged his father to make his best friend his brother-in-law too.

"Michal loves David, and David loves her," he argued.

Yet the king, haunted with his dreads, could not bear to think of giving his daughter to David, whom he sometimes loved as a son but more and more rejected as a threat to his throne. His informants had brought him the incredible report that once, years ago, Samuel had gone to Bethlehem and anointed David as he had once anointed him. There could be no two meanings about this. Saul kept a watch on the young man for fear that he might attempt to overthrow him at any moment. When he also heard the gossip of the court that David was openly and scandalously showing his love for his daughter, the king grew grim. One day he had David brought to him. Merab stood blushing beside the throne.

"Behold my elder daughter, Merab," the king said. "Her will I give to you as a wife. I ask only that you be valiant for me and fight the Lord's battles."

David was shocked. The king was offering him the daughter he did not love! But he dared not show his heart.

"Who am I," he asked, "and what is my life or my father's family in Israel, that I should be son-in-law to the king?"

David's modesty touched the king's heart, but his fear of the youth did not lessen. He told David that if he would raid Philistia (fih-LISS-tee-uh) and bring back proof of one hundred dead enemies, he would give him Merab in marriage.

For a long moment David studied the king's face. This bloody dowry was not to his liking, nor was the bride; but he felt he could do nothing but accept the royal bargain.

In the field, David's genius as a commander again asserted itself. He won a brilliant success, easily killing more than the number of Philistines demanded by Saul. After he returned at the head of his troops, he learned to his astonished pleasure that Jonathan, when he had found his father in a happy frame of mind and untormented for the time by his melancholy, had persuaded the king to give Michal to David, instead of her sister.

Saul welcomed David to his palace, embraced him, and gave him his daughter. To David, who since his first boyhood glimpse of Michal had loved her passionately, it seemed far too good to be true. Now she was actually his wife! He sank to his knees before her and covered her outstretched hands with kisses.

Saul's Treachery

IN THE DAYS THAT FOLLOWED, David knew a bliss that appeared to have no bounds. All over the kingdom peace reigned, and David, son-in-law to Saul and the fourth ranking man of the kingdom, was a popular figure at the court and throughout the realm.

Saul's happy mood lasted for a time. He looked upon his kingdom with open-hearted good humor. But then, at first occasionally and later more and more, he fell back into his brooding silences, breaking them only to fly into violent anger. All the courtiers and even Jonathan suffered, but David was the particular object of his outbursts. One moment he would show David every sign of affection; next he would scorn him.

Then one day the court was stunned to learn that, for the first time in years, Saul had gone into another of his dreaded trances. His memory of the prophet Samuel's condemnations once again had smothered his reason.

It was only natural that David should be asked to sing again to help dispel the king's sickness. David had no choice but to do so, although he knew that, no matter how sweetly he sang now, he was a grown man and would not have the same effect as he once had as a fresh-faced boy.

David went to the king's chamber and found him in one of his gloomy moods, furtively peering at the faces of strangers and members of his family alike, as if he would find in them confirmation of his fears. David sang softly the songs he knew the king loved best, and at first it seemed as if once again he might restore the king to serenity. At least Saul's reason regained control, and his eyes ceased their frantic wandering.

But with reason's return there came a glitter in his eyes which David was quick to understand. He saw the king's gaze rest for a moment on his spears stacked in the corner, and when Saul stood up and began to pace the chamber, David realized that he was drawing ever closer to his weapons, preparing to seize one.

Saul did just that, but David was ready for it. Agile as ever, he leaped aside as the king hurled the spear at his head. The sharp point smashed into the wall, and David sprang out of the room.

Within a few days the king had recovered fully from his latest fit of depression, and the ranking officials of the kingdom hurried to him, David among them. Saul treated David as if nothing had happened. But in the following weeks, David saw that the king now planned to do in cold blood what he had tried to do as he emerged from madness. Courtiers who had been his apparent friends now avoided David. Only Jonathan remained faithful, as did Joab and his brother Abishai (uh-BISH-ay-eye), who were bound to him by blood and had little alternative in a day when the fall of a great man almost always took his relatives with him.

Joab anxiously urged David to flee before it was too late, but David refused. He had no wish to quit his high rank and roam homeless in the wilderness. Above all, he drew back at the idea of leaving Michal, who at first would not believe that her father could be preparing the death of her husband.

But soon Michal also realized that David was doomed if he did not escape at once. Her fear for him haunted her eloquent eyes when David kissed her. At night she would bolt up in her bed at the slightest noise in the street, terrified that soldiers might be coming to kill her sleeping husband.

The Testing of the King

DAVID still determined that before he gave up everything—his beautiful wife, his high position, and his bright hopes for the future—he must know for certain that the king planned his murder. He sent word to Jonathan to meet him that night outside the city walls, at a favorite spot where the two friends had often walked and talked in those happy days when the prince was helping him win Michal's hand.

Jonathan came, and David clasped his friend's arm in the darkness. Tensely, he told him of the fear he had for his life.

At first Jonathan would not take him seriously. Why would his father want to kill David, whom he loved? David gripped his arm harder and cried, "As the Lord lives and as your soul lives, there is but a step between me and death!"

Jonathan was convinced. "Whatever your soul desires," he said quietly, "I will do for you."

David had a plan to test the intentions of Saul. The Festival of the New Moon began on the following day, and David was expected to sit down to a state dinner with Saul, Jonathan, and Abner. David now told Jonathan that he planned to hide near a great rock a few miles from the city. When he did not come to the feast, Saul would doubtless want to know why. Jonathan was to say that he had given his friend leave to go to Bethlehem to celebrate the holiday with his family. How the king took this news might well betray his plans. The two friends talked long that night, for if David's fears were well founded, they might never have another such chance.

At the Feast of the New Moon, Saul sat down to table with Jonathan and Abner. He glanced often at David's empty chair but said nothing. The next night the three men sat down to dinner again. Once again David was absent.

"Why," demanded the king, "does the son of Jesse not come to eat—neither yesterday nor today?"

When Jonathan explained, Saul flamed into instant rage. He cursed Jonathan for his wicked friendship for David, who was trying to steal the very throne from him.

"Now bring him to me," raged the king, "for he shall surely die."

Jonathan, with the same bravery he had often shown on the battlefield, replied, "Why should he be put to death? What has he done?"

Saul choked with fury. He caught up a spear and threw it wildly at Jonathan. The prince dodged, jumped up from the table, and raced from the room.

At dawn, armed with his bow and arrows, he set out for the large rock outside the city where David was hiding. As the two friends had arranged, he brought a small boy with him. Jonathan was to shoot three arrows as if he were practicing. If, as the boy ran to pick up the arrows, Jonathan shouted that he had passed the arrows by, it meant that death was passing David by. But if he shouted that the boy had not gone far enough, then David too must go farther and hide from the king's anger. Jonathan loosed his three arrows as if firing at a target. The boy ran to retrieve them.

"Aren't the arrows farther on?" he called, as if to the boy. "Hurry! Make haste! Keep going!"

But even then David stayed for a last farewell with Jonathan, whom he feared he would never see again.

Michal fools the king's soldiers with a dummy of David

Flight

D AVID FLED that morning while Saul's troops were marching to Bethlehem to arrest him there. When the soldiers returned with the news that he had not been in Bethlehem, Saul fumed.

At this point Michal slyly let it be known that her husband was sick at home. Saul immediately sent men to seize David, but Michal, summoning all her royal presence, refused to admit them to the house. When at last they made a forced entrance, she showed them David's bed, where she had carefully placed the image of a man with a pillow of goat's hair for a head. This was David, she told them, and they were satisfied when they saw the bed clothes humped as if by a sleeping man. They could make the arrest at their leisure.

But Saul was not to be put off longer. He demanded that the sick David be brought to him, bed and all. When the bed was carried before him, he pulled back the covers and discovered that only a dummy slept in it. As he stormed, his daughter laughed. In hatred for David and anger at Michal, he told her that he would now marry her to somebody else.

David, traveling tirelessly on foot, jogging at a shepherd's trot or walking, headed toward the priests' city of Nob, where he hoped that the priests might shelter him. He knew the chief priest, Ahimelech (uh-HIM-uh-leck), and he recalled that the priests had never made peace with Saul after his break with Samuel.

Arriving at the largest dwelling in the town, David asked for bread for his party, which he claimed was camped not far away. At first Ahimelech would not help the son-in-law of the king, for he had heard nothing of the rift between the two. But David was too persuasive to be resisted, and Ahimelech sent for loaves of unleavened holy bread. An evil-faced man named Doeg (DOE-eg), whom David remembered as a former servant of Saul, brought the bread. There was no escaping the man's crafty eyes. David knew that he had been recognized and would be reported.

"I have brought neither my sword nor my weapons with me, because the king's business required haste," David said boldly. He needed a sword or spear if he were safely to make his way through the wild country.

"The sword of Goliath the Philistine, whom you slew in the vale of Elah, is here wrapped in a cloth." said Ahimelech. "If you need a sword, take that, for there is no other one here."

"And no other like that one," said David grimly. "Give it to me."

For weeks David, an outcast, fought to survive. He had bread but only enough to last for a short time. If he were to live, he must find supporters. A lone fugitive would never be given food and shelter by the king's loyal subjects. Sending a message to Bethlehem for his brothers to join him, he hurried to Adullam (uh-DULL-um), a rocky hill where he knew deep caves near the summit which could hide an army.

One by one, relatives and friends who remained loyal to David joined him at his fortress on the rocky hill. His aged parents, of course, could not endure the hardships of life in the caves, and David arranged that the king of Moab (MOE-ab) should keep them safe in his country, from which Jesse's grandmother, Ruth, had come.

Sometimes larger parties arrived to join David, among them the sons of Zeruiah (zeh-ROO-yuh)—Joab, Abishai and their gifted young brother Asahel (AY-suh-hel), who reminded many of David himself at his age. David knew that he had in them three first-class lieutenants for the guerrilla warfare he must now wage against the king.

How ruthless the king was in his manhunt for David became evident when an exhausted young priest, Abiathar (uh-BYE-uh-thur), arrived at the caves and pitifully told the outlaws that he was the last of the house of Eli (EE-lye). It was a tragic tale. The vicious Doeg had told Saul how Ahimelech had given food and Goliath's sword to David. Saul then had the priests brought before him and accused them of helping the fugitive. He ordered them put to death, but none of his soldiers would raise a hand against the holy men. Doeg, however, sprang forward to do the king's bidding. One by one he murdered the eighty-five unarmed priests—all but one of the inhabitants of Nob. Only Abiathar had escaped.

The Kingdom of Saul

DAVID PLAYS THE HARP FOR SAUL

RIVER JORDA

ISRAEL

Endor

PLAIN OF ESDRAELON

MOUNT GILBOA

GREAT
(Mediterranean)
SEA

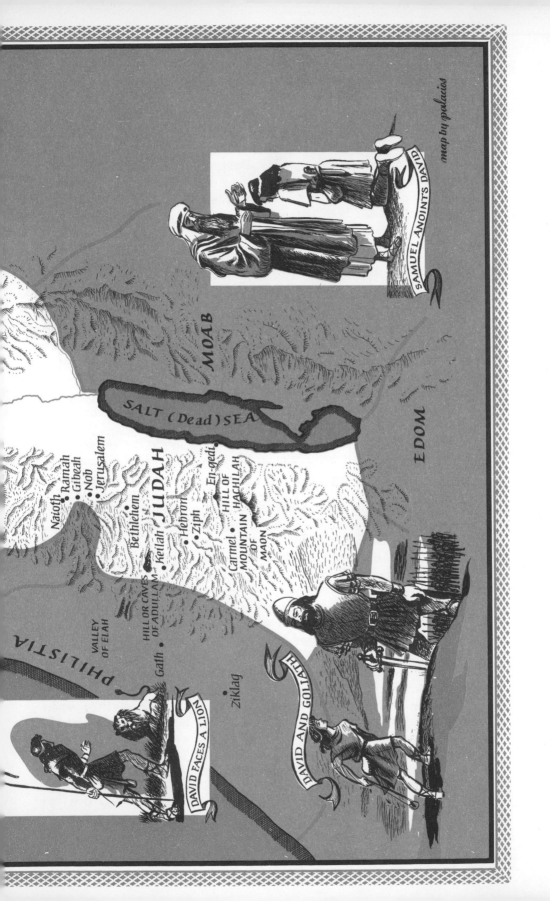

map by palacios

SAMUEL ANOINTS DAVID

MOAB

EDOM

SALT (Dead) SEA

Naioth
Ramah
Gibeah
Nob
Jerusalem

Bethlehem

JUDAH

Keilah
Hebron
Ziph

En-gedi

HILL OF
HACHILAH

Carmel
MOUNTAIN
OF
MAON

PHILISTIA

VALLEY
OF ELAH

HILL OR CAVES
OF ADULLAM

Gath

Ziklag

DAVID FACES A LION

DAVID AND GOLIATH

David was stricken with remorse. "I am responsible for the death of all these innocent people," he mourned to Abiathar. "Stay with me, and fear not. Anyone who would take your life will have to take mine first. Stay with me; you will be safe."

Soon afterwards David also heard the bitter news that Saul had given Michal in marriage to a certain Palti (PAL-tye), son of Laish (LAY-ish). In the dark cave on his mountain top, David wept. For all the suffering that had marched with him through his life, he could not help but feel that he would have done well to stay a shepherd boy. Was it for heartbreak and tragedy that he had been set aside from other boys of Bethlehem by his talents? Was this the way God treated those He marked for greatness?

Guerrilla Warfare

IN THE MORNING David rose to welcome another messenger. The nearby town of Keilah (keh-EYE-luh) was under siege by the Philistines. To show his countrymen that he was not a bandit but still a patriot, David led his six hundred seasoned fighters in an attack upon the invaders. He surprised the much larger Philistine army and routed them. The people of Keilah loudly welcomed David, and for the moment he and his men found shelter in a city.

When Saul heard the news that David had come to the aid of one of his cities and was even then resting within it, he exclaimed, "God has delivered him into my hands! He is trapped in a town that has gates and bars."

Saul knew what a master of guerrilla warfare his one-time commander was, and he felt relief to learn that David had come out of the hills to a city where his hit-and-run tactics would do him no good. He hurried an army to Keilah, but his soldiers found that David and his men had fled.

David raided the countryside south of Hebron (HEE-brun) for provisions for his starving men. Food was hard to find in this sparsely settled countryside, but at last he happened upon the prosperous village of Carmel. Abigail, the lovely wife of Nabal (NAY-bul), a rich but niggardly man of the place, brought him a gift of two hundred loaves of bread, two bottles of wine, five sheep, five measures of parched corn, a hundred clusters of raisins and two hundred cakes of figs. This generosity so incensed her husband that he died in rage, speechless. David not only gladly accepted the lady's gifts, but when he learned of her husband's death, he married her as well.

Now the harried men retreated into the wilderness of Ziph (ZIF), where it became still harder to find supplies. To make matters more critical, the few inhabitants of the country reported David's every movement to Saul. High on the hill called Hachilah (hah-KYE-luh), David planned to build a new fortress, but Saul and a huge army marched against him. Fleeing before the king, David and his men climbed the rocky mountain of Maon (MAY-un), which was separated from Hachilah by the deep but narrow Valley of Rocks. A man could shout across this gorge, although it took six miles of treacherous, roundabout trails to go from one side to the other.

David discovers Saul asleep and defenseless

That night David was checking the outermost defenses with Abishai and a Hittite (HIT-yte) follower when he noticed that he could make out the lights of Saul's camp on the far side of the valley. He was struck with an idea. "Who will go down with me to Saul's camp?" he asked.

"I will go down with you," replied Abishai, always brave.

David and Abishai crept down the precipitous mountain unseen and crossed the valley to climb Hachilah. Saul's sentries, not realizing that David's band was near, were not alert. They did not see the shadowy figures slip between them into the camp. David and Abishai had no trouble finding the sleeping Saul among his baggage carts. They stood staring down at the king, who slept with his spear stuck in the ground by his head.

"God has delivered up your enemy into your hand tonight," whispered Abishai. "Let me spear him to the earth with one stroke, I pray you. I won't have to stab him a second time!"

David looked upon the sleeping king with pity.

"Don't destroy him," he said. "What man can raise his hand against the Lord's anointed and be guiltless?"

David took Saul's spear, together with a jar of water which stood beside him. Leading the glowering Abishai, he safely made his way out of the camp and back across the gorge. By the time he reached his own camp it was dawn.

Once there, David turned, threw back his head, and shouted in his piercing voice across the chasm. In the dawnlight he called the names of Saul and his commander, Abner.

It was Abner who shouted back, "Who is calling the king?"

Even with his life in danger, David decided to play a little joke at the general's expense. "Are you a brave man?" he demanded. "The bravest in Israel? Then why don't you keep watch over your lord, the king? Go and see what became of the king's spear, and the jar of water that was at his head."

In a few minutes Saul's camp was in an uproar at the disappearance of the jar and spear.

"Is this your voice, my son David?" shouted the king, who immediately guessed the man whose cool bravery had carried out such a daredevil exploit.

"It is my voice, my lord. Why does my lord pursue his servant? What have I done? What evil is in my hand?"

Saul felt deeply moved to hear the once beloved voice from across the ravine.

"I have sinned," cried Saul. "Come back, my son David. I will do you no more harm. Today you spared my life."

But instead of returning, David told the king to send a man for his spear. The king, who loved him when he was sane, would surely try again to kill him when madness crept over him. Meanwhile, however, Saul again shouted his good wishes. "Blessed be you, my son David!" he cried. "You shall do many things, and will succeed in them."

This was the last time David ever heard the voice of Saul. He did not go to the king's camp, and Saul sadly marched away.

When Saul had gone, David knew that he had no other course of action than to take his hungry men into Philistia. There Achish (AY-kish), king of Gath, welcomed him and made him governor of the town of Ziklag. From there David plundered the ancient foes of Israel, all the while persuading Achish that he was from time to time attacking *his* enemy, Judah, as well. It was a trying position for a patriotic Israelite to be in, but within two years David was to find himself in an even more difficult predicament.

Saul's Last Battle

IN TWO YEARS' TIME David's new lord, King Achish, and the lord of his own people, King Saul, went to war once again. In the van of the Philistine army marched David. He who in his day, according to the old song, had slain tens of thousands of Philistines, now went with his old enemies to attack his native land.

On the desolate plain of Esdraelon (ess-druh-EE-lun) in the north, the Philistines found Saul's army holding a strong position on Mount Gilboa (gil-BOE-uh). As the armies prepared for battle, David now had to choose between making war on his own people or breaking his word to a king who had given him shelter and a command.

But before the armies came together, Achish called him to his side.

"My lords refuse to go into battle with you on their side," he said. "I have not found you doing anything wrong since the day of your coming to us, but the lords do not trust you." The king therefore ordered David to take his men and march back to Ziklag.

There, while he awaited news of the vital battle in the north, David carried on a campaign against the Amalekites (uh-MAL-uh-kytes), who had struck the defenseless town in his absence and burned it. By forced marches David overtook the Amalekite raiders and destroyed them in one of his shrewdly planned surprise attacks.

Even as David was winning this victory, the Philistines and the Israelites had started their bloody fight. Before the battle began, Saul had gone in humility to a soothsayer to talk through her with the dead Samuel.

The prophet's words shattered the king. As terrifying as in life, Samuel told Saul that his kingdom was lost and that he and his sons were to perish.

When the Philistines attacked in the morning, Saul fought doggedly though he had no hopes of victory. His soldiers fell back around him, but still he fought on. Then the report was brought to him that Jonathan and two of his other sons had been killed.

Knowing that the battle was now lost and that his kingdom was indeed overthrown, Saul called upon his armor-bearer to kill him. The soldier refused to kill his beloved king. To escape the fate of captive kings, Saul fell upon his sword and died.

A soldier brings David Saul's crown and bracelet

Three days later a young Amalekite came to David at Ziklag with the crown and bracelet of Saul. Confidently expecting a reward, he concocted a story to the effect that he had helped the king take his own life. But David gave him a terrible look and ordered him put to death for raising his hand against the Lord's anointed.

Then David tore his clothes and mourned. From his poet's heart came sorrowing words which today still call back the tragedy of Saul and Jonathan:

> Ye daughters of Israel, weep over Saul,
>> who clothed you daintily in scarlet,
>> who put ornaments of gold upon your apparel.
>
> How are the mighty fallen
>> in the midst of battle!
>> Jonathan lies slain upon thy high places.
>
> I am distressed for you, my brother Jonathan;
>> very pleasant have you been to me;
>> your love to me was wonderful,
>> passing the love of women.
>
> How are the mighty fallen,
>> and the weapons of war perished!

Abner made Ish-bosheth (ish-BOE-sheth) king of Israel, but in the land of Judah there was chaos. One day David left Ziklag in charge of a deputy governor and marched to Hebron, the leading city of the south. There the royal crown of Judah was placed upon the still unfurrowed brow of David, son of Jesse of Bethlehem—and honored ancestor of the Redeemer to come.

(continued from page 506)

Yet soon after this, David lapsed into a series of failures (Mephibosheth's appearance [II Sam. 9] could not have preceded 995 B.C. [9:12, 4:4], nor could Solomon's birth [12:24] have been long subsequent). He slew seven innocent descendants of Saul (but not Mephibosheth, 21:7) to enforce a promise rashly made to pagan Gibeonites (contrast Num. 35:33). He committed adultery with Bath-sheba and murdered her husband to conceal his crime (II Sam. 10-11). When exposed by Nathan, he humbly confessed his sin (the great penitential psalms 32 and 51); but the testimony of God's people had suffered compromise, and Nathan condemned the king to corresponding punishments (II Sam. 12:10-14). David also became

David's place of sacrifice and the very house of God (I Chron. 22:1; Ps. 30 title). David subsequently undertook massive preparations for the temple (I Chron. 22); he received in writing from God's Spirit the plans for its construction (28:12, 19); and he solemnly charged Solomon and the princes with their execution (I Chron. 22, 28-29). As David became increasingly incapacitated by age, his oldest surviving son, Adonijah, attempted to usurp the throne from Solomon, the divinely designated heir. Nathan, however, aroused David to proclaim Solomon's coronation (I Kings 1). Thus in 970 B.C., after a final charge to his son (2:2-9), David died. His last words were a prophecy of the future Davidic Messiah and of his own salvation, springing from this covenant (II Sam. 23:5).   J.B.P.

THE AGING DAVID ordered the priest Zadok and the prophet Nathan to go with the young prince Solomon to Gihon, a sacred spring on the east side of Jerusalem, and there to anoint him as the future king.

guilty of ineffective control over his sons. Thus in about 990 B.C. Amnon, following his father's shameful example (13:1-14), raped his sister Tamar; and two years later Absalom avenged Tamar by murdering Amnon (13:23-29). Until about 983 B.C. (13:38; 14:28) David shunned Absalom's presence; and four years later (15:7 ASVmg) Absalom revolted, driving his father from Jerusalem (cf. Pss. 3, 63) and specifically fulfilling Nathan's curses (II Sam. 16:20-22). Through fatal delay, Absalom was defeated and slain by Joab, though only the latter's stern rebuke could shake David from irresponsible grief over the death of his son (18:33-19:8). Even after David's restoration to Jerusalem, inter-tribal jealousies led Sheba of Benjamin to prolong the disorder (II Sam. 20).

David's last years (975-970 B.C.) were occupied with Philistine wars (21:15-22) and with a military census, motivated by David's pride in his armed forces (24:3,9; Ps. 30:6). Plague resulted. But when the destroying angel halted at Araunah's threshing floor on Mt. Moriah, just N of Jerusalem (II Chron. 3:1), this area became marked as

DAVID, CITY OF, a part of the Jerusalem plateau, 2500 feet above sea-level. This plateau is bounded on the E by the Kidron Valley and on the W and S by the Hinnom, which show a 500 ft. drop to their southeastern junction. It is connected on the N with the central ridge of Palestine and is bisected by a smaller valley, the Tyropoeon. Western Jerusalem, the "Upper City," is larger and higher and, since the fourth Christian century, has been designated (erroneously) the City of David. The eastern half, however, the peak of which is called Ophel or Zion (I Kings 8:1; II Chron. 33:14), possesses Jerusalem's chief water-supply (the Gihon spring, in the Kidron Valley) and marks the true City of David (II Chron. 32:30).

Mixed Canaanite settlement on Zion (Ezek. 16:3) dates back to the third millennium. The area occupied was small, about 1250 x 400 ft.; but a Jebusite wall, 27 feet in width, rendered the natural cliffs almost impregnable (cf. the "descent" noted in Neh. 3:15-16; 12:37). David, however, scaled the stronghold in 1003 B.C., made it his capitol, and called it and the surrounding town the "City of David" (II Sam. 5:9, 6:10; I Chron. 11:7).

SITE of the City of David at Jerusalem, showing the walls of Zion and the Citadel in the background. David's birthplace, Bethlehem, is also called the City of David.

He is known to have constructed fortifications, palaces and other government houses, and a tent for God's ark (II Sam. 5:11; I Kings 3:1, 9:24; I Chron. 11:8, 15:1,29; II Chron. 8:11); but no certainly Davidic structures have been recovered. David and his successors were buried in the City of David (I Kings 2:10, 11:43; 15:8; II Chron. 16:14, 21:20, 24:16, etc.).

Solomon enlarged Jerusalem beyond the City of David to include Mt. Moriah, for the temple and other buildings, on the N (I Kings 8:1) and probably part of the western plateau opposite Ophel. In the eighth century, Hezekiah seems to have ex-

MOSQUE marking the Tomb of David, so called, on Mount Zion. David's tomb was for long the general sepulcher of the kings of Judah.

tended the City of David southward to include the new Pool of Siloam, for his water tunnel from Gihon (II Chron. 32:4-5,30; II Kings 20:20; Isa. 22:9-11). By the time of Josiah, 621 B.C., Jerusalem also included the *mishneh* or "second quarter," W of the temple (?) (Zeph. 1:10; II Kings 22: 14); but it was the old City of David which the Greeks chose to fortify as their citadel during the Maccabean wars (I Macc. 1:33, 7:32). Simon reoccupied this "Lower City" in 139 B.C. (14:36-37). He partially leveled the ridge so that it should not rival Moriah to the north (Jos. *Ant.* XIII, vi,7), and the name Ophel (Ophlas) was shifted to the area between the old City and the temple. After A.D. 70 the original City of David was abandoned and now lies outside the walls of Jerusalem.

In Luke 2:11, the Christmas angels identified David's native town of Bethlehem as "the city of David." J.B.P.

DAY (Heb. *yôm*, Gr. *heméra*), a word often misinterpreted because of its various uses in the Bible. It often denotes time from sunrise to sunset (Gen. 1:5; Ps. 74:16). At an early date it was divided into three parts—morning, noon, and evening (Ps. 55:17; Dan. 6:10). Probably due to Medo-Persian influence after the Exile, it was divided into 12 hours (John 11:9). Early morning was the first hour; the sixth hour was noon. Time could not be determined by clocks, so the length of an hour depended upon the time of the year. The word also refers to time in general (Judg. 18:30; Obad. 12; Job 18:20). It is also used figuratively, referring to the day of judgment (Isa. 2:12; Joel 1:15; Amos 5:18; Rom. 13:12), the length of life (Gen. 5:4), the time of opportunity (John 9:4), and any time (Prov. 12:16 ASV, note 3). J.D.F.

DAY OF ATONEMENT (Heb. *yŏm hakkipūrîm*), the annual day of atonement when the high priest offered sacrifices for the sins of the nation (Lev. 23:27; 25:9). It was the only fast period required by Mosaic law (Lev. 16:29; 23:31). It came in August and was preceded by special sabbaths (Lev. 23:24). Instituted in recognition of man's inability to offer full atonement for his sins (Heb. 10:1-10), it was a day of great solemnity and strictest conformity to the law. The elaborate ritual, given in Leviticus 16, was as follows: 1. The high priest sanctified himself by a ceremonial bath and putting on white garments (v. 4). 2. He made atonement for himself and the other priests by sacrificing a bullock (Num. 29:8). 3. A goat was chosen by lot for a sin offering and sacrificed before the congregation (Lev. 16:8,9); blood from the bullock first and then the goat, was sprinkled on and about the mercy seat after the Holy of Holies had been sanctified by incense (vv. 12,14,15); a scapegoat was sent into the wilderness, the anti-type of the promised "Sin-bearer" (vv. 20-22); the high priest changed his garments, after a second ceremonial bath, and made the final offering (vv. 23-28). J.D.F.

DAY OF CHRIST, a term used in the NT to indicate the redemptive ministry of Jesus, both while in the flesh and upon His return. Sometimes it is called "that day" (Matt. 7:22) and "the day" (I Cor. 3:13). It refers to the return of Jesus for his own and for the judgment of unbelievers (I Cor. 1:8; 5:5; II Cor. 1:14; Phil. 1:6,10; 2:16; II Thess. 2:2,3). It is for the completion of the redemptive work (II Thess. 2:1,13). It is the day of triumph

(Phil. 2:9-11). Paul's epistles, especially, are suffused with the longing for the day of Christ when He will manifest Himself in glory and establish His kingdom.

DAY OF THE LORD, an eschatological term referring to the consummation of God's kingdom and triumph over His foes and deliverance of His people. It begins at the second coming and will include the final judgment. It will remove class distinction (Isa. 2:12-21), abolish sins (II Pet. 3: 11-13) and will be accompanied by social calamities and physical cataclysms (Matt. 24; Luke 21: 7-33). It will include the millennial judgment (Rev. 4:1-19:6) and culminate in the new heaven and the new earth (Isa. 65:17; 66:22; Rev. 21:1).

DAYSMAN (dāz'măn, Heb. *yākhah, to act as umpire*), a mediator or arbitrator—one who has set a day for hearing a dispute. As used in Job 9:33, the word means an umpire or referee who hears two parties in a dispute and decides the merits of the case. In eastern lands it was the custom for the judge to put his hands upon the heads of the two parties in disagreement to show his authority and desire to render an unbiased verdict. Job means that no human being is worthy of acting as a judge of God.

DAYSPRING (dā'sprĭng, Heb. *shahar, to break forth*), a poetic name for dawn (Job 38:12). It describes the advent of Messiah (Luke 1:78).

DAYSTAR (Gr. *phosphóros, light-giving*), the planet Venus, seen as a morning star, heralding the dawn. The prophet compared the splendor of the king of Babylon to Lucifer, son of the morning (Isa. 14:12; in RV daystar). Jesus calls Himself "the bright and morning star" (Rev. 22:16). In II Peter 1:19 the word daystar is applied to Christ.

DEACON, DEACONESS (dē'kŭn, dē'kŭn-ĕs, Gr. *diákonos, servant*). Paul called himself a deacon (I Cor. 3:5; Eph. 3:7). Jesus was declared to be a deacon of the circumcision (Rom. 15:8). He said, "If anyone will serve me" (*Emoí tis diakoné*) . . . "where I am, there shall also my servant (*diákonos*) be" (John 12:26). Household servants were *diakónoi* (Matt. 22:13). Paul told Timothy how to be a good *diákonos* (I Tim. 4:6). The diaconate, as a church office, is based by inference upon Acts 6:1-8, but at least two of the seven men were evangelists. Ignatius, a contemporary of the Apostle John, declared that the deacons were not mere servers of meat and drink. But they did serve (*diakonein*) tables, so that the apostles could give themselves to the ministry (*diakonía*) of the Word. Their successors came to be recognized as church officers. Qualifications given in I Timothy 3 show that they were not considered ordinary lay members of the church. Paul's mention of deacons in connection with bishops (Phil. 1:1) supports the view. Clement of Rome based the office upon the two classes of synagogue workers given in Isaiah (60:17,LXX translation) where pastors and helpers are named. *Deaconess* is from the same Greek word. Phebe was named by Paul as a deaconess (Rom. 16:1). Certain women ministered (*diekónoun*) unto Jesus (Luke 8:2,3). It does not appear from the Scripture or early church literature that deaconesses were ever church officers. J.D.F.

DEAD SEA, called in Scripture the Salt Sea (Gen. 14:3), Sea of the Arabah ("plain," Deut. 3:17), or East(ern) Sea (Joel 2:20; Zech. 14:8 ASV). It has the earth's lowest surface, 1290 ft. below sea-level. Occupying a geologic fault that extends from

COLOSSAL SALT SLABS in the cliffs of Jebel Usdum (the Hill of Sodom) at the southern end of the Dead Sea. Scripture refers to the Dead Sea as the Salt Sea.

Syria through the Red Sea into Africa, it measures 47 x 10 miles (approximately 300 sq. mi.). Cliffs rise 1500-2500 ft. on either shore. North of Lisan, "the tongue" (Josh 15:2 ASVmg), the water's depth attains 1300 ft., though southward it averages less than ten. The Sea is slowly expanding, as the muddy Jordan extends its northern delta. Salt concentration reaches 25%, four times that of ocean water. Magnesium bromide prevents organic life; the climate is arid, and the heat extreme.

Though man's historical access to the Dead Sea has been slight, five streams S of Lisan recom-

SALT PANS and mud flats where the Jordan River enters the Dead Sea at the north. The mountains of Moab are in the distance.

537

QUMRAN RUINS AND EXCAVATIONS, less than a mile from the northwestern shore of the Dead Sea. These are the remains of the mon- astery of the Essene Community of the first cen- tury B.C. The community has been dated within the limits of 140 B.C. and A.D. 67.

mended the Plain of Siddim to Lot as a "well-watered garden," 2090 B.C. (Gen. 13:10). Yet writing some 600 yrs. later Moses explained, "The same is the Salt Sea" (14:3 ASV), a fact suggested by the known growth of the Sea (once crossable at Lisan), by his mention of "slime pits" (bitumen, 14:10 ASVmg) now active on the Sea's floor (cf. Josephus' name, "Lake Asphaltites," *Ant.* i, 9,1), and by contemporaneous ruins discovered on Lisan (BA 5, May 1942). God's destruction of Sodom in 2067 B.C. may thus reflect the area's combustibleness (19:24,28); and Jebel Usdùm, "mountain of Sodom," still identifies an extensive rock-salt formation opposite Zoar (cf. 19:26; Luke 17:32).

The Dead Sea constituted Israel's eastern border (Num. 34:12; Ezek. 47:18). At En-gedi, which terminates the principal descent from Judah, a spring provided refuge for David, 1015 B.C. (I Sam. 24:1). The Valley of Salt, S of the Sea, witnessed the victories of David and of Amaziah, 790 B.C., over Edom (I Chron. 18:12; II Kings 14:7) and countermarches in the days of Jehoshaphat (II Chron. 20:1-2; II Kings 3:8-9; the "Moabite Stone"). On the E shore above the Arnon, the springs of Callirhoe served Herod the Great during his final illness (4 B.C.); and at Machaerus

his son Herod Antipas imprisoned John the Baptist (Mark 1:14; 6:17). On the W shore, above En-gedi lies Khirbet Qumran, site of the NT Essene community with its famous scrolls; and opposite Lisan rises Masada, Palestine's finest natural fortress, the refuge of Herod against Parthians in 42 B.C., and the last stand of Jerusalem's zealots in A.D. 70 (Jos. *Wars* VII, x,1). In modern times the Dead Sea has produced potash; but Ezekiel predicts a healing of its waters, granting abundant life in God's kingdom-age (47:8-10).

J.B.P.

DEAD SEA SCROLLS, discovered, probably in 1947, by Arabic Bedouin and brought to the attention of the scholarly world late that year and early in 1948. The discoveries were made in caves located in the marly cliffs, a mile or so W of the northwestern corner of the Dead Sea, at a place known by the modern Arabic name of Qumran, which is near a copious spring of fresh water known as Ain Feshkha. This location is at the eastern edge of the Wilderness of Judah. Accordingly, alternate names for the discoveries including "Qumran," "Ain Feshkha," or "Wilderness of Judah" are sometimes used.

The scrolls were seen by several scholars in the latter part of 1947, some of whom have admitted

QUMRAN CAVES, where the Dead Sea Scrolls were discovered. In the foreground is cave No. 4, where the main library of the Essenes was found. The scrolls were discovered by an Arabic Bedouin, and brought to the attention of scholars late in 1947.

that they passed them up as forgeries. One of the scholars who recognized the antiquity of the scrolls was the late Professor Eleazar L. Sukenik of Hebrew University, who was subsequently successful in purchasing some of them. Other scrolls were taken to the American School of Oriental Research in Jerusalem, where the Acting Director *pro tempore*, Dr. John C. Trever, convinced of their value, arranged to photograph the portions which were brought to him. One of his photographs was sent to Professor William F. Albright, who promptly declared that this was *"the most important discovery ever made* in Old Testament manuscripts."

The scrolls which were purchased by the Hebrew University included *the Hebrew University Isaiah Scroll* (1QIsᵇ), which is a partial scroll of the book, the *Order of Warfare,* also known as the *War of the Sons of Light against the Sons of Darkness* (1QM), and the *Thanksgiving Hymns* or *Hodayot* (1QH). The scrolls purchased by the Syrian archbishop and published by the American Schools of Oriental Research included the *St. Mark's Isaiah Scroll* (1QIsᵃ) which is a complete scroll of the book, the *Habakkuk Commentary* (1QpHab) which contains the text of chapters one and two of Habakkuk with a running commentary, and the *Manual of Discipline* (1QS), which con-

tains the rules for the members of the Qumran community. These all have subsequently come into the possession of the State of Israel and are housed in a shrine in the Hebrew University, Jerusalem, Israel. They have been published in numerous editions and translated into many languages, and are readily available for anyone who wishes to study them either in translation or in facsimile.

Following the discovery of these important scrolls, which are now all but unanimously accepted as having come from the last century B.C. and the first century A.D., the region from which they came was systematically explored. Numerous caves were found, and so far eleven caves have yielded materials from the same period as the original scrolls. Most of these materials have come from the fourth cave explored (known as Cave Four or 4Q); others of significance come from Cave Two, Five, and Six. According to recent reports the most significant discoveries are those from Cave Eleven (11Q).

At least 382 manuscripts are represented by the fragments of Cave Four alone, about 100 of which are Biblical manuscripts. These include fragments of every book of the Hebrew Bible except Esther. Some of the books are represented in many copies: e.g., 14 different manuscripts of Deuteronomy, 12

OPENING OF CAVE No. 4. Most of the Dead Sea Scroll fragments came from this cave. Remains of the Essene monastery can be seen in the distance.

manuscripts of Isaiah, and 10 manuscripts of Psalms are represented in Cave Four; other fragments of these same books have been found in other caves. Almost complete scrolls of Psalms and Leviticus have been found in Cave Eleven, but these have not yet been published. One of the significant finds, which may turn out to have importants bearing on the theories of date and authorship, concerns the Book of Daniel, fragments of which have been found with the change from Hebrew to Aramaic in Daniel 2:4 and from Aramaic to Hebrew in 7:28-8:1, exactly as in our modern texts of Daniel.

In addition to Biblical books, fragments of Deuterocanonical writings have been found, specifically Tobit and Ecclesiasticus, as well as fragments of several noncanonical writings. Some of these latter were already known, such as Jubilees, Enoch, the Testament of Levi, etc.; others were not previously known, such as the peculiarly Qumranian documents: the Thanksgiving Psalms, the Book of Warfare, the commentaries on portions of Scripture, etc. These last give us insights into the nature and beliefs of the community at Qumran.

Near the cliffs on an alluvial plateau overlooking the shore of the Dead Sea is the site of an ancient building complex often referred to as the "Monastery." This was thoroughly excavated over several seasons, and has yielded important data about the nature, size, and date of the Qumran community. From coins found there, together with other remains, the community has been dated within the limits of 140 B.C. and A.D. 67. The members were almost all male, although the literature contains provisions for the admission of women and children. The number of living there

FRAGMENT of the Dead Sea Scroll of the Habakkuk Commentary, found in cave No. 4 at Qumran. The Habakkuk Commentary was published by the American School of Oriental Research in Jerusalem, whose acting director was one of the first to recognize the value of the scrolls. At cave No. 4 were found fragments of every book of the Hebrew Bible except Esther.

at any one time was in the neighborhood of two to four hundred. A mile or so S at Ain Feshkha were found the remains of other buildings, the nature of which is not exactly clear. The fresh water of the spring probably was used for the growing of crops and other needs of the community.

From the sect's literature we know that the people of Qumran were Jews who had split off from the Jerusalem or main stream of Judaism, and indeed were quite critical of and even hostile toward the priests at Jerusalem. The fact that they used the name, "The Sons of Zadok" has suggested to some scholars that they should be connected with the Zadokites or Sadducees; other scholars believe that they are rather to be identified with the Essenes, a third sect of Judaism described by Josephus and Philo. It is not impossible that elements of truth are to be found in both of these theories and that there was originally a split in the priestly or Saducean line which first joined the movement known as the Hasidim, the forerunners of the Pharisees, ultimately to split again and form a narrow separatist group part of which located at Qumran. We must await further discoveries before we attempt to give a final answer to this entire problem.

The community devoted itself to the study of the Bible. The life of the community was largely ascetic, and their practices included ritual bathing, sometimes referred to as baptism. This has been understood by some to be the origin of the baptism of John the Baptist. A study of John's baptism alongside that of the Qumranians shows, however, that the two practices were quite distinct; hence, if John did come from this community (which is not yet proven and may never be), he must have developed important distinctions in his own doctrine and practice of baptism.

Some scholars believe that Zoroastrian elements are to be found in the Qumran writings, particularly with reference to dualism and angelology. The problem is extremely complex. Zoroastrian dualism developed greatly in post-Christian times, and therefore it is precarious to assume that the Zoroastrian beliefs as we know them represent the beliefs a century or two before the time of Christ.

The discoveries at Qumran are important for Biblical studies in general. The matter of the canon is not necessarily affected, since the group at Qumran was a schismatic group in the first place, and, moreover, the absence of Esther does not necessarily imply that they rejected this book from the canon. In the matter of the text of the Old Testament, however, the Dead Sea Scrolls are of great importance. The text of the Greek Old Testament (or the Septuagint), as well as the quotations of the Old Testament in the New, indicate that there were other texts beside the one that has come down to us (the Masoretic Text). The study of the Dead Sea Scrolls makes it clear that at the time of their production, which would be about the time of the production of the Scriptures used by the New Testament authors, there were at least three texts in existence: one we might call the ancestor of the Masoretic Text; the second was a text closely related to that used by the translators of the Septuagint; the third was a text differing from both of these other texts. The differences are not great and at no point do they involve doctrinal matters; but for careful textual study of the Old Testament it is important that we free ourselves from the notion that the Masoretic Text is the only authentic text. As a matter of fact, the quotations of the Old found in the New Testament rather imply that it was not the Masoretic Text which was most commonly in use by New Testament authors. These statements should be qualified by pointing out that the quality of the text varies from book to book in the Old Testament, and that there is much more uniformity in the text of the Pentateuch than in some of the other portions of the Hebrew Bible. The Dead Sea Scrolls have particularly made great contributions to the study of the text of Samuel.

In relation to the New Testament, the Dead Sea Scrolls are likewise of importance. There are no New Testament texts in the discoveries at Qumran, obviously, since the earliest book of the New Testament had been written only very shortly before the destruction of the Qumran community. Moreover, there was no reason why any of the New Testament writings should have reached Qumran. On the other hand, there are certain references and presuppositions found in the New Testament, particularly in the preaching of John the Baptist and Jesus Christ, and in the writings of Paul and John, which are placed against a background now recognizably similar to that furnished by the documents from Qumran. Thus, for example, the Gnostic background found in certain Pauline writings and formerly thought to be second century Greek Gnosticism—thus requiring a late date for the composition of Colossians—is now recognized as a Jewish Gnosticism of the first century or earlier. Similarly the Fourth Gospel is shown to be Palestinian and not Hellenistic.

A great deal has been written concerning the relationship of Jesus Christ to the Qumran community. There is no evidence in the Qumran documents that Jesus was a member of the sect, and nothing in the New Testament requires such a position. Rather, the outlook of Jesus with reference to the world and particularly toward His own people is diametrically opposite that of Qumran, and it can be safely asserted that He was not a member of that group at any time. He may have had some disciples who had come out of that background, particularly those who were formerly disciples of John the Baptist—though this is far from proven. The attempt to show that the Qumran Teacher of Righteousness was the pattern for the Gospel portrayal of Jesus cannot be established on the basis of the Dead Sea Scrolls. The Teacher of Righteousness was a fine young man with high ideals who died untimely; there is, however, no clear statement that he was put to death, certainly no indication that he was crucified or rose from the dead or that the Qumranians expected him to return. The difference between Jesus and the Teacher of Righteousness stands out clearly at several points: the Teacher of Righteousness was never referred to as the Son of God or God Incarnate; his death was not sacrificial in its nature; the sacramental meal (if such it was indeed) was not viewed as a memorial of his death or a pledge of his return in any way connected with the forgiveness of sin. Obviously in the case of Jesus Christ, all of these things are clearly asserted, not once but repeatedly in the New Testament, and indeed form a necessary basis without which there is no Christian faith.   W.S.L.S.

DEATH. In the Bible the word is used in various senses.

It refers to cessation of natural life: Abraham (Gen. 25:11), Aaron's wicked sons (Lev. 16:1), Moses (Deut. 34:5), a woman in travail (1 Sam. 4:20), a father (Matt. 8:22), David's child (II Sam. 12:23), a thief (Mark 15:27), even the son of Man (Mark 15:37), from every age and class death takes its victims. It is pic-

BEFORE DAVID'S DEATH, he called the people around him. In their presence, he charged his son Solomon with the great task of building the Temple. When he received Solomon's willing promise, he burst into a joyful hymn thanking God for letting him begin the great work. It was David's last song.

tured as the departure of the spirit from the body (II Tim. 4:6), as being inevitable (Josh. 23:14), as laying aside the body (II Cor. 5:1), as the return to the former natural state (Eccl. 3:20; 12:7). It is pictured as a sleep (Jer. 51:39; Dan. 12:2; John 11:11; Acts 7:60). It is a state in which God is not seen (Isa. 38:11; Job 35:14), nor praised (Ps. 6:5; Isa. 38:18). It is the result of sin (Gen. 2:17; Rom. 5:21; 6:23; I Cor. 15:56; Heb. 2:14; James 1:15). In the spiritual sense death is a separation from God, or spiritual night (Luke 1: 79; I John 3:14; Rom. 5:12, 6:23; John 3:36; Eph. 2:1,5; Rev. 2:11). The righteous and wicked go on forever, the righteous to everlasting good (Isa. 35:10, 45:17; Dan. 7:14, 12:2; Rev. 7:17), the evil to eternal torment (Jer. 20:11; Dan. 12:2; Matt. 25:46; Mark 3:29; II Thess. 1:9; Jude 7).

Confusion has arisen in some minds regarding the meaning of passages which seem to teach total destruction of man, whether good or bad. David's plaint over the death of his child (II Sam. 12:21, 22) is cited, but that David knew that death was not the end of rational existence is attested by numerous expressions such as Psalm 23; 62:2,7; 89:26; 116:14, etc. Job's question (14:14) is readily answered by himself (Job 19:25-27). Matthew 10:28 must be interpreted in the light of the discourse which contains it. Such passages as Job 7:9,10; and Psalm 6:5 must be interpreted in the light of other statements by their authors, none of which teaches that sin ultimately annihilates the wicked. Death to the righteous is a glorious experience (Num. 23:10; Ps. 116:15; Rev. 14:13). Jesus has conquered death and removed from it the awful sting (Isa. 25:8, 26:19; Hos. 13:14; John 5:24; I Cor. 15:53-57; I John 5:12; Rev. 1:18).

The second death has been misinterpreted by many, yet the revelation regarding it is plain. It is definitely final separation from God. God's law of the wages of sin included the penalty of death (Gen. 2:17). While physical death was involved, the special penalty was spiritual death, or separation from fellowship with the Creator. Expulsion from Eden typified this. So spiritual death is at first broken fellowship with Jehovah, with its consequent penalties. Paul so interpreted it (I Cor. 15:21-23). They who are victorious in their faith will not be hurt by the second death (Rev. 2:11), because He who has power over it will never forsake his inheritance (Ps. 94:14). Consummation of the judgment ushers in the second death, eternal and absolute separation from God in the lake of fire and brimstone (Rev. 20:6,14).   J.D.F.

DEBIR (dē'bêr), a city of Judah, once a center of culture for the Canaanite people. Probably it took its name from the pagan temple in which the oracle occupied the holy place (see I Kings 6:5, where *Debhir* is translated "oracle" — Holy of Holies in margin). It is called *Kirjath-sepher*, or "town of books" (Josh. 15:15). It could have been "town of scribes" (*sopher*). In Joshua 15: 49 it is called *Kirjath-sannah*. It was SW of Jerusalem, some ten miles west of Hebron and was occupied by the Anakim (Josh. 11:21; 15:14). It was captured by Joshua (10:38,39), evidently retaken by the Canaanites, and captured a second time under Caleb, who gave his daughter as reward to its captor, Othniel being the winner (Josh. 15: 13-17). It later became a priestly possession (Josh. 21:15; I Chron. 6:58).

2. *Debir*, a king of Eglon, who made an alli-

TELL BEIT MIRSIM, ruins of Debir, ancient Kirjathsepher in southern Palestine. Once a center of Canaanite culture, Debir took its name from the pagan temple, in which an oracle occupied the holy place.

ance with the king of Jerusalem against Joshua and was defeated at Gibeon (10:1-11).

3. *Debir*, a town on the border of Gad near Mahanaine (Josh. 13:24-26).

4. A town on the border between Judah and Benjamin (Josh. 15:7), on the road between Jerusalem and Jericho.

DEBORAH (děb'ō-rà, Heb. *devôrâh*, bee). 1. Rebekah's beloved wet-nurse (Gen. 24:59, 35:8), who accompanied her former nursling to Palestine — she became attached to Jacob's household and died at great age (c. 2065-1909 B.C.; cf. Gen. 25:20, 35:8) near Bethel, the tree under which she was buried being called '*Allôn-bākhûth* (oak of weeping).

2. The fourth and greatest (with Gideon) of Israel's judges, a prophetess, a wife of Lappidoth (Judg. 4-5). She resided near the border of Benjamin and Ephraim, probably belonging to the latter tribe, and administered justice under "the palm-tree of Deborah" (4:4-5). Like most Hebrew "judges," however, Deborah served primarily as a divinely-appointed deliverer and executive leader of Israel.

After the death of Ehud, God's people had lapsed into apostasy, with the result that He subjected them to the Canaanitish king Jabin II of Hazor, whose commander, Sisera, "had 900 chariots of iron; and 20 years he mightily oppressed Israel" (4:2-3; cf. James B. Pritchard, *Ancient Near Eastern Texts*, Princeton Univ. Press, 1950, p. 237). This period (c. 1240-1220 B.C.) coincides with the unrest that followed upon Hittite collapse and the death of Egypt's Rameses II, the treaties under which had preserved order in Palestine since the days of Seti I, 80 years before (3:30; cf. John Garstang, *Joshua-Judges*, London: Con-

543

stable, 1931, pp. 278-283). Rameses' successor, however, was the elderly Merneptah. Despite his claim to have pacified both Canaanites and Israelites (cf. his famous "Israel-stela," Pritchard, *op. cit.,* pp. 376-378), disorder became rampant: "The highways were unoccupied, and . . . was there a shield seen in Israel?" (5:6-8)

Then arose Deborah, "a mother in Israel," (5: 7). Summoning Barak of Naphtali, she prophesied that an offensive from Mt. Tabor at the northeastern limit of Esdraelon would lure Sisera and Jabin's army to annihilation on the plains below (4:6-7). Barak agreed, provided Deborah's inspiring presence should accompany the troops, though Deborah predicted Sisera's death by a woman (4:8-9). Barak and Deborah then scouted Esdraelon around Kedesh (Tell Abu Kudeis, E of Megiddo? Garstang, *op. cit.,* p. 301); they mustered 10,000 men of Naphtali and Zebulun; and, together with princes of Issachar (5:15), they occupied Tabor (4:12). Deborah also summoned Dan and Asher in the N (cut off by Hazor) and Reuben and Gad in Transjordan, who failed to respond (5:16-17; Simeon and Judah in the far S remain unmentioned). But Benjamin, Ephraim, and Machir (Manasseh) answered the call (5:14), probably massing at Jenin at the southeastern edge of Esdraelon (*Ibid.,* pp. 299-300). Deborah thus accomplished Israel's first united action since the conquest, 175 years before.

Sisera, meanwhile, advanced from Harosheth in western Esdraelon, forded the Kishon southward to marshal the Canaanite kings from Jokneam, Megiddo, and Taanach (5:19), and pressed inland along its southern bank. But God in heaven's courses fought against Sisera (5:20). A providential storm (cf. 5:4), which turned the plain into a morass, rendered Sisera's chariotry unmaneuverable, and they were cut to pieces by Israel's wildly charging foot-soldiers. The routed Canaanites, cornered at the Kishon ford, were then swept away by a flash-flood (5:21). Sisera was slain in single flight, by the woman Jael at Kedesh (4:11,17-22); Jabin was destroyed (4:24); and the land rested 40 years (5:31), corresponding to the reign of Rameses III, the last great Pharaoh of Egypt's XXth dynasty. After the battle, Deborah and Barak sang Deborah's song of victory (5:2-31. cf. v. 7), the contemporaneous authenticity of which is universally recognized from its archaic language, vivid descriptions, and ringing faith (v. 31).

Yet Deborah's record has occasioned manifold criticism against Scripture. 1. Textually, her song's admitted antiquity has been used to discredit the reliability of Scripture's earlier prose narratives (ICC, p. 110). But while poetry does tend to preserve archaic forms, the "modernized" Hebrew of the Pentateuch need not affect true Mosaic authorship (cf. R. Laird Harris, "On a Possible Revision of the Biblical Text During the Monarchy," Evangelical Theological Society, *Annual Papers, 1953,* pp. 18-24).

2. Confusion, futhermore, is alleged between Joshua II and Judges 4-5, as two garbled accounts of one actual battle against Jabin (IB II:683, 712). Yet Joshua's opponent, in 1400 B.C., may have been a predecessor of Deborah's; or "Jabin," a hereditary title in Hazor.

3. Contradictions are discovered between the prose and the poem: fewer tribes fighting in chapter 4, and Sisera killed in his sleep (ICC, pp. 107-

108). But the poetry intentionally singles out the tribes; and Sisera's sleeping, in 5:26, is apparently understood; and his "bowing and falling," in 5:27, simply describes his subsequent death-agonies.

4. Within the prose, a conflation is surmised between a King-Jabin story in Kedesh-Naphtali and a King-Sisera story in Esdraelon (ICC, pp. 108-109). Yet the Kedesh of 4:9-11 fits Esdraelon, not Naphtali; and Scripture never designates Sisera "king," only "captain" (an Aegean or Hittite mercenary-adventurer?) of Jabin.

5. The Biblical date of Deborah is lowered a full century by Albright to 1125 B.C. (BASOR 62 (1936), p. 29), but only because of his theory that no Philistines (cf. 5:6, 3:31) could reach Palestine before the 1100's; yet see Genesis 21:34, 26:1!

6. Morally, the charge that the scriptural account of Jael is "reprehensible . . . cannot be justified" (IB II:716). But while we question this Gentile's treacherous methods, Deborah's insight into her fearless and unsolicited devotion to God's people renders her "blessed above women" (5:24).

J.B.P.

DEBT (Heb. *neshî,* Gr. *opheílema, a sum owed, an obligation*). Under Mosaic law Jews were not allowed to exact interest (usury) from other Jews (Exod. 22:25). Special laws protected the poor against usurers (Exod. 22:25-27; Deut. 24:12,13). After the Exile cruel practices arose in collecting debts (II Kings 4:1-7; Isa. 50:1). A debtor had to make good his obligation, so land that was pledged (mortgaged) could be seized, but had to be restored during the Jubilee year (Lev. 25:28). A house so pledged could be sold, or held in perpetuity if not redeemed during a year, unless it was an unwalled town (Lev. 25:29,30). In NT times the Mosaic code was disregarded. We read of bankers, money-changers, interest, usury (Matt. 25:16-27; John 2:13-17). Debtors were often thrown into prison (Matt. 18:21-26). Jesus taught compassion towards those in debt (Matt. 18:23-35). The prayer of Jesus, "forgive us our debts," implies guilt from unpaid moral obligations to God (Matt. 6:12).   J.D.F.

DECALOGUE (děk'à-lŏg, Gr. *déka, ten* and *logós, word*), the basic laws of the Hebrew state. They were given by God to Moses at Mt. Sinai (Exod. 20). The laws were inscribed on tablets of stone (.Deut. 4:13) and were afterwards carried in the ark of the covenant (Deut. 10:2). There is a slight difference between the record in Exodus '20:1-17 and that in Deuteronomy 5:6-21. Catholics and Lutherans unite 1 and 2 and divide 10; Eastern (Greek) Catholics and most Protestants accept the order given in the KJV. Jesus approved the law (Matt. 5:18; 22:40), fulfilled it (Matt. 5:27-48; 23:23), and became the end of the law for righteousness to all who believe (Rom. 10:4; 8:1-4).

DECAPOLIS (dē-kăp'ô-lĭs, Greek *déka,* ten, and *pólis,* city), a region E of Jordan that had been given to the tribe of Manasseh (Num. 32:33-42). A league of ten cities, consisting of Greeks who had come in the wake of Alexander's conquests, was established after the Romans occupied the area (65 B. C.). According to Ptolemy, the number was later increased to 18. They had their own coinage, courts, and army (Jos. XIV:4:4). Ruins of temples, theaters and other buildings tell of the

high degree of culture which developed in these cities. Jesus drove the demons into swine near Gadara, one of these cities (Mark 5:1-20), and became popular in the Decapolis (Matt. 4:24,25; Mark 7:31-37).

RUINS OF GERASA (modern Jerash), one of the principal cities of the Decapolis, showing the Forum, above, and a general view of the ruins, below.

DECISION, VALLEY OF, where God will some day gather all nations for judgment (Joel 3:2,12). It is called the Valley of Jehoshaphat (*Jehovah judges*), and has been identified by some with the valley of Kidron, but this is only conjecture. Perhaps no particular valley is intended, and the name may be only a symbol of the event.

DECREE, an official ruling or law. It translates various words in the OT such as *'ēsār, interdict* (Dan. 6:7); *gezērāh, decision* (Dan. 4:17); *dāth, law* (Dan. 2:9), In general it refers to any fiat of an official nature. In Esther 1:20, Daniel 3:10, Jonah 3:7, the word refers to laws governing special occasions. In Acts 16:4 the Greek *dogma* means rules for Christian living. God's decree is His settled plan and purpose (Ps. 2:7-10; Dan. 4:24; see also Exod. 32:32; Rev. 13:8).

DEDAN (dē'dăn), an Arabian people descended directly from Noah (Gen. 10:6,7). They established themselves in the region about the northwestern end of the Persian Gulf. They were also related to Abraham by his concubine Keturah (Gen. 25:3). Mention of these people occurs fre-

545

quently in the Chaldean and Assyrian tablets. Israelites of later generations considered them kinsmen. Dedanites were warned by Jeremiah to flee to the back country (Jer. 49:7,8). They were an important commercial people. Isaiah called the Dedanites traveling tradesmen (21:13). Ezekiel wrote of their connection with Tyre (27:3,15, 20), and foretold that the destruction of the Dedanim was to accompany that of the Edomites (Ezek. 25:13).   J.D.F.

DEDICATION (Heb. *kādhēsh, to sanctify, hănukkâh, to consecrate*), an expression denoting dedication to holy ends. Often used of the consecration of persons, but usually of the setting apart of things for God's use. Consecration of the tabernacle (Num. 7) was an elaborate ceremony, as was that of the temple (I Kings 8). Among various dedicated things were: the city wall (Neh. 12:27), private dwellings (Deut. 20:5), the temple treasure (I Chron. 28:12), the child (Exod. 13:2), people (Exod. 19:14; I Sam. 16:5), and booty of war (II Sam. 8:10,11). The dedication of Nebuchadnezzar's image (Dan. 3:2,3), and of Herod's temple (Jos. XV:11:6), were elaborate occasions.

DEDICATION, FEAST OF, an annual festival of the Jews held throughout the country for eight days, celebrating the restoration of the temple following its desecration at the hands of the Syrians under Antiochus Epiphanes (I Macc. IV; 52-59; II Macc. X:5), of which Josephus gives a graphic picture (Ant. XII:5:4). The feast came on the 25th of Kislev (December). Josephus called it the "Feast of Lights." Like the Feast of Tabernacles, it was a time of pageantry and joy. It was at this feast that Jesus delivered in the temple the discourse recorded in John 10:24ff, at Jerusalem.   J.D.F.

DEEP, a translation of Hebrew and Greek words of varying meaning. Hebrew: *metsûlâh, the ocean* (Neh. 9:11; Job 41:31; Ps. 107:24; Isa. 44:27); *metsôlâh, torment* (Ps. 88:6); *tehôm, chaos* (Gen. 1:2; 7:11); *subterranean water* (Gen. 49:25; Deut. 33:13); *ămîq, mysterious* (Dan. 2:22); *āmōq, depth,* or *power* (Lev. 13:4,31; Job 11:8). Greek: *báthos,* of *water* or *condition* (Luke 5:4; John 4:11; Acts 20:9; II Cor. 8:2); *buthós, sea* (II Cor. 11:25) or *abyss* (Luke 8:31; Rev. 9:1, 11:7).

DEFILE (dē-fīl'). There are a number of Hebrew and Greek words which in general mean *to profane, pollute, render unclean.* In the OT, defilement was physical (S. of Sol. 5:3), sexual (Lev. 18:20), ethical (Isa. 59:3; Ezek. 37:23), ceremonial (Lev. 11:24; 17:15; etc.), and religious (Num. 35:33; Jer. 3:1). In the NT it is ethical or religious (Mark 7:19; Acts 10:15; Rom. 14:20). In the NT the idea of ceremonial or ritual defilement does not exist. In OT times God's purpose in issuing laws regarding ceremonial defilement was clearly an educative one—to impress the Israelites with His holiness and the necessity of their living separate and holy lives.

DEGREE (dē-grē, Heb. *ma'ălâh, a going up* or *ascent,* Gr. *tapeinós, low*). The word *degrees* occurs in the titles of 15 psalms, Psalms 120 to 134, which are called Songs of Degrees. The common opinion regarding the meaning is that they were sung by the pilgrims as they went up to Jerusalem (cf. I Sam. 1:3; Ps. 42:4; 122:4; Isa. 30:29). The word is also used in II Kings 20:9,10, where Hezekiah is told that the sign that the Lord would heal

him would be that his sundial would go back ten degrees, and in a secondary sense of rank or order (I Chron. 15:18; 17:17; Ps. 62:9; Luke 1:52; James 1:9).

DEGREES, SONGS OF, the title given Psalms 120-134. Uncertainty exists as to the origin of the title. Some Jewish authorities attributed it to the use made of fifteen steps leading from the court of men to the court of women in the temple. The Levitical musicians performed with these steps as the stage. It is possible that originally the songs were part of a ritual which required the Levities to advance up the steps as they played or sang. Some scholars attribute the title to the way in which the thought advances from step to step, as seen in 121:4,5; 124:1,2,3,4, but all these songs do not do this. Because Ezra (7:9) used the word *hammă'lâh, a going up from Babylon,* some have thought that the title originated when exiles were returning to Jerusalem during the reign of Artaxerxes in Babylon. The most logical explanation is that the title was given the series of hymns because they were used by pilgrims during the annual journeys to the three required feasts in Jerusalem. One tradition has it that Solomon wrote Psalm 132 and the others were written later. They are songs of penitence (120,131), praise (121,128,133, 134), and praise and prayer (122,123,129,132).
J.D.F.

DEKAR (dē'kàr), the father of one of Solomon's twelve purveyors (I Kings 4:7-9).

DELAIAH (dē-lā'yà, *raised* or *freed by Jehovah*). 1. A descendant of David (I Chron. 3:1,24).

2. A priest of David's time and leader of the 23rd course of temple service (I Chron. 24:18).

3. A prince who besought Baruch not to burn the sacred roll containing the prophecy of Jeremiah (Jer. 36:12,25).

4. Head of a tribe that returned under Zerubbabel from captivity (Ezra 2:60; Neh. 7:62).

5. The father of Shemaiah who advised Nehemiah to flee (Neh. 6:10).

DELILAH (dē-lī'là, *dainty one*), a Philistine woman from the valley of Sorek, which extends from near Jerusalem to the Mediterranean. By her seductive wiles she learned the secret of Samson's strength and brought him to his ruin (Judg. 16:4-20).

DELUGE (See Flood)

DEMAS (dē'măs, Gr. *Demás, popular*), a faithful helper of Paul during his imprisonment in Rome (Col. 4:14). Paul called him a "fellow laborer" (Philem. 24). He was probably a citizen of Thessalonica to which place he went upon deserting Paul (II Tim. 4:10).

DEMETRIUS (dĕ-mē'trĭ-ŭs, Gr. *Demétrios, belonging to Demeter*). 1. The disciple whom John praised in his letter to Gaius (III John 12).

2. The jeweler of Ephesus who raised a mob against Paul because his preaching had resulted in damage to his lucrative business of making silver images of the goddess Diana (Acts 19:23-27). The name of one Demetrius, a warden of the Ephesian temple, has been found by modern explorers; he probably was the silversmith. Three kings of Syria bore the name: Demetrius Soter or Saviour (Jos. *Ant.* XII:10;1-4); D. Nikator, or Conqueror (*ibid.* XIII:5,2,3,11); D. Eukarios, the fortunate, (*ibid.* XIII:13;3 and XIV:1;3).

DEMONS (Gr. *daimónion*), evil spirits (Matt. 8: 16, Luke 10:17,20; Matt. 17:18 compare with Mark 9:25). The immaterial and incorporeal nature of both Satan and his demon hosts is graphically set forth by the Apostle Paul in describing the believer's intense conflict as being "not against flesh and blood," but against "principalities," "powers," "world-rulers of this darkness," and "spiritual hosts of wickedness in the heavenly places" (Eph. 6:12). Again the non-material and incorporeal character of demons is hinted in the expression "The prince of the powers of the air, the spirits that are now at work in the hearts of the sons of disobedience" (Eph. 2:2, Weymouth).

The Apostle John likewise stresses the incorporeality of demons in his reference to the three unclean spirits issuing out of the mouth of the dragon, the beast, and the false prophet as the "spirits of demons" (*pneúmata daimoníon*, Rev. 16:14). The construction is patently a genitive of apposition, more particularly defining the general term "spirits," which may be either good or bad, as in this case, bad, or "demon-spirits."

As purely spiritual beings or personalities, demons operate above the laws of the natural realm and are invisible and incorporeal. The Bible presents them as such, and thus free from magical rites and exorcistic rigmarole, which contaminate ethnic and rabbinic demonology. The Word of God however, does recognize the principle of miracle where natural law may be temporarily transcended and denizens of the spirit world glimpsed (II Kings 6:17; 2:11). On this principle John in apocalyptic vision *saw* the awful last-day eruption of locust-demons from the abyss (Rev. 9:1-12), as well as the three hideous frog-like spirits which emanate from the Satanic trinity (the dragon, the beast and the false prophet) in the Tribulation to muster the world's armies to their predestined doom at Armageddon (Rev. 16:13-16).

As spirit personalities demons have an intellectual nature through which they possess superhuman knowledge. Plato's etymology of *daimon* from an adjective meaning "knowledge" or "intelligent" (*Cratylus* I, 389) points to intelligence or knowledge as the basic characteristic of demonic nature. Scripture features the perspicacity of demons. They know Jesus (Mark 1:24), bow to Him (Mark 5:6), describe Him as "the Son of the Most High God" (Mark 5:7), entreat Him (Luke 8:31), obey Him (Matt. 8:16), vitiate sound doctrine (I Tim. 4:1-5), conceal the truth of Christ's incarnate deity and sole Saviourhood (I John 4:1-3) and comprehend prophecy and their inevitable doom (Matt. 8:29).

Because of their superphysical knowledge, demons are consulted in spiritistic oracles through spiritistic mediums, who allow themselves to get under the control of evil spirits for oracular purposes (I Sam. 28:1-25; Acts 16:16), as is seen in both ancient and modern spiritism, erroneously called "spiritualism."

In their moral nature all demons (as fallen angels) are evil and depraved, in distinction to the good spirits (the unfallen angels), who are sinless. The moral turpitude of demons is everywhere evidenced in Scripture by the harmful effects they produce in their victims, deranging them mentally, morally, physically and spiritually, and by the frequent epithet of "unclean," which often describes them (Matt. 10:1; Mark 1:27;

Luke 4:36; Acts 8:7; Rev. 16:13). Fleshly uncleanness and base sensual gratification are the result of demon control of the human personality (Luke 8:27). Demons figure in the moral collapse of a people who yield to gross carnality and sexual sin, so rampant in the world today (II Tim. 3:1-9; Rev. 9:21,22).

In addition to their superhuman intelligence and moral turpitude, demons possess terrible strength, imparting it to the human body (Luke 8:29), and binding their victims as with chains and with physical defects and deformities (Luke 13:11-17), such as blindness (Matt. 12:22), insanity (Luke 8:26-36), dumbness (Matt. 9:32,33) and suicidal mania (Mark 9:22).

Demons under the leadership of Satan seek to oppose God's purposes and to hinder man's welfare. So intimately bound up are they with their prince leader that their work and his are identified rather than differentiated. Thus the earthly life of our Lord is said to have consisted in going about "doing good, and healing all that were oppressed of the devil" (Acts 10:38). Certainly much of this so-called oppression by the devil was the work of Satan's minions, the demons, as a cursory examination of the Gospel records will show.

Demons are of two classes — those who are free with the earth and the air as their abode (Cor. 1:13; Eph. 2:2; Eph. 6:11-12) and those who are imprisoned in the abyss (Luke 8:31; Rev. 9:1-11; Rev. 20:1-3). The abyss is only the temporary prison house of evil spirits, which must surrender its doleful inhabitants to Gehenna or the "lake of fire" (Matt. 25:41), the eternal abode of Satan, demons, and unsaved men.   M.F.U.

DENARIUS (See Money)

DEPRAVITY (dē-prăv'ĭ-tē), a theological term not found in Scripture, although the reality expressed by the word is certainly there. Negatively, it means that man, as a result of the fall, has lost his original righteousness and love for God. Positively, it means that man's moral nature has become corrupted, and that he has an irresistible bias toward evil. The corruption extends to every part of his nature and every faculty of his being. In his depraved state man can do nothing perfectly pleasing to God. This does not mean that he has no qualities pleasing to men, that he is as bad as he can be, or that he is as opposed to God as he can possibly be. The image of God in which he was created has not been completely obliterated; some vestiges of it remain. He cannot, however, no matter how hard he tries, love God with all his heart or his neighbor as himself; nor can he change his supreme preference for himself, or so radically transform his character that he can live according to God's law. Arminian and Calvinistic theologians differ on the extent of depravity, but they are agreed that without the saving grace of God no salvation is possible.   S.B.

DEPUTY (dĕp'ū-tē, Heb. *nitstsāv*, Gr. *anthúpatos*), one appointed to rule under a higher authority, as a regent in place of a king (I Kings 22:47) or a Roman consul or proconsul (Acts 13:7; 18:12; 19:38). Roman proconsuls were appointed by the Roman senate to govern senatorial provinces, usually for one year. They exercised judicial as well as military power in their province. During their term of office their power was absolute, but when it expired they were accountable for what they had done.